TWAYNE'S WORLD AUTHORS SERIES

A Survey of the World's Literature

Sylvia E. Bowman, Indiana University

GENERAL EDITOR

FRANCE

Maxwell A. Smith, Guerry Professor of French, Emeritus
The University of Chattanooga
Visiting Professor in Modern Languages
The Florida State University

EDITOR

Émile Zola

TWAS 10

TWAYNE'S WORLD AUTHORS SERIES (TWAS)

The purpose of TWAS is to survey the major writers —novelists, dramatists, historians, poets, philosophers, and critics—of the nations of the world. Among the national literatures covered are those of Australia, Canada, China, Eastern Europe, France, Germany, Greece, India, Italy, Japan, Latin America, New Zealand, Poland, Russia, Scandinavia, Spain, and the African nations, as well as Hebrew, Yiddish, and Latin Classical literatures. This survey is complemented by Twayne's United States Authors Series and English Authors Series.

The intent of each volume in these series is to present a critical-analytical study of the works of the writer; to include biographical and historical material that may be necessary for understanding, appreciation, and critical appraisal of the writer; and to present all material in clear, concise English—but not to vitiate the scholarly content of the work by doing so.

Émile Zola

By ELLIOTT M. GRANT

TWAYNE PUBLISHERS
A DIVISION OF G. K. HALL & CO., BOSTON

Library of Congress Catalog Card Number: 66–21744

ISBN 0–8057–2996–8

MANUFACTURED IN THE UNITED STATES OF AMERICA

Contents

Preface

If we ask how Émile Zola appeared to his contemporaries, the answer can be readily found. His friend Paul Alexis states that in his maturity Zola was a stocky, square-set man with dark brown hair, closely trimmed beard, small hands and feet, near-sighted but reflective eyes, high forehead, and a sensitive nose. According to Edmond de Goncourt, Zola possessed "a pointer's nose, aimed inquiringly at things and quivering like a mucous membrane twitching at the touch of a fly." However that may be—for Goncourt is far from a reliable guide—Zola's physical appearance was suggestive of the inner man whose curiosity and determination were universally recognized.

He quickly became a controversial figure. He remained so throughout his life, and he has not ceased to arouse controversy since his death. He was rarely free from attack: his work was often labeled crude or obscene; his ideas were judged absurd, or wrong, or even subversive. These hostile criticisms had no effect. He calmly went his way; and, because of his determination not to be swayed from his course, French literature broadened its scope. It had never been as prudish as English literature in the Victorian age, as the work of Balzac, Stendhal, Flaubert, and Goncourt demonstrates. But Zola depicts on a larger scale than his predecessors the lower layers of the social structure as well as the less attractive aspects of human nature.

His work is voluminous, and the present study is primarily concerned with that work. While I have included enough facts about Zola's life to help in understanding the published texts, my aim is less biographical than literary.

Zola wrote a good many short stories, some of which are very good, but in the following pages these and other genres are less emphasized than the novels. It is on the novels that Zola's reputation rests. In a book limited in length, the decision to concentrate on them was unavoidable.

E. M. G.

Lyme, New Hampshire
February 1965

Acknowledgments

I have naturally made use of the work done by previous workers in this particular vineyard. Among biographies, those by Denise Le Blond-Zola and Armand Lanoux have been useful. Among literary studies of a general nature, those by F. W. J. Hemmings and M. Turnell have been extremely valuable. More specialized studies have also contributed their share; to these I have tried to make proper acknowledgment in appropriate notes. I should add that I have made use of material—and occasionally a bit of the phraseology—from my own work on Zola done over the past twelve to fifteen years.

I am indebted to The New American Library of World Literature for permission to use excerpts from Mr. A. H. Townsend's translation of Zola's *L'Assommoir.*

I am grateful to my son, Richard B. Grant, and to my wife Evelyn, for reading my chapters as I penned them. Their criticisms have often been helpful.

Finally, I am much indebted to the Baker Library of Dartmouth College which has given, as always, unstinting use of its resources and services.

E. M. G.

Chronology

	April	*La Faute de l'abbé Mouret* (Vol. V).
1876	February	*Son Excellence Eugène Rougon* (Vol. VI).
	April	Zola becomes a dramatic critic for *Le Bien public*.
1877	February	*L'Assommoir* (Vol. VII).
1878		Zola buys a property at Médan.
	June	*Une page d'amour* (Vol. VIII).
1879	January 18	First performance at the Ambigu of *L'Assommoir*.
1880	March	*Nana* (Vol. IX).
	May	*Les Soirées de Médan*.
	September	Zola begins a series of articles for *Le Figaro*.
	October 17	Death of Zola's mother.
	December	*Le Roman expérimental*.
1881		*Les Romanciers naturalistes; Nos auteurs dramatiques; Documents littéraires*.
1882	April	*Pot-Bouille* (Vol. X).
1883	March	*Au bonheur des dames* (Vol. XI).
1884	March	*La Joie de vivre* (Vol. XII).
1885	March	*Germinal* (Vol. XIII).
1886	April	*L'Œuvre* (Vol. XIV).
1887	August 18	"Le Manifeste des cinq," a manifesto hostile to Zola, published in *Le Figaro*.
	November	*La Terre* (Vol. XV).
1888	April 21	*Germinal*, the play.
	October	*Le Rêve* (Vol. XVI). Before the year ends Jeanne-Sophie Adèle Rozerot becomes Zola's mistress.
1889	September 20	Birth of Denise, daughter of Jeanne Rozerot and Zola.
1890	March	*La Bête humaine* (Vol. XVII).
1891	March	*L'Argent* (Vol. XVIII).
	April	Elected president of the Société des Gens de Lettres.
	September 25	Birth of Jacques, son of Jeanne Rozerot and Zola.
1892	June	*La Débâcle* (Vol. XIX).
1893	July	*Le Docteur Pascal*, the twentieth and final volume of *Les Rougon-Macquart*.

Chronology

1894	August	*Lourdes,* first novel of *Les Trois Villes.*
	December 22	Captain Dreyfus condemned by a court martial.
1896	May	*Rome,* second novel of *Les Trois Villes.*
1897	November 25	Zola begins the publication in *Le Figaro* of *La Vérité en marche.*
1898	January 13	"J'accuse," published in *L'Aurore.*
	February 23	Zola condemned by the Cour d'Assises to a year in prison and 3000 francs fine.
	March	*Paris,* the third of *Les Trois Villes.*
	July 18	Zola goes into exile in England.
1899	June 5	Zola returns to France.
	October	*Fécondité,* the first of *Quatre Évangiles.*
1901	May	*Travail,* the second of *Quatre Évangiles.*
1902	September 29	Zola killed by coal gas.
	October 5	Public funeral of Zola.
1903	March	Posthumous publication of *Vérité,* the third of *Quatre Évangiles.*
1908	June 4	Zola's ashes transferred to the Pantheon.

CHAPTER 1

Childhood and Youth

THE early 1840's were not, perhaps, as exciting a period in human history as some—the 1790's or the 1940's, for example —but they were nevertheless marked by a number of notable events. In 1840, Victor Hugo, the recognized leader of the Romantic school, continued his series of lyrical volumes with *Les Rayons et les Ombres.* His contemporary, Honoré de Balzac, added in these years an incredible number of stories to an already large output, giving in 1842 to his gigantic structure the grandiose but not inappropriate title of *La Comédie humaine.* Although Balzac's novels contained a wide streak of Romanticism, they pointed undeniably in a new direction. Much the same can be said of Stendhal, whose *Chartreuse de Parme* missed the new decade by only a few months. In 1840, the first volume of Sainte-Beuve's history of Port-Royal came off the press, and indicated that an impressive work was in the making. Auguste Comte's *Cours de philosophie positive,* launched in the previous decade and continued into the 1840's, began to have an important effect on men's minds. Across the Channel, Charles Dickens was busily at work. After having composed in quick succession *Pickwick, Oliver Twist,* and *Nicholas Nickleby,* he now in 1840 issued *Barnaby Rudge.* This same year witnessed the marriage of young Queen Victoria to Prince Albert of Saxe-Coburg-Gotha. It was also marked by a diplomatic crisis over the Near East, which momentarily threatened the peace of Europe. Such were some of the literary and historical events which surrounded the birth on April 2, 1840, of Émile-Édouard-Charles-Antoine Zola, destined to become a famous novelist and one of the most controversial figures of the Third Republic.

Émile was born in Paris, the son of a French mother, Émilie-Aurélie Aubert, and an Italian father, François Zola,[1] forty-five years old, whose family came from Zara in Dalmatia. François

Zola was an engineer; and what is equally important, he was an exuberant, ambitious man, full of ideas, and endowed with enormous energy. He had developed schemes for the fortification of Paris and was seeking to have them adopted. He also had plans for a water system for which Aix-en-Provence had dire need. So, when his ideas on the defense of Paris were not adopted, he turned to the other. Taking his young wife and infant son to Aix, he was able in 1843 to make a temporary agreement with the municipality; and the following year he succeeded in obtaining a royal declaration of the public utility of his project. This carried with it the right of expropriation of property. A company was finally formed in 1846 with a capital of six hundred thousand francs, and François Zola began work on the enterprise which involved the construction not only of a canal but of a dam. Unhappily, he caught cold while working in the hills and failed to shake it off when he went on a business trip to Marseilles. There, in a hotel room, he died prematurely on March 27, 1847, of pneumonia. Years later, Émile Zola included this sudden death in a second-class hotel room in one of his novels, *Une page d'amour*.

As a young widow of twenty-seven or eight, Émilie Zola found herself in a precarious situation. Her husband's estate consisted of shares in the canal company and a claim on the municipality. Apart from that, she and her parents, who had come to live with her in Aix, had only some modest savings. Before long, she found herself involved in lawsuits as she tried to salvage something from her husband's estate. Soon, her diminishing resources forced her to leave her rented house in the Impasse Sylvacanne and take up increasingly less expensive quarters.

I *School Days in Aix-en-Provence*

While she struggled during the next few years with financial problems, Émile began his schooling. He was first sent as a day pupil to a little private school, the Pension Notre-Dame, conducted by an indulgent man with the name of Isoard. His earliest lifelong friendships were formed there. Philippe Solari, who in later years became a well-known sculptor, and Marius Roux, a future popular novelist and editor of *Le Petit Journal*, were his principal comrades. Then, in 1852, young Émile entered the Collège of Aix-en-Provence, called at that period the Collège Bourbon, a public school which corresponded roughly to an

American high school plus a year or so of an American college. Because of the poor training of the Pension Notre-Dame, he was behind the others by a full year or two and was obliged to work unusually hard in consequence. That he did so is indicated clearly by the fact that in 1853 and other years he won several awards. In fact, in 1856–57, the last year he spent in this *collège,* he carried off most of the prizes.

During this period he made the acquaintance of Paul Cézanne and Baptistin Baille. Cézanne, who was a year older, earned Zola's gratitude and friendship by protecting him from the torments of other students who mocked him for an accent which was less Southern than theirs because of the daily influence of his mother and grandmother. Nor were these students slow in taking advantage of the fact that he was behind others of his age. Cézanne's intervention was extremely welcome. Baptistin Baille was a bright lad who became in later life a professor at the École Polytechnique. Then there were a lawyer's son, Marguery, who had a passion for music, and Antony Valabrègue, the future poet and art critic. The latter was four years younger, and Zola did not see a great deal of him at this time, but their correspondence several years later is of importance. Marius Roux and Philippe Solari were not forgotten. They still contributed to Zola's enjoyment of life.

The three truly inseparables, however, were Zola, Baille, and Cézanne. Because of their passionate interest in literature and art, hardly a day passed without lively discussions. Romanticism may have begun at this date to decline in Paris, but it was still potent in the provinces; and the three youths were devotees of the great Romantic poets. Cézanne seems at this period to have been as interested in poetry as in painting. Baille dreamed of winning fame as an epic poet. They discovered Alfred de Musset whom they came to admire even more than Victor Hugo. As young Zola tramped the hills of Provence, sometimes alone, often with his bosom friends, Musset was a frequent companon. "I carried him with me in my game-bag," he wrote in later years, "and leaving my gun forgotten on the grass, I read his poetry in the warm shade of the South, perfumed with sage and lavender. To him I owe my first sorrows and my first joys. Today still, [. . .] whenever I feel a sudden surge of youth, I think of Musset in his despair and thank him for having taught me to weep."[2] In time,

Zola ceased to be influenced by the author of "La Nuit de mai," but he never forgot him.

Nor did he forget his rambles along the streams, the valleys, and over the hills of Provence. The Mont Sainte-Victoire, the almost bottomless pit of Le Garagay, the old castle of Vauvenargues, the nearby plain watered by the Arc or the Torse, the gorges of Infernet—these are some of the scenes of nature which the area around Aix provided and which the three friends visited in their expeditions. Glimpses of these hills and dales, of these streams and torrents, are to be found in more than one of Zola's novels. The vision of that beautiful, rugged country never left him, nor did his love for it.

But beautiful scenes of nature and emotional, stirring poetry were not the only experiences of these years. Zola and his companions, like all maturing boys, were increasingly aware of girls. The Collège d'Aix, of course, was sexually segregated, so that they were not, like most young Americans, thrown into immediate association with the opposite sex; and in nineteenth-century France the adolescent girl, the *jeune fille,* was guarded and chaperoned to an incredible extent. Nevertheless, the boys—and the girls—had eyes. Philippe Solari had a sister Louise whom Zola found attractive. Armand Lanoux not only believes that young Émile had surreptitious dates with his friend's sister but identifies her with "a little girl in a pink hat" whom the boy had admired for some time.[3] There is little evidence in support of Lanoux's conjectures. It is doubtful whether Zola ever approached Louise Solari except in the most conventional way, for from all that is known or can be deduced, it appears that Zola was unusually timid in his relations with the other sex, despite the fact that his work reveals a certain obsession with sexual matters. He had undergone in his childhood, at the age of five, an experience at the hands of a domestic servant[4] that may have been traumatic in its consequences and may possibly account for his timidity and his obsession, though little is known about it. In any case, we may reasonably conclude that the boy's experience with girls was very limited.

II   *First Years in Paris*

Unfortunately, Émile Zola was soon forced to leave his friends and his accustomed joys. In the autumn of 1857 ruin came upon his family. His grandmother, Mme Aubert, tried her best to keep the wolf from the door, raising money by selling whatever furniture or clothing could be deemed at all superfluous. Worn out by this struggle and by old age, she fell ill and died in November. Her daughter, seeing that existence was rapidly becoming impossible in Aix, left in December for Paris in the hope of obtaining some sort of assistance from friends of her late husband. In February, she wrote Émile to sell what was left and buy tickets for his grandfather and himself with the proceeds. In the middle of the school year, after taking a goodby tramp with his comrades to Le Tholonet, a village on the road to the Infernet gorges, Émile grimly took the train for Paris where his mother had found quarters at 63, rue Monsieur-le-Prince on the left bank, not far from the Luxembourg gardens and palace. Some friends had come to her aid, including a prominent lawyer by the name of Labot who had known and esteemed her husband and who now obtained a scholarship at the Lycée Saint-Louis for her son. Émile entered the school on March 1, 1858.

At the Collège of Aix, the boys had made fun of his accent for not being sufficiently southern; in Paris, on the contrary, they thought it obviously and amusingly Provençal. Moreover, most of the students came from wealthier families than his. Feeling in a sense *déclassé* and perhaps a little like a foreigner in this group of four hundred young Parisians, he found it difficult to concentrate on his work as he had done in Aix, with the result that he obtained only a second prize in French composition. He had forecast in a letter to Cézanne that he could not hope for more, and in the same missive he contrasted the two cities. "Paris is big, full of amusements, monuments, and charming women. Aix is small, monotonous, petty, full of . . . women (God keep me from slandering the women of Aix). And despite all that, I prefer Aix to Paris." And to Aix he returned for a visit during the summer vacation. How his mother managed that financially is a minor miracle still unexplained.

On his return to the north, he fell ill and was forced to stay at home for the first two months of the school year. In August he presented himself for the baccalaureat. He did well on the written examination but failed on the oral. Still optimistic, he went south for another vacation which his mother, again miraculously, arranged. In November, a second attempt at the "bachot" ended more disastrously than the first, for this time he failed to pass the written examination.

Until this second failure occurred, the year 1859 had been reasonably happy in spite of poverty with all its restrictions. Zola had done a good deal of reading, doubtless enjoyed himself while at Aix, and had composed a number of things. The year before, he had penned a comedy in verse entitled *Enfoncé, le pion* (*The Schoolmaster worsted*), the text of which has not been preserved; its title suggests that it may have been intended as a rollicking farce. He had also written a couple of poems, "A mon ami Paul" and "A mes amis," published much later by Paul Alexis in his *Émile Zola, Notes d'un ami.* In 1859 he wrote more: "Ce que je veux," "Nina," "Vision," "Le Diable ermite," "Religion," and "Rodolpho." He informed Baille that he had finished *Les Grisettes de Provence* (*The Shop-girls of Provence*),[5] and that a fairy tale, *La Fée Amoureuse* (The Fairy named Amoureuse, a sort of patron saint of lovers), had been accepted by *La Provence,* a newspaper published in Aix. Some of these texts, as well as a few letters that have come down to us, indicate that his spirits were by no means low, that he had romantic notions about life and love, that he was filled, in short, with the kind of idealism possessed by many at the age of nineteen.

The problem of everyday existence now pressed heavily upon him. His schooling was ended, his financial position desperate, his mood, for the moment, pessimistic. He obviously needed a job, and for a short time, during the second quarter of 1860, he had one. M. Labot, his father's friend, helped out again and found him a clerkship in the office of the Paris docks. But the wages were derisory and the work was indescribably dull. Zola endured it for a couple of months, but the day came when he failed to appear at his desk.[6] Meanwhile, he and his mother had taken cheap lodgings on the seventh floor of no. 35 rue St. Victor, on the slope of the "Montagne" Ste Geneviève. The best that could be said for it was that the view from their tiny terrace embraced nearly all Paris. He was buoyed up during most of this year, particularly after quitting his job, by the hope of a trip to the south in the late summer or early fall; consequently his letters do not sound, on the whole, too gloomy. They are full of comments on literature, art, and life. On March 25, while still at the Docks, he wrote to

Cézanne: "What do you mean by this word 'realistic'? You boast of painting only subjects devoid of poetry! But everything has its poetic quality, manure as well as flowers." A month later he discussed the relative importance of form and subject in painting. In July a long letter to Baille includes reflections on Shakespeare, stating that what was important to the great dramatist was "man in general, not individuals. [. . .] Othello is not a jealous man, he is jealousy; Romeo, love; Macbeth, ambition and vice; Hamlet, doubt and weakness; Lear, despair. No petty or freakish exceptions, but a grandiose generalization, no realistic or idealistic tendencies, but a true conception, containing like life itself, the real and the ideal."

In August, another long letter demonstrates beyond dispute the depth of Zola's idealism at this date. He believes that to save men from vice it is more effective to give them a picture of goodness than to try to frighten them by a portrayal of evil, that "celestial splendors are more capable of saving sinners than is hell." He conceives of the modern poet as a soldier who "fights in the name of God for everything that is great." His mission is to "reveal the soul to those who think only of the body." It is also to serve humanity, for "art should be above all useful, either directly or indirectly." In this same letter, young Zola expresses some anticlerical sentiments, but states categorically his belief in God and immortality. "I believe in a good, just, and omnipotent God. I believe that this God created me, that he guides me here on earth, and that he awaits me in heaven. My soul is immortal . . . ." As for Christ, the young man hesitates to recognize his divinity, but declares the man of Nazareth to be a "sublime legislator, a divine moralist." He concludes that "if Christian means disciple of Christ," he accepts the name. Christ's precepts, he says, "are mine, his God mine." Early in September[7] he writes again to Baille, partly to announce his arrival in Aix-en-Provence on the 20th, partly to discuss Victor Hugo's *Le Dernier Jour d'un condamné*, partly to propose the formation of an artistic association with Baille, Cézanne, Pajot (a new friend), and himself as founders. In this letter his idealism is again revealed. There is also ambition, for he says: "If I take up definitely a literary career, my watchword will be: *All or nothing!*"

During this year, Zola finished the trilogy he had started in 1859 with *Rodolpho*. He now wrote *L'Aérienne*[8] and *Paolo*. The three parts formed *L'Amoureuse Comédie,* the first section depicting the inferno of love; the second, the purgatory; and *Paolo,* the paradise. He began a play in verse entitled *La Mascarade* with "a young and melancholy" hero named Hermann, but he never completed it. He planned a new trilogy on *La Chaîne des êtres* of which the first canto was to represent the creation of animals leading to the appearance of man; the second, the development of man; the third, the formation of new and more perfect beings after the extinction of the human race. This ambitious project, possibly inspired by the work of André Chénier, was never realized. A story called "Un coup de vent" was apparently finished, though, as far as is known, never published; but "Le Carnet de danse," written this year, was destined to appear in his first published collection of short stories.

The optimism from which much of Zola's youthful idealism sprang was severely jolted at the end of the summer. He did not have the money for the trip to Aix, and this time his mother was unable to find it. On the contrary, mother and son were obliged to separate, Mme Zola going to a boarding house at 21 rue St. Étienne-du-Mont, where she may have partly earned her subsistence, Émile taking a room at no. 24 in the same street. This particular room, on the top floor as usual, was a kind of belvedere which Bernardin de Saint-Pierre, the author of *Paul et Virginie,* had once inhabited.

A change of tone in Zola's letters to his friends is clearly perceptible after the abandonment of the trip to Aix. His poverty is essentially responsible for it, and his poverty remained constant for many months. November, 1860 to February, 1862 is the grimmest period of his existence. The winters of 1860–61 and 1861–62 were severe, and often, to keep warm in his fireless room, he had to stay in bed. Many of his few belongings went to the pawnshop. Sometimes his food consisted of a bit of bread and cheese or an apple, sometimes of bread alone dipped in oil. In April of 1861, unable to pay his rent, he had to move to no. 11 rue Soufflot where his room was, if anything, worse than any he had known. Other rooms in the building were occupied by poor students or by prostitutes. Nocturnal raids by the police were fairly frequent. During the summer of 1861, Zola could escape into the parks or the surrounding area of Paris; but in the wintertime no such solution was possible. His clothing was quite inadequate for any prolonged period out-of-doors.

Sometime between October, 1860 and February, 1861, he had an affair with a girl. Not much is known about it except that it seems to have been a disillusioning experience. In 1859–60 he had written idealistic pages to his friends about love. But in February, 1861 he tells Cézanne in a letter written in bed because of the cold that he had just graduated from the harsh school of reality, that he is much depressed, and that he now possesses new views on love. A few days later a letter[9] to Baille confirms this, for he writes that the heart-breaking truth is that "the prostitute is irremediably lost, the widow frightens me, the virgin does not exist." By virgin, he means a girl pure and innocent in both body and mind. He has clearly been cured of some of his earlier romanticism.

April, 1861 signifies for an American the outbreak of the Civil War, but for Émile Zola it meant the arrival of Paul Cézanne in Paris. During the weeks that followed, they saw a good deal of each other, but were not as inseparable as in the days of old. Cézanne, who received a respectable allowance from his banker-father, soon took up quarters in the rue des Feuillantines, not far from Zola to be sure, but in a more comfortable building. Paul could not stand the cheap little restaurant which dire necessity forced Zola to patronize when he could find the few necessary pennies. But more important was the fact that their temperaments began to clash. Cézanne was unstable, unsure of himself. He soon discovered how much he had to learn about painting. Zola, in spite of his material circumstances, was filled with ambition. He could not understand his friend's hesitations or his reluctance to discuss artistic problems. Exasperated, he wrote to Baille: "To prove something to Cézanne would be like trying to persuade the towers of Notre-Dame to dance a quadrille." When Paul began to talk of leaving Paris and returning home, Zola was appalled. One day in late July or early August, 1861, he found Cézanne packing to go home. Paul had started a portrait of Émile and had been working on it for some time. "What about my portrait?" asked the future novelist. "I've destroyed it," Cézanne replied, and confessed how upset he was at his inability to paint it as his inner vision dictated. They went to lunch, and during the afternoon,

Zola succeeded in calming his friend and persuading him to stay in Paris; but he realized that Paul would probably leave soon and concluded that it would be best. "Paul may have the genius of a great painter," he wrote to Baille, "he will never have the genius to become one. The slightest obstacle causes him despair." He ended his letter with a word that was meant both for himself and Baille: *"courage!"*

During these grim days, Zola displayed his perseverance by finishing *L'Aérienne,* by discussing—in an otherwise personal and melancholy letter—the question of versification, by reading and commenting on Montaigne whom he found much to his taste and whose work was certainly an element in Zola's growing detachment from Romanticism.[10] He also composed in this difficult time an essay on "Progress in Science and in Poetry," [11] and planned, according to Paul Alexis, a vast poem in three parts on *La Genèse:* the creation of the world, the history of humanity, and the humanity of the future. It sounds much like *La Chaîne des êtres* of which he had thought the year before; in any case, only eight lines were actually composed. But it is clear from his letters and projects, and particularly from his essay, that he believed that truth and reality should be the prime inspiration of the writer, who should not ignore the world of science. These preoccupations testify to the strength of his spirit in a time of adversity.

Zola's letter to Baille concerning Cézanne's departure contained the news that he hoped to have a job soon. He was to have it, with the publishing house of Hachette—ultimately. But for four or five months, his terrible ordeal continued. At the end of the year he was in such desperate straits, so obviously in need of help, that M. Boudet, his backer for the job at Hachette's, employed him to distribute the visiting cards customarily left at friends' residences on New Year's Day. Fortunately this period of unemployment and destitution did not continue much longer.

CHAPTER 2

The First Rungs of the Ladder

I Work in the Publishing House of Hachette

ON February 1, 1862, Émile Zola began work in the shipping department of Hachette & Cie at a salary of one hundred francs a month. The work was far from exciting and the salary far from munificent, but he was saved from destitution, and assured of food, clothing, and shelter. His evenings and his Sundays were his own, and he used them to labor on literary projects. Baille had come to Paris in January, so for the next six or seven months Zola was able to renew this valued friendship, to talk instead of write. Cézanne was back in Aix, but no letters were addressed to him till September. The correspondence of this year and the next is scanty and furnishes little information. We know that Zola continued to work on his poetry and that he composed three prose stories: *Le Sang, Simplice,* and *Les Voleurs et l'âne.* In May, Zola suggested to his employer the creation of a new series of books to be called "La Bibliothèque des débutants." [1] He was convinced that the presentation of new authors would be an admirable thing for French literature, and would also be a financial success. Louis Hachette decided against it, but he was sufficiently impressed by Zola's enterprise and intelligence to promote him to the advertising department with an increase of salary. It was a fine chance for a young man with literary ambitions, for not only did he see and sometimes meet authors like Taine, Michelet, About, Littré, and others whose work was published by Hachette, but he came into contact with newspaper editors. This entrance, however limited and modest, into the literary and journalistic world of Paris was to stand him in good stead.

Louis Hachette appears to have been responsible for Zola's decision to abandon poetry. The story goes that Émile left his manuscript of *L'Amoureuse Comédie* on his employer's desk one Saturday night and that on Monday morning Hachette informed him of his decision.[2] It was a negative one, but at the same time he encouraged his young employee to continue—in prose. As Zola had already written several stories and had already thought of making up a collection for publication, the decision to concentrate on this plan was not difficult. From 1862 to 1864 much of his energy went into it.

During this same period other events of importance occurred. In October 1862, Zola became a naturalized French citizen, a step made necessary by the fact that his father had been a foreigner. He then had to register for military service. Luck was on his side, for he drew a number that was not called and, consequently, according to the system then in vogue, was exempt. Early in 1863, Paul Cézanne returned to Paris and through him Zola developed his contacts with the world of painting, which was thrown into turmoil in April by the Salon des Refusés. Manet's "Déjeuner sur l'herbe" was prominently displayed there and at once became the talk of Paris. Zola was deeply interested in this discussion. In all probability he also owed to Cézanne his introduction during the summer or autumn of this year to Gabrielle-Alexandrine Meley, who was to become his mistress and ultimately his wife. Not much is known about her humble origins. Her mother was dead when Zola made her acquaintance, and she apparently saw her father rarely, if at all. A year older than Émile, she was endowed with a robust type of beauty, a Juno, as Lanoux puts it, rather than a Venus. One suspects that it was she who made the necessary advances.

Zola spent the rest of 1863 and the first months of 1864—outside of working hours at Hachette's—on the volume of short stories he projected; he also continued his reading and his reflections on literary problems. In a letter to Valabrègue dated July 6 he says that he must close in order to get back to Stendhal. Did he read Darwin's *Origin of the Species,* the French translation of which appeared in 1862? [3] He certainly did sooner or later, but it is difficult to pinpoint the exact time of this contact. On the other hand, we know that he perused Taine's Introduction to the *Histoire de la littérature anglaise,* which came out in 1863. A reference to Taine in a letter written to Valabrègue in the summer of 1864 leaves no room for doubt. This letter, moreover, is important, for in it Zola included a short essay on what he called *L'Écran* (*The Screen*). "Every work of art," he wrote, "is like a window open on creation; set in this window is a kind of transparent screen through which may be seen objects more or less deformed." The deformations "are due to the nature of the screen." He goes on to say that absolute realism is impossible in a work of art; there has to be an element of falsehood. Zola defines the classical, romantic, and realistic "screens," and states his preference for the realistic, which claims to transmit images with complete accuracy. But he contends that even the realistic "screen" cannot avoid a little deformation. His final preference is for "the screen which, staying close to reality, is satisfied with lying just enough to make me feel the presence of a man in an image of creation." This is already fairly near the famous formula: "A literary work is a corner of nature seen through the temperament of the writer" ("Une œuvre est un coin de la nature vu à travers un tempérament").[4]

II   Contes à Ninon

The letter to Valabrègue disclosing Zola's interest in Stendhal contained the information that his volume of stories had been accepted. The *Contes à Ninon*, a curious combination, were published in October, 1864. The Romantic dreamer of 1858–60 is still in evidence, for the volume contains "La Fée Amoureuse" and "Le Carnet de danse," written before the age of twenty-one, while Zola was still under the influence of the Romantic poets. The same can be said of other stories in the collection, of *Simplice*, for example, with its theme of a handsome young man who takes refuge from the world in a virgin forest where he meets a beautiful nymph whose love is fatal to them both. In this charming, naïve tale there is a touch of Victor Hugo, the Hugo of the Feuillantines or of certain poems of *Les Contemplations. Le Sang* also reveals the influence of Victor Hugo, but the longest tale in the collection, *Aventures du grand Sidoine et du petit Médéric*, stems rather from Voltaire's philosophical stories like *Micromégas, Zadig,* and *Candide. Celle qui m'aime,* a tale of disillusionment, is apparently completely original.

Reality, including even contemporary politics, is not absent from the *Contes à Ninon*. The correspondence of 1859–61 with Baille could easily give the impression that young Zola was totally unconcerned about such matters. Only his essay on "Progress in Science and in Poetry" and, in 1864, his comments to Valabrègue on classicism, romanticism, and realism suggest that he might have been interested in the real world. The *Aventures du grand*

Sidoine et du petit Médéric proves that he was by no means indifferent. Zola's giant, Sidoine, is stupid, but his dwarf, Médéric, is highly intelligent. They undertake, in the tradition of the philosophical tale, a long journey in search of the Realm of the Happy, in the course of which Sidoine becomes king of the Egyptians and, through Médéric, announces his program: "War abroad and peace at home." But since their neighbors are not harming or provoking them, they will "always fight for others, never for themselves." The allusion to the policy of Napoleon III is evident, for at this date he had not taken on an adversary like Prussia, but had sent his soldiers to the Crimea, to Italy, and to Mexico, to fight, in a sense, "for others." Médéric goes on to say that the policy of peace at home is more difficult to achieve, but it can be done by choosing mediocre ministers, by muzzling the press, by abolishing liberty of thought. One thinks inevitably of some of the measures adopted after the coup d'état which gagged the newspapers very effectively and deprived university professors of much of their academic freedom. By 1862–63 a little relaxation had been permitted, but not enough to vitiate Zola's satire. When Médéric states that the "true supporters of our throne, the glories of our reign, will be the stone-cutters and the masons," when he says that "we shall demolish more than build," that the city will be "razed, levelled, cleaned, whitewashed," and adds that naturally this will entail enormous cost, but that since "I am not the one to pay, the expense does not worry me," the allusion to Baron Haussmann's activities in the remodeling and the embellishing of Paris is perfectly clear. There is then in this particular *conte à Ninon* a glimpse of the future author of the *Rougon-Macquart*. Indeed, these early tales contain not only ideas which recur in Zola's later work, but themes and images as well. The forest in "Simplice" announces Le Paradou in *La Faute de l'abbé Mouret*. The role of the moon and the stars in "Sœur-des-Pauvres" forecasts certain passages in later novels. The giganticism of "Sidoine et Médéric" will be one of the sources of imagery in several of the *Rougon-Macquart*.[5]

III *Journalism*

About this time Zola became a "chroniqueur" and a literary critic. "Chroniques" were compositions written in a chatty tone on topical subjects and varied greatly with the talent and interests of the writer. Zola wrote a good many for *Le Petit Journal* and *Le Courrier du monde*. His literary criticisms appeared fortnightly in *Le Salut public* of Lyons. His purpose was twofold. He needed to make money, but he also viewed journalism as a "powerful lever," as an opportunity to make himself better known.[6]

The article devoted to *Germinie Lacerteux* in *Le Salut public* brought him into contact with the Goncourt brothers, for it constituted a vigorous defense of this "gutter-novel," as some critics had labeled it. Zola upheld the authors' right to depict the depraved side of human nature and praised them for doing it with honesty and skill. The Goncourts, of course, were delighted and wrote him a warm letter of gratitude.

This article and others in *Le Salut public*, published the following year in volume form under the provocative title of *Mes haines*, show that Zola was still reflecting fruitfully on literary and artistic questions. Indeed, it is in a discussion of Proudhon and Courbet that he first formulated the doctrine that "a work of art is a corner of nature seen through the temperament of the artist or writer."[7] This word "temperament" is emphasized in Zola's articles at this date fully as much as "realism." He understood that no two men view human existence with exactly the same eyes, and he made this fact an integral part of his literary and artistic conceptions.

IV La Confession de Claude

Meanwhile, he labored on a novel, *La Confession de Claude*, which appeared late in 1865. The first chapters were probably written in 1862, not long after the disillusioning experience with a woman of which he had written to Cézanne and to Baille in February 1861. Claude's confession is, therefore, to some extent Zola's own confession. Fiction, of course, plays its part in the composition of the novel, but the autobiographical element is considerable, a combination of the subjective and the realistic. The poverty of Claude is the poverty Zola endured, portrayed with grim realism. When the hero sends his overcoat to the pawnshop, and later has to pawn his trousers, he is doing what Zola was compelled to do in the early winter of 1861–62. The bohemian life depicted in this book is no light opera à la Puccini, but a somber episode leading to complete disillusionment. It is relieved at one point, in Chapter XXI, when Claude and Laurence, lured by the springtime, walk to Fontenay-aux-Roses and spend the night at the

Coup du milieu. For a moment, Laurence seems to respond to her lover's affection, and Claude thinks himself really loved. The chapter is based partly on the personal experience already mentioned, partly on a different and later one. Laurence is still the unknown woman of 1860–61, but in 1864 or 1865 Zola made an excursion to Fontenay-aux-Roses with Alexandrine Meley; the descriptions of external nature in the text were inspired by that episode and indicate clearly that these pages were written much later than the first few chapters.

While the book, like its two principal characters, emerges from Zola's personal life, it has literary antecedents. Michelet's volumes on *L'Amour* and *La Femme*, with their idealistic views on women and love, help to explain Claude's early idealism. Musset's *Lorenzaccio* and *La Confession d'un enfant du siècle* are obvious sources, especially in the light of Zola's well-known fondness for his work. One should add Hugo and Dumas *fils* who treated the theme of the rehabilitation of the courtesan through love. References in the novel to Marion Delorme and Didier leave no doubt that Zola had such a theme in mind. He gives it a new twist, however, for Laurence is not purified, and in the end Claude returns to Provence cured of his madness, ready to face the future with confidence. Zola, too, is mirrored in this conclusion.

Although the subject matter of this novel is realistic, the form provides as much poetry as straightforward, objective prose. Philippe Dauriac, one of the reviewers of *La Confession de Claude,* saw this quite clearly. "In spite of his frequent excursions into realism," he wrote in *Le Monde illustré,* "the author's imagination is purely poetic. Fundamentally, M. Zola is an enemy of reality. However hard he tries to reproduce the conversation of the most vulgar and abject creatures, he cannot help putting into their mouths the honey and flowers of poetry." [8] Hallucinatory and nightmarish effects confirm Dauriac's opinion. Claude's balcony view of the dancers at the ball to which he has taken Laurence is an example of the first; the window scenes in which he finally perceives the shadows of Laurence and Jacques in an embrace, of the second. Interestingly, this window scene announces a famous moment in *Nana* when Count Muffat watches Fauchery's lighted window for proof of his wife's infidelity.

During this year, Zola managed to write two plays, *La Laide* and *Madeleine.* The first appears to have been what we should call today "pure corn." Rejected by the Odéon, it was never performed or published. The other was refused by two theaters, then transformed into a novel, the original play remaining unproduced until 1889. Apart from these ventures and a short story, "La Vierge au cirage," published in *La Vie parisienne*, the year is chiefly notable for the sketches in *Le Petit Journal*, the articles in the *Salut public*, and the novel just discussed.

V   *The Free-lancer*

As 1865 came to a close, Zola faced a new problem. He was working a ten-hour day at Hachette's, and although the contacts his position gave him were extremely valuable, the hours consumed left him insufficient time for his literary labors. Furthermore, since the death of Louis Hachette in 1864, he had felt somewhat less at ease in the organization. *La Confession de Claude* was being harshly criticized; the office of the state's attorney had concerned itself with the book and had even sent a man to Hachette's to make inquiries. According to Maurice Le Blond,[9] Zola's employers were upset. Zola was also, even though the state's attorney decided that there was no reason to prosecute. For a variety of reasons, then, Zola decided to give up his position and henceforth rely on his pen. He ended his association with the publishing house on January 31, 1866. It had been a valuable experience in more ways than one, for, quite apart from the contacts provided, he had learned much about selling books while he was beginning to learn how to write them.

Before leaving Hachette's he entered into negotiations with Bourdin, the son-in-law of Villemessant. The latter was the great mogul at *Le Figaro*, then a weekly publication, and had decided to launch a daily paper to be called *L'Événement*. Zola, writing to Bourdin, suggested that he would be glad to undertake for the new publication a "Chronique bibliographique" which would announce and describe new books with interesting side lights on the authors. Villemessant and Bourdin accepted the idea. On February 1, 1866, the first of Zola's *Livres d'aujourd'hui et de demain* appeared in print.

His articles there, his long study of Taine already referred to, which appeared in *La Revue contemporaine* in February 1866, and was republished in *Mes haines*, his criticisms in *Le Salut public*, and his discourse on the novel addressed to the "Congrès scientifique de France" held in 1866 at Aix—all testify to his growing attachment to realism. Although in *L'Événement* he complimented Hugo for excluding social theories and philosophical beliefs from *Les Travailleurs de la mer,* and stated in another article that "nothing encumbers an action like a shovelful of politics or social science thrown into its midst," he also said (*L'Événement,* May 8, 1866) that he was "hard on works of pure imagination, being unable to understand the necessity for dreams when reality offers such a human and gripping interest." [10] His article on Taine emphasizes, on the one hand, the importance of individual talent: "A work of art or literature, for me, is a man; I want to find in this work a temperament, a special and unique accent"; but, on the other, it quotes with approval Taine's view of science: "science neither proscribes nor pardons, it observes and explains." Zola clearly protests against the mechanical rigidity of Taine's determinism, and he just as clearly accepts the critic's enthusiasm for the scientific method; in a later article (July 25), he declares himself to be Taine's "humble disciple."

It is, then, increasingly evident, in spite of reservations about some aspects of Taine's doctrine, that for Zola reality is the proper field for the novelist. In December of that year he offered in his communication to the scientific Congress the example of Balzac, whom apparently he had discovered only a year or two before. Balzac's "only concern is with truth, and he exhibits our heart to us on the operating-table. Modern science has presented him with the instrument of analysis and the experimental method. He proceeds like our chemists and our mathematicians: he decomposes men's acts, determines the causes, explains the effects; he operates according to fixed equations, in a factual study of the influence of environment on individuals." [11] The word "naturalistic" does not appear, but it is clearly implied.[12] It is also evident that the romantic dreamer of yesteryear has given way to the observer of life as it is, not life as it should be.

How, then, do we explain the composition of *Le Vœu d'une morte* and *Les Mystères de Marseille,* the first bearing the date of 1866, and the second, 1867? They are, particularly the latter, potboilers, written primarily to meet a financial need. The *Mystères* were published serially, at two cents a line, in the *Messager de Provence.* Zola doubtless gave as little time to it as his conscience would permit, yet the book contains occasional revelations of his literary gifts. Among other things, it includes his first description of a mob in action.[13]

Meanwhile, Zola's contacts with the world of painting had multiplied. Cézanne was in Paris, and in his studio Zola met others: Guillemet, Pissarro, Monet, as well as the art critic, Théodore Duret. Guillemet and the novelist Duranty introduced him to Manet. As early as February, 1866, Zola had begun to frequent the café Guerbois where many of this group met on Fridays. He himself received artists and writers on Thursdays in his apartment, no. 10 rue de Vaugirard, where he now lived with his mother. His association with painters was perhaps closer at this period than with novelists and poets. This doubtless explains why he got the idea of asking Villemessant to let him do some articles on the Paris *Salon*. Villemessant agreed, and Zola's first article appeared on April 27 under the transparent pseudonym of Claude. This article and the next contained a violent attack[14] on the jury system which put the fate of young artists into the hands of men unsympathetic to novelties. "What I ask of the artist," he wrote in a third *Salon*, "is not to give me tender visions or frightful nightmares; but to give himself, heart and soul, flesh and blood, to give clear evidence of a powerful and individual mind, a sharp, strong character which will boldly seize on nature and will put it frankly on his canvas as he sees it." And in his fourth and most famous *Salon* of this year, he praised Manet—the laughingstock of the conservatives, rejected by the jury—as an artist who truthfully painted reality as he saw it, in contrast to men like Gérome, Dubufe, Cabanel, who, in his view, failed to do so. The series continued with praise for Monet and acid remarks for artists like Ribot, Vollon, and Bonvin. Even Roybet, whom he liked better, he tended to damn with faint praise.[15] He summed up his ideal with his formula about a work of art being a corner of nature interpreted by the artist—a formula rapidly becoming famous.

However right Zola was, and posterity has upheld his approval of the work of Manet and Monet, many protests flowed into the offices of *L'Événement*. Villemessant finally capitulated and told Zola that the remaining articles would have to be divided with Théodore Pelloquet who was willing to compliment the painters whom Zola had attacked or ignored. So in a final *Salon*, after praising Pissarro, he said goodby to his readers, still declaring his allegiance to truth and reality. "I shall always be on the side of the vanquished," he added in a prophecy that was to be more accurate than he realized.

From early in May until perhaps September, Zola, accompanied in all probability by Alexandrine Meley, spent much time at Bennecourt on the Seine with some of his artist friends. It was a delightful experience which Zola greatly enjoyed and which he never forgot. His whole association with these men was to furnish an important section of one of his novels, L'Œuvre, nearly twenty years later; and the sojourn at Bennecourt was the inspiration of a charming chapter of the same volume.[16] The summer of 1866 was not lacking in productivity, for he spent a portion of the time on the long study of Manet which he wrote and saw printed on January 1, 1867 in the Revue du xixe siècle.

VI Thérèse Raquin

Much of this new year, 1867, was devoted to Thérèse Raquin, a novel of lust, murder, remorse, and suicide.[17] It focuses attention on a small cast of characters: on Mme Raquin, a widow with a son, Camille, a colorless frail young man, almost entirely lacking in virility, and on Mme's niece, Thérèse, whom she has taken in and brought up. The girl is healthy, robust, and sensual. When Mme Raquin succeeds in marrying the two, it is obvious that the stage is well set for drama, for here are two essentially incompatible temperaments. Mme Raquin, yielding to her son's demand to leave their provincial town for the capital, buys a small-wares shop in the Passage du Pont-Neuf, a dismal hole on the left bank in Paris, the same quarter that Balzac evoked in the first part of La Rabouilleuse.[18] Mme Raquin and Thérèse run the shop and keep house in the rooms overhead. Camille finds a job as a clerk in the offices of the Orleans railroad. The young husband one night introduces into this mediocre milieu an old acquaintance, Laurent. After pretending to study law while he dabbled in art, Laurent had finally taken a job with the same railroad, though in a different office. A vigorous, lusty young animal, his only ambitions are to work as little as possible and to enjoy the pleasures of the flesh as much as he can. The inevitable happens. One evening, while Camille goes on an errand, and Mme Raquin is downstairs in the shop, Laurent and Thérèse find themselves alone. They virtually fall into each other's arms.

With this man Thérèse finds the sexual satisfaction that her husband had been totally unable to give her. And Laurent receives from her the kind of response that previous women had failed to offer him. For a while Laurent is able to get away from the office where he works and join Thérèse in her room, but soon that becomes impossible. The idea of Camille's death then comes into their minds.

The murder is accomplished in a sham boating accident at Saint-Ouen on the Seine. It makes one think of the scene in Dreiser's *American Tragedy*, for in both books everything hinges on the "accident." Laurent and Thérèse succeed completely in their suddenly decided upon plan; the rest of the novel is devoted to a study of the effect of murder on the pair. However insensitive they may have appeared, however lacking in religious or moral restraints, murder is something so completely outside the norm, that they cannot—any more than most people—remain unaffected by it. They discover that sexual desire has vanished, drowned, as it were, in the waters of the Seine. As time goes on, fear and horror become their daily, or rather their nightly companion. In Laurent's case, the horror is enhanced by the memory of his daily visits to the morgue, immediately after the crime, until the body of Camille finally appears on the slab. He is unable to free his mind of that vision.

After months of prudent waiting, they maneuver in such a way that Mme Raquin proposes their marriage. Apparently they have achieved their aim, but they discover that fear and horror remain with them. Little by little recrimination and hatred creep in. A new horror begins with Mme Raquin's suffering when, wholly paralyzed, unable to move a muscle or say a word, she overhears their conversation and learns the truth. Soon, each sees a possible solution in murdering the other, but in a sudden though not improbable denouement, they jointly commit suicide, while Mme Raquin sits there motionless, "feasting her eyes" on their downfall.

This far from complete summary may give some slight indication of the tension that grows ever more acute in the novel. It may also suggest what Zola attempted to do. As he said in the preface he wrote in April, 1868, for the second edition: "I tried to study temperaments not characters. That is the whole of the book. I chose persons dominated by their nerves and their blood, deprived of free will, led into every act of their lives by the fatalities of their flesh." He goes on to say that his aim was "scientific above all," and explains that "given a powerful man and an unsatisfied woman," he sought by throwing them into a violent drama "to note scrupulously their sensations and their acts." He simply performed "on two living bodies the analytical work that surgeons perform on corpses." These words were written in defense of the book, for reviewers threw up their hands in dismay, notably Louis Ulbach who cried: "Putrid literature." [19] The chapter on the morgue was one important element in their reaction. But Zola was able to get consolation from a letter written by Sainte-Beuve. In spite of some harsh criticisms, the famous critic gave him encouragement and let him see that he thought him an author of talent with a promising future.

That *Thérèse Raquin* has affiliations with Flaubert's *Madame Bovary* is evident. Camille Raquin is as ineffectual as Charles Bovary and perhaps even more lacking in virility. Thérèse, like Emma, is sensual and romantic. She is even influenced by the reading of novels in somewhat the same way as was her predecessor. Sainte-Beuve said of Flaubert that in writing *Madame Bovary* he wielded his pen as a surgeon does a scalpel, and the same can be said of Zola in *Thérèse Raquin*. The differences, however, are obvious and great. Adultery in *Madame Bovary* causes trouble enough, but it does not lead to murder. By seizing on this ultimate violence, Zola is enabled to make a profoundly interesting and powerful study of its aftermath. It is even more moral in its conclusion than *Madame Bovary*, though it is no more likely that Zola planned to write a moral lesson than Flaubert did. The style, too, is different. To be sure, both writers rather frequently use the three-part periodic sentence (*la phrase ternaire*) and the so-called creative *and*, which is not a mere connective but lends a new impetus to the sentence or paragraph (known in French as the *"et" de mouvement*). But Flaubert's work contains more imagery and above all reveals that extraordinarily rhythmic, melodious, poetic style over which he labored so long. Zola's prose is clear, straightforward, and vigorous, but not musical. Sainte-Beuve reproached him for the excessive use of *vautrer* (wallow) and *brutal*. He might have added *nerfs* (nerves), *sang* (blood), *frisson* (shudder), and *chair* (flesh) to those two. All suggest a certain obsession on Zola's part with sex, tension, and violence, particularly in view of the fact that they had appeared with some frequency in *La Confession de Claude*. In *Thérèse Raquin* they testify perhaps even more to his desire to depict with accuracy a neurotic condition, for he shows us people in the grip of disorders which apparently they cannot control. But even admitting that this vocabulary is overemployed, the style in general is appropriate and adequate for the purpose.

In a sense Zola placed his novel under the shield of Taine by using as an epigraph for the second edition that famous formula: "Vice and virtue are products like vitriol and sugar." And he emphasized in the preface quoted above the scientific aim. Here and there he departs from that aim, as when he interjects, at the beginning of Thérèse's liaison with Laurent, the remark that "she knew she was doing evil"; or when, at the end, the pair burst into tears, "thinking of the filthy life they had led and would go on leading, if they were cowardly enough to stay alive." Yet, on the whole, the presentation is objective; and Zola is justified in placing himself in the category of Naturalistic novelists.

Over and above the Naturalistic method and manner, the book contains literary phenomena worthy of note. The part played by light and dark is only partially Naturalistic. The dim daylight in the Passage du Pont-Neuf and the shadowy effects there at night under the gaslights create a sort of devitalized place where gloom and horror can easily reign. The comparison of the Thursday evening guests in the fourth chapter to a collection of mechanized corpses in a cave moving their arms and legs on strings is striking in itself, and made more so by the yellow light cast on them by the dining-room lamp. The comparison reinforces the notion of death already suggested in the early presentation of Camille as sickly and almost moribund. The whole chapter on the morgue goes far beyond the absolute requirements of the narrative and helps create the mood of terror and dread which the author needed. In the eighteenth chapter the image of the prison chain binding the murderers together, though more banal, is effective. The role of the cat, François, first as witness of the liaison, then as an observer of the murderers' nuptial night, inspiring in Laurent the hallucination that Camille had entered into the animal, and the violence finally committed on the poor beast—all this is an invention beyond the Naturalistic. As much can be said of Laurent's paintings. Before the murder he had done from life a portrait of Camille which gave him the "greenish face of a drowned man." Like the cat, this portrait is present during the nuptial night and helps to make it a night of horror. The pair are so affected by this experience as well as by the memory of the murder that a few nights later, when they finally get into bed together, they have the sensation that Camille's corpse is actually present between them. Then, some portraits painted later by Laurent, not intended as portraits of Camille, superior artistically to the earlier one, all recall his drowned victim. It takes other gifts than those of mere realism or naturalism to successfully include material of this type. Perhaps the most noteworthy phenomenon of all is that involving the wound inflicted on Laurent by Camille as his supposed friend hurled him into the waters of the Seine. The scar is magnified by the author so that it becomes in the latter part of the book something awful and frightening, almost a living thing boring, biting into Laurent, filling him with fear and terror. This, like the role of the cat and like the portraits, is the invention of a poet rather than a Naturalistic novelist. The wound may also be viewed, as Professor Lapp suggests, as a "stigma" or "brand of guilt" of the type found in the Gothic novel of the last century.

Thérèse Raquin, while not quite the masterpiece that some critics have called it, represents a tremendous advance over Zola's previous writings. One may already say of it what Anatole France said of one of Zola's later novels: "It is not an agreeable book, but it is a powerful one."

VII   Madeleine Férat

Madeleine Férat, Zola's next novel, is not particularly "agreeable" either. Although it is not lacking in power, it is much less successful than *Thérèse Raquin.* Perhaps the reason is that Zola, rather surprisingly, had not got Michelet's *L'Amour* out of his system. His dislike of promiscuity and lewdness, revealed in his early letters, led him, as has been shown, to respond to Michelet's idealism concerning love. At the same time, the obsession with sex which underlies the two previous novels underlies *Madeleine Férat* also. But the new novel is built on a special theory which Zola found in *L'Amour,* namely, that when a woman has given herself to a man and especially when she has been impregnated by him, she belongs to him for all time. Even his death and her remarriage will not destroy the physical bond. "Impregnation transforms her permanently," wrote Michelet. "Frequently a widow gives her second husband children who resemble the first." [20] Michelet claimed to have found this notion in Dr. Lucas' work on heredity.[21] Whether Zola turned to Lucas at this date is not known; he certainly perused the book not much later. In any case, if we examine the section in Lucas' volume cited by Michelet, we discover that Lucas was far from positive about the application of this principle of impregnation to higher animals and to human beings. It seems likely, therefore, that Zola took Michelet's statement on faith without checking his source.

Madeleine Férat is Zola's first attempt to apply science to the novel. Unfortunately for him, the concept adopted was neither credible nor scientific. But even if the theory were true, *Madeleine Férat* would still not be a good novel; for the coincidences on which the action is based seem to the reader beyond the bounds of probability. That Madeleine's former lover, Jacques, should turn out to be the intimate friend of her second lover and husband, Guillaume; that Guillaume and Madeleine should become lovers in exactly the same room of a country inn on the outskirts of Paris where she had slept with Jacques; that after their marriage Madeleine and Guillaume should find themselves at a critical moment in a hotel bedroom she had once occupied with Jacques—such coincidences support the contention of the French classicists, which they attributed to Aristotle, that tragedy should treat only what the public will accept as credible. When we add that Madeleine's child by Guillaume resembles her former lover Jacques—by whom, incidentally, she had never been impregnated —and that the child dies at the precise moment when Madeleine, irresistibly drawn to her former lover, finally gives herself to him, the unbelievable theory combined with the unlucky coincidence makes it quite impossible to view the book as a piece of scientific realism.

This novel, interestingly, has affiliations with the legend of the temptation of Saint Anthony, for, through the eyes of the old Calvinist Geneviève, Guillaume's aged housekeeper, Madeleine appears as a Temptress. In fact, Geneviève owns an engraving of the Temptation of Saint Anthony, in which one of the women who seek to lead the hermit astray somewhat resembles Madeleine. In Geneviève's view the poor girl becomes Lubrica, the Fatal Woman, the devourer of men.[22] The old woman, formidable in her austerity, tortures Madeleine and forecasts her doom. The denouement, which brings the suicide of Madeleine and the insanity

of Guillaume, is as terrible as many of those found in the history
of drama, from Aeschylus to Shakespeare and Racine.

Madeleine Férat was the reworking and the expansion in novel
form of *Madeleine,* a play mentioned earlier in this chapter. First
published serially in *L'Événement illustré* in 1868 under the title
of *La Honte,* the novel caused more trouble than *La Confession
de Claude.* Subscribers to the paper protested, and the state's attorney's office threatened to prosecute the forthcoming book. Zola
defended himself and his work in *La Tribune* (Nov. 29, 1868)
and in a private letter to Lacroix, his publisher, who wanted him
to agree to certain eliminations. He denied, quite justly, that the
novel was in any way immoral and stood his ground against all
pressure.

During the period when he was working on these two novels,
he continued to interest himself in art, and sought to continue his
journalistic career. The latter had its ups and downs. It had supported him well in 1866, but in November of that year
L'Événement (the daily) was abandoned, absorbed into *Le Figaro.* In December Zola was dropped from *Le Salut public.* The
year 1867 was, therefore, difficult. He had an occasional sketch or
story published by *Le Figaro, L'Illustration,* or *La Rue.* An article
on the exhibition of paintings at the great Exposition universelle
of that year was taken by *La Situation.* But without *Les Mystères
de Marseille*[23] he would have starved. In fact, he more than once
had to borrow money from friends. Fortunately, the government
of Napoleon III began to ease restrictions on the press. *Le Globe,*
founded in January, 1868, was short-lived, but before disappearing on February 16 took several articles by Zola, including a review of *La Physiologie des passions* by Charles Letourneau, a
book of some importance in Zola's intellectual development. In
April, he began to write a "chronique" for *L'Événement illustré,*
and in June he made his debut in *La Tribune* to which he was to
contribute a weekly article.[24] One important achievement of 1868,
outside the field of fiction, was the series of articles composed on
the Salon of that year, published from May 2 to June 16 in
L'Événement illustré, republished (1959) by Professors Hemmings and Niess. One whole article was devoted to Manet, and in
it Zola did not hesitate to discuss his own portrait which Manet
had painted during the preceding winter and which, with "La
Femme au perroquet," was exhibited. In the following articles Zola

eulogized Pissarro, Monet, Bazille, Jongkind, Corot, the Morisot sisters, Courbet, Boudin, and Degas. There was no mention of Cézanne, whose offerings had been refused by a jury more liberal than its predecessors. The only defense in print that Zola made of his friend had occurred the year before when Cézanne's "Grog au vin" and "Ivresse" had been rejected by the jury of that year. In 1868 the question of Cézanne was not placed before the public.

If one scans the years since Zola, an unknown youth, entered the employ of Hachette & Cie as an underling in the shipping department, his achievements in six short years are impressive. They testify to his industry, his enormous capacity for work, his pride and ambition, his determination and perseverance, his strength. Jules Vallès recalled his first meeting with Zola in 1864 at Hachette's. They talked, among other things, of the future, and Zola asked him bluntly: "Do you feel yourself to be a power?" Whatever Vallès may have replied is not recorded, but Zola then said: "Speaking for myself, I feel I am one." [25] This is surely a key to Zola's character as well as an explanation of his extraordinary transformation in the 1860's. The discouraged youth observed in the correspondence of 1861 has been replaced four years later by the confident young man who writes to Valabrègue: "I am in this feverish period when events sweep you along; every day, my position is better outlined; every day, I take a step ahead." Again, in 1867, which was not a good year for him, he writes: "I like difficulties, impossibilities. Above all, I like life, and I believe that production of any kind is always preferable to repose. These are the thoughts which will cause me to accept all the struggles that may be offered me, struggles with myself, struggles with the public." [26]

In these short years he had met Taine, Michelet, About, Duranty, Vallès. In December of 1868 he finally made the acquaintance of the Goncourt brothers who recorded in their *Journal* that from this "ultra-nervous," "anxious" fellow there burst forth "a vibrant note of bitter determination and raging energy." He had made more friendships among the artists than among the writers. But by the end of 1868 he was well known in Paris and viewed as a man to be reckoned with. He had begun his climb up the ladder.

The transformation that had come over his personality is reflected in his work. The poet has become a writer of prose. The author of fairy tales has turned to adultery and murder for themes. From "La Fée Amoureuse" to *Thérèse Raquin* the distance in time is short, but in mood and presentation, immeasurable. The young man's theories about literature have moved more and more clearly in the direction of realism. In *Thérèse Raquin* he sought to analyze his characters truthfully, to show how their behavior responded to essentially physiological stimuli. What he needed to do now, he said in the illuminating preface composed for the second edition, was "to view society with a wider vision," to "paint it in its multiple and varied aspects." This final step he was soon to take.

CHAPTER 3

Theories—Plans—Methods

FOR Émile Zola, full of passion and energy, determined to make his way to the top, the winter of 1868–69 was a period, not only of journalistic activity, but of reflection and decision. Instead of continuing to produce isolated novels, he paused to take stock. He wanted to do something much more significant, something large scale, something spectacular, "de grandes machines," as he expressed it to Edmond and Jules de Goncourt on December 14, something that would be as impressive as Balzac's achievement, yet different. With the example of the *Comédie humaine* before him, he evolved the concept of *Les Rougon-Macquart, histoire naturelle et sociale d'une famille sous le Second Empire.*

The influences he had undergone were now to bear fruit. That of Balzac scarcely needs elaboration. It has been noted that in 1866 he had held Balzac up for admiration. In May, 1867 he wrote to Valabrègue: "Have you read all of Balzac? What a man! I am re-reading him. He overwhelms the entire century. Victor Hugo and the others, as far as I am concerned, shrink in comparison." Flaubert's *Madame Bovary* naturally pleased him. In 1866, disappointed by a book he was reviewing, a book which bore the subtitle *Scènes de la vie réelle,* he reread a bit of *Madame Bovary,* explaining that he "had been promised a real-life story" and "was not to be cheated of one." In another article published that year (August 25, 1866), there is a eulogy of Flaubert as a skilful analyst who has probed the depths of human nature.[1] By 1868 he had also come under the spell of Stendhal whose clear-sighted logical analysis he admired. He even, in a moment of infidelity to Balzac, called him France's "greatest novelist."[2] But other influences contributed to Zola's evolution. Hippolyte Taine was still an important force in his thought; for his doctrines, disavowing the older concepts of spontaneity and inexplicable genius, declared that psychological characteristics are not miracles or mysteries, but explainable phenomena. In later years the novelist spoke of the impact that Taine's writings had made on him: "When I read him the theorist and positivist within me was developed. I can say that I have used his theory on heredity and environment, that I have applied it in the novel." [3]

By 1868 he had surely dipped into Darwin whose ideas on selectivity and evolution impressed him as they did many of his generation. He had recently reviewed Letourneau's *Physiologie des passions*. Maintaining that the mysterious of today is the known of tomorrow, Letourneau defined passion as being "violent and enduring desire," and gave striking quotations from the letters of Héloïse and Abélard and from those of Mlle de Lespinasse to her lover which showed the extreme lengths to which passion could go.[4] The book undoubtedly reinforced the notion that psychological traits are explicable; from that point of view it could not fail to impress the planner of the *Rougon-Macquart*. Nor could its pages leave indifferent a man who later described himself as a "passionné." [5] But Zola was even more interested in Dr. Lucas' *Traité de l'hérédité naturelle*, which he had first heard of, it will be remembered, in connection with his reading of Michelet's *L'Amour*. As will shortly be seen, he now turned to it in earnest. Whether or not he read Auguste Comte, he could not fail to be influenced by the latter's positivist philosophy, which by this date had won wide acceptance and was part of the intellectual atmosphere.

Paul Alexis relates that Zola went almost every day to the Imperial Library where he diligently read books on physiological and natural history. He had long been impressed by science, as the little essay on "Progress in Science and in Poetry," mentioned in the first chapter, indicates, and held the opinion that science should not be ignored in the creation of truth. In 1868, he was less attracted by Cuvier and Geoffroy Saint-Hilaire, the famous natural scientists who had interested Balzac, than by Darwin and Lucas, especially the latter. Lucas' treatise seemed to buttress and support the scheme that was forming in his mind. Since heredity could be made to play an interesting role, he gradually came to the decision that he would relate the history of a single family rather than try, like Balzac, to depict all of society in innumerable volumes. His work would thus have greater cohesion and concentration than the *Comédie humaine*, where the multiple volumes were tied together, to be sure, by a number of recurring characters and by a specific historical period, the Restoration and the reign of Louis-Philippe, but nevertheless produced a less unified effect than the author perhaps intended. At the same time, Zola proposed to achieve breadth by not limiting himself to one generation of his chosen group. Through descendants, direct and collateral, he would be able to evoke much of France during the period selected for study: the reign of Napoleon III. The worlds of politics, art, commerce, labor, and religion could be scrutinized while he recounted the career of a given member of the Rougon-Macquart tribe. In comparison with Balzac's, it was an original scheme.

Theories

Zola's thoughts on his project are contained in three manuscript documents preserved in the Bibliothèque Nationale: "Notes on the general trend of the work," "General notes on the nature of the work," and "Differences between Balzac and myself." [6] In the second of these he tells himself that he should "choose, above all, a philosophical tendency, not in order to exhibit it, but so that it may link my books together. The best would perhaps be materialism, that is to say the belief in forces about which I need never be explicit. The word *force* does not compromise me. But I must not use the word *fatality*, which would be ridiculous in ten volumes." The force chosen by Zola is heredity, modified, however, by the influence of environment. His series will have "two elements: (1) the purely human, physiological element, the scientific study of a family with the inevitable consequences and the fatalities of its lineage; (2) the effect of the modern era on this family, its breakdown through the ravaging passions of the epoch, the social and physical action of the environment." [7]

As for Balzac, Zola was thoroughly aware of the gulf that existed between his work and his conservative principles. Two articles published in 1869, one in *Le Rappel* (May 13), the other in *La Tribune* (Oct. 31), call attention to this dichotomy. "Balzac, the royalist and the Catholic, worked for the Republic, for the free societies and religions of the future. [. . .] Balzac chastises the aristocracy ruthlessly. He shows it on every page as impotent, dying, rotting. [. . .] [He] is no gentler toward the middle class. [. . .] A hundred times he has shown the limited, narrow mentality of this class, he has implied that by itself it was incapable of founding anything of enduring value." [8] Zola clearly saw that, for all of Balzac's admiration of the *Ancien Régime* with its privileged classes, his pitiless picture of the upper strata of society led to their condemnation in the mind of the reader. No such conflict, even unconscious, bothered the budding novelist of 1868. He was already republican in sympathy and humanitarian in outlook. Yet in his third document, "Differences between Balzac and myself," he claimed that he intended to avoid all propaganda: "My work will be less social than scientific. [. . .] Instead of having principles (royalty, Catholicism), I shall have laws (heredity, innateness[9]). I do not want, like Balzac, to influence the affairs of men, to be political, philosophical, moralistic. [. . .] A simple exposition of the facts concerning a family, showing the inner mechanism which makes it function."

But he recognized that he could not, indeed, would not avoid the exceptional. In the "General notes on the nature of the work" he said as much: "In the studies I wish to undertake, I shall scarcely be able to depart from the exceptional. These special creations are, besides, more those of an artist, using the word in its modern sense. It seems too that in abandoning the universal, the work acquires superiority (Julien Sorel); there is personal creation, artistic effort. The work gains in human interest what it loses in current reality. I ought, therefore, to create exceptional characters as Stendhal does, avoiding extreme monstrosities, but choosing particular cases of psychological and physiological interest." Balzac's exceptional characters, like Grandet, Goriot, and Hulot are not produced by their environment. They were born with the capacity or trait which, feeding on itself, becomes a kind of madness, whereas Stendhal's heroes and heroines, as F.W.J. Hemmings suggests, "are made to behave extraordinarily by the stresses of their environment." [10] Zola appears to prefer the Stendhalian hero, but in fact both types will make their appearance in his saga. Nor, as will be seen, will he always avoid "extreme monstrosities." Furthermore, these characters will often be presented in highly dramatic situations, for he adds: "Don't forget that drama catches the public by the throat. Readers get angry, but they do not forget. Always give them, if not nightmares, at any rate excessive books which stick in their memory." By "excessive" Zola clearly meant books that go to extremes, that are frequently violent, and magnify beyond the average and the normal.

These reflections, aided by his reading of Dr. Lucas, account for some of the structure and nature of the *Rougon-Macquart*. The family stems from a hysterical ancestress, Adélaïde Fouque, who marries a gardener by the name of Rougon. She has a son by him, is promptly widowed, and soon after takes a lover, the smuggler Macquart. She ultimately dies in an insane asylum in 1873. Some twenty descendants of Adélaïde cross the pages of Zola's novels. He classified these people according to the information that he culled from Lucas' *Traité de l'hérédité naturelle*, which declared that the complex phenomenon of heredity manifests itself in diverse ways. Sometimes a child will inherit his physical or moral traits exclusively from his father, sometimes from his mother. Lucas' term for this type of heredity is *election*. Again, there may be *mixture* (*mélange*), achieved by *fusion, dissemination,* or *soldering* (*soudure*). But now and then, through *combination* (*combinaison*), a new type is formed. When that happens we are in the presence of *innateness* (*innéité*). The phenomenon of *innéité* is in a class by itself; but the others may logically occur either in the direct line or collaterally, and sometimes they may skip a generation. All this and more is discussed in Lucas' work, which fills two thick volumes. Zola noted the basic concepts, but he was a good enough artist to avoid using Lucas' jargon in his novels, except for a passage in *Le Docteur Pascal*, the last of his series. With that noteworthy exception, he rarely uses such words as *election, dissemination, soldering*. In most of the novels they do not appear at all. On the other hand, he does make full use of them in the family tree which he concocted and which was first published in *Le Bien public* on Jan. 5, 1878. Heredity is of importance in the *Rougon-Macquart*, but it must not be forgotten that environment is equally so. Indeed, in several cases environment seems much more powerful.

Treated also in these preliminary reflections is the artistic question. Zola tells himself that since other writers have successfully used "analysis of detail," he must adopt the "solid construction of masses." His chapters must be logical and full of driving power, "piling up on each other like superimposed blocks." The given novel, and indeed the whole series, must be animated by "the breath of passion, running from one end of it to the other." [11] Here in germ are the notion and the technique which will impart tremendous power to the series and give to some of the volumes their epic quality.

Combined with what he had written earlier, these preliminary notes contain essential elements of the Naturalistic novel. The word "Naturalistic" does not appear in them, nor is there any reference to "experimentation." He had used "Naturalism" sparingly till now. From this date on it comes more frequently to his pen. He later explained that he adopted it because he felt that "the word *naturalism* widened the domain of observation." [12] As for experimentation, it was several years later in 1880 that Zola published *Le Roman expérimental,* in which he made use of Claude Bernard's *Introduction à la médecine expérimentale* (1865). In all probability he had not read that book until 1878 and by then he had published seven novels of his series. It is, however, worth while at this point to anticipate matters a bit and summarize the views contained in that famous, perhaps too famous essay. Like Bernard, Zola states his belief in both observation and experiment. "The novelist," he writes, "is part observer, part experimenter. As observer he collects the facts, sets the point of departure, establishes the solid ground on which the characters will walk and the phenomena be developed. Then the experimenter appears and institutes the experiment, I mean, causes the characters to move in a given story in order to show that the succession or order of facts will be such as is required by the determination of the phenomena under study." [13] Zola goes on to say that Balzac, whom he inevitably invokes, for he viewed him as the father of the Naturalistic novel, gives in *La Cousine Bette* a good example of the kind of experimentation in which the Naturalistic novelist is interested. "The general fact observed by Balzac is the destruction caused in himself, in his family, and in society by a man's sensuality. As soon as he chose his subject, he (Balzac) set forth from the observed facts, then instituted his experiment, subjecting Baron Hulot to a series of tests, placing him in certain situations to show the functioning of the mechanism of his passion." *La Cousine Bette* is "simply the written report of an experiment which the novelist conducts in full view of the public."

Furthermore, Zola then states, "the idea of experiment involves the idea of modification. [. . .] To show the mechanism of the facts we must produce and direct the phenomena; there lies our share of invention and genius." [14] The novelist "operates on characters," as "the chemist and physicist operate on inanimate bodies and the physiologist on living ones."

But what about heredity, which has, according to Zola, "a great influence in the intellectual and emotional manifestation of man"? Can anything be done about it? Zola does not go into the details of genetics, but his essay implies that if men are aware of hereditary laws, they can, by arranging appropriate marriages, improve the race. And environment, which he also judges to be of capital importance, must not be neglected. It not only helps to shape man, but it can be modified in turn. "Man is not alone," he writes, "he lives in society, in a social setting, and therefore for us novelists this social setting continually modifies the phenomena. Indeed our great study lies there, in the *reciprocal* effect of society on the individual and of the individual on society." [15] The Naturalistic novel, after explaining man on the basis of his heredity and his environment, will show him "living in the social setting which he himself has produced, which he modifies every day, and in the bosom of which he experiences in turn a continual transformation." [16] Therefore, says Zola, the Naturalistic novelist is an "experimental novelist," a "practical sociologist." [17] He is, in short, far more than a laboratory technician; he becomes a social reformer. This seems to be in conflict with his earlier statement that he did not wish to influence men. What Zola presumably means is that, whereas he does not wish to preach or propagandize in the fashion, say, of Dumas *fils*, he hopes his work will have a social effect, that by its presentation of a given situation, social action may follow.

The notion of applying the methods of the natural sciences to the novel is easy enough to criticize. The scientist observes phenomena which he does not create. Even when he is experimenting, he is using something which existed before he entered his laboratory. On the other hand, both environment and human beings are created by the novelist, even allowing for the fact that he may have carefully collected observable data beforehand. Few scholars and critics have been willing to accept the doctrines set forth in *Le Roman expérimental*. And, in truth, Zola did not let himself be bound by them. Fortunately, he was much more independent than this essay would imply. While he sought to integrate reality into his literary work, using for that purpose observation and documentation, the role of temperament which he had emphasized in his earlier writings remained as important as ever. *Les Rougon-Macquart* are not the product of a machine-like creature functioning in a laboratory; they are the work of an artist.

I *The Plan*

In 1866–68 Zola was naturally armed with the theories of 1866–68, not those of 1878–80. Guided by the earlier notions, he drew up a fairly detailed plan, which he submitted to his publisher Albert Lacroix. He proposed to write two novels a year so that the series could be completed in five. The first of his ten novels would have as subject the coup d'état of 1851 as it affected a provincial town. It would be followed by a novel on the stupid, dissolute life of the gilded youth of the time. The third would deal with the shady, unbridled financial speculations of the Second Empire and would center on Auguste Goiraud (later, Aristide Rougon). The fourth would have as its setting the world of politics and as its hero Alfred Goiraud (later, Eugène Rougon). This would be followed by a book on the religious hysteria of the period. Numbers six and seven would deal respectively with the Italian war and with the proletariat, the latter concentrating on the degradation of the Paris worker under the influence of drink. Then would come a novel on the demimonde, the heroine of which would be Louise Duval (later, Nana). The last two would be devoted, in the first case, to the world of art, with Claude Duval (later, Claude Lantier) as hero, and in the other, to the courts and the question of hereditary crime.[18] As anyone who has ever dipped into *Les Rougon-Macquart* knows, this ambitious scheme was to be profoundly modified and greatly expanded. By 1871 he had added seven more books, though one of these was never to be written.[19] In its final, revised, and again expanded form, the series contains twenty novels, the last being published in 1893. But for the moment Lacroix was favorably impressed and agreed to advance Zola five hundred francs a month for a trial period of two years.

II *The Method*

So Zola set to work. This brings us to the question of method. Much has been written about it, and there has been a tendency to attribute to Zola a greater rigidity of method than really existed. One can say that by and large Zola began with a very general subject and a character from his chosen family. He put down on paper statements about this character and this subject, introducing additional characters as he wrote, developing the action of the novel, even including some of the scenes and episodes he ultimately used, but insisting above all on the general theme and its social implications. This first, primitive outline he called the *Ébauche*. In that of *La Curée*,[20] after sketching his principal character, Aristide Rougon, later dubbed Saccard, as a speculator and spender on the grand scale, Zola tells himself not to forget that his novel is "the vigorous picture of the unleashing of appetites and rapid fortunes." He then proceeds to rough in the relations of husband, wife, and stepson, leading to the fact of incest. In the *Ébauche* of *Le Ventre de Paris* he states that "the general idea is the belly, the belly of Paris" and by extension that of the bourgeoisie digesting its pleasures and achievements.[21] One of the principal characters will be a Macquart, Lisa Macquart, who embodies this bourgeois self-satisfaction. *Germinal* is presented in its *Ébauche* as being "the uprising of the wage-earners, the blow dealt to a society which for a moment breaks apart: in a word the struggle between capital and labor."[22] Here the chief character is to be Étienne Lantier, with a tainted heredity from the Macquarts; his rivalry with another wage-earner for a girl will constitute one of the important, though not major, actions of the book. The preliminary outline of *Nana* forecasts that this novel is to be the "poem of male desire," and this descendant of the Macquarts, the ferment which brings about the "decomposition of our society."[23] The word *poem* is again used by Zola in the *Ébauche* of *La Terre* when he says that he wants to write "the living poem of the land."[24] He even uses it in connection with his department-store novel: "I want to compose the poem of modern activity."[25] In general, therefore, the various *Ébauches* set the theme and to some extent the atmosphere, introduce characters, suggest some of the lines of action and even some detailed incidents; often they contain a statement or hint of a symbol or myth which may be developed in the finished work. The poet and the realist in Zola are both visible in his *Ébauches*.

Zola frequently began his documentation before the *Ébauche* was completed, and occasionally interrupted these labors to visit the area which he had chosen for the locale of his book. Direct observation plays a considerable part in the composition of *Les Rougon-Macquart*. His firsthand knowledge of Aix-en-Provence and the surrounding villages buttresses *La Fortune des Rougon*, *La Conquête de Plassans*, *La Faute de l'abbé Mouret*, and *Le Docteur Pascal*. Plassans, where the action of three of these novels takes place, is the town where Zola spent his youth; and the setting of *La Faute de l'abbé Mouret* is in the nearby area. When he was planning *Le Ventre de Paris*, he visited the central markets (*les halles*) of Paris, notebook in hand. A strike which broke out at Anzin on Feb. 21, 1884 led him to drop his *Ébauche* of *Germinal* and go to see what was happening in that mining section. In preparing to write *La Terre* he spent five days in La Beauce, one of the important agricultural regions of the country. Before writing *La Bête humaine*, he got permission to ride in a locomotive from Paris to Mantes. He paid a visit to the battlefield of Sedan while planning his great war novel, *La Débâcle*.

The dossiers of *Les Rougon-Macquart* preserved in the National Library contain the *Ébauches* and a great many other notes, as well as the manuscripts of the novels. One set of notes bears the label, *Personnages*. They are preliminary portraits of the characters, some of which had been mentioned in the *Ébauche*, sometimes by name, sometimes anonymously. Occasionally they were not created until after the *Ébauche* was completed, and the portraits were usually not penned till somewhat later. The portraits give the physical appearance, the age, the character, the health, the past history of each person. In the case of members of the Rougon-Macquart family, hereditary traits are included. They even contain now and then references to some action or incident to be incorporated in the novel.

The dossiers also include a brief Plan and then, as a rule, two detailed Plans, chapter by chapter. The brief plan gives only thumbnail outlines of individual chapters. The substance of each chapter is usually found in the first detailed plan, though the material is often set down without regard for the exact order in which it will appear in the finished product. The second plan rearranges and coordinates the data of the earlier plan, correcting it, and adding new material when desirable. While both sets represent a labor of organization more than of creation, there is nearly always, naturally enough, an advance toward perfection from the short, summary outline through the first detailed plan into the later one.

Zola's documentation, as distinct from direct observation, was achieved in two ways, by personal research and by the exploitation of friends and acquaintances. More than once Paul Alexis, Gabriel Thyébaut, and Henry Céard[26] put special information at his disposal. As Zola acquired fame, other persons volunteered factual details for his forthcoming novel, for after his first great successes, the general subject of the next book of the series was frequently announced in the press. But the bulk of the documentation was done by Zola himself, the principal sources being technical studies and the newspapers. Hours were spent in the National Library, still more in his own study where he pored over books which he had bought or borrowed, taking rapid notes, which carefully included page numbers for ready reference. Some of the novels are heavily documented, but there is no indication in the work-sheets or in the finished product that the original concept of the novel was seriously modified by the documentation. The *Ébauche* told him what to look for in the works and newspapers he consulted, so that in general he took from them only what he needed. While now and then he was led by his source material to incorporate into his novel something that he otherwise might not have thought of, it is fair to say that he was not enslaved by his research. Any modification of his earliest concept of a novel was usually due to second thought and sounder judgment. Furthermore, what emerges above all from the work-sheets is Zola's concern for the novel as such. In any conflict between theory or documentation on the one hand, and art on the other, the latter wins out. It can again be said that even after 1879 Zola did not let himself be bound by the doctrines of *Le Roman expérimental*.

If he was methodical in the planning and composition of his novels, he was equally so in his daily life. Avoiding the fantastic ways of Balzac who wrote after midnight for hours on end, stimulated by large quantities of strong black coffee, Zola set himself a more rational schedule. By half past nine or ten o'clock in the morning he was at his desk where he labored steadily till twelve-thirty or one. Sometimes he was taking notes, writing an *Ébauche*, or outlining a chapter; sometimes he was writing his novel. In the latter case he produced three to five pages a day of modest format. He early adopted the old Latin maxim, *nulla dies sine linea,* and stuck to it scrupulously. The afternoon was occupied by his journalistic commitments. These ceased after a number of years, but he still spent a portion of the afternoon on his correspondence. Late in the day he exercised, usually going for a walk. After dinner, reading and conversation filled the evening.

All his careful planning and his systematic work schedule certainly helped in the final redaction of his novels, which was nevertheless by no means an easy or mechanical task. It was here that the true work of creation took place, here that characters took on life, here that dialogue was written, here that the setting was evoked with whatever color and form were required, here that symbols were developed. Qualities of pace, vision, insight, imagination, and balance were needed to give the novels literary value, qualities which fortunately Zola possessed. As more than one critic has seen, he was endowed with power, and he was able to impart this power to his text. Not all of the *Rougon-Macquart* are great, but few are negligible; and the series contains a half-dozen masterpieces.

III *Journalism Again*

Meanwhile, Zola had to earn his living, and for this he depended on his journalistic articles. Apart from his *Salons* in *L'Événement illustré,* mentioned in the preceding chapter, his contributions were welcomed in *Le Gaulois, La Tribune,* and *Le Rappel.* All three were organs of the opposition to the government of Napoleon III, especially the last two; *Le Gaulois* was only mildly critical. Among the articles written by Zola are many on literary topics: shrewd comments on Sainte-Beuve, Balzac, and Flaubert; a long analysis of the Goncourts' most recent novel, *Mme Gervaisais;* a discussion of moral literature in which he, not surprisingly, takes the position that people are not likely to be either saved or corrupted by the fiction they read; a treatment of the question of poetic inspiration which places him squarely on the side of those who wish poets to seek their subjects, not in the remote past, however magnificent, but in the modern world. Beside these articles are others that forecast in one way or another aspects of his future novels. His attacks on the activities of Baron Haussmann, who had been entrusted by Napoleon III with the task of renovating Paris, foreshadow *La Curée;* his discussion of contemporary novels which treat the problem of the priest who has the misfortune to fall in love announces *La Faute de l'abbé Mouret;* an article on the decadence of society anticipates pages of *Nana* by twelve years; a review of Blache's *Histoire de l'insurrection du Var en décembre 1851* contains sentiments similar in tone to those expressed in *La Fortune des Rougon.* While he wrote a number of *chroniques* without social or literary significance, which merely evoked some aspect of Paris, the Tuileries gardens, for example, or the squares and cemeteries of the capital, others, like the review of Blache's book, clearly revealed his political and religious liberalism. When Queen Fatouma of Moheli, one of the Comore islands near Madagascar, visited Paris in 1868, Zola addressed an open letter to her in which he satirized, among other things, standing armies, the recent ill-fated Mexican adventure, the administrative departments of the government, censorship, the extravagant construction of the Opera house; he advised her to go incognito to the working-class quarters of the city where she would see much poverty as well as courageous endurance. An article composed in May of 1869 concerning the suggested canonization of Joan of Arc is both satirical and anticlerical in tone and phrasing.[27]

These contributions of 1868–69 reveal not only greater social and political liberalism on Zola's part than was perceptible five years earlier, but a firmer style. Any detailed discussion with supporting evidence would entail the use and analysis of the text in French. To treat style by means of a translation is impossible. It is, therefore, necessary simply to say that by 1868–69 Zola had made notable progress as a writer. He was learning when and how to be concise, when and how to use the hammer or the pinprick; he was learning to be mocking or serious, cynical or nostalgic; he was discovering when to use the periodic sentence and when not to, when to be literary and when popular, even colloquial. He had learned the value of epithets and much about their effective use. These reviews, "chroniques," and sketches show that in the closing years of the Second Empire, the mature, passionate, robust style of Zola was being forged on the anvil of journalism.

CHAPTER 4

Frustrations and Accomplishments

From La Fortune des Rougon to Son Excellence Eugène Rougon

DURING the last two years of the Second Empire, Zola continued his journalistic labors, writing for such papers as *Le Gaulois, La Tribune, Le Rappel,* and, most important of all, *La Cloche.*[1] But he also began work on his newly planned series. In all probability he started to write *The Rise of the Rougons* in May, 1869. By September, when Antony Valabrègue brought Paul Alexis to meet his old friend, the bulk of the novel was completed, and Zola charmed them both by reading the opening pages aloud. *Le Siècle,* a paper with a much larger circulation than those to which he was contributing, had agreed to print the book in serial form. It was hoped publication would begin in October, but one delay after another ensued, so it was not till June 28, 1870, that the first instalment appeared.

Meanwhile, private preoccupations were giving way to anxiety about public events. Difficulties between France and Prussia led unfortunately to war, which was declared on July 19, 1870. Both before this declaration and after, Zola's newspaper articles left no doubt of his attitude. He was clearly hostile to the policies of Napoleon III, and, as war came closer, he expressed his views with increasing violence. Finally, on August 5, in an article entitled "Vive la France," published in *La Cloche,* he openly declared that "fifty thousand soldiers on the banks of the Rhine" had rejected the Empire, that "they wanted no more of this terrible power which puts the fortunes and the life of the nation into the hands of one man." He denounced the "fops of official journalism who have stolen the *Marseillaise* and defiled patriotism." This was too much for the government. Two days later, Zola was ordered to court to answer charges of incitement to civil disobedience. He was saved by events which led first to the postponement of his case and then, after the defeat of Sedan and the overthrow of the *régime,* to its abandonment.

These events and the journalistic situation explain Zola's departure, accompanied by his mother and Alexandrine, from Paris in September. With military news filling the press, Zola saw that he might have difficulty in placing his "chroniques" and his book reviews. The war was going badly; the Prussians were threatening more alarmingly than before. Alexandrine was becoming terrified,[2] so Zola decided to take the two women to the South where they would be in greater security. Alexandrine had become his wife on May 31. After a liaison of nearly four years he made an "honest woman" of her. On September 7, the three left for Marseilles where he hoped to find employment if he were unable to return to the capital. As the only son of a widow he was exempt from military duty; with these two women to support, and nearsighted as he was, he could scarcely think of volunteering for the armed services. In Marseilles and in Aix he had relatives and friends to whom he could appeal.

Ambitious as ever, Zola's first decision was to found, with the help of Alfred Arnaud and the collaboration of his old schoolmate Marius Roux, a daily newspaper, *La Marseillaise*. It lasted two and a half months, from September 27 to December 16, 1870. Unfortunately no copies have survived, but other sources show that its editorial policy was vigorously republican. Foreseeing its demise, Zola sought other employment and tried to get an appointment as an assistant prefect, but he settled for a post in Bordeaux as secretary to Glais-Bizoin, one of the members of the Government of National Defense. Once again he was saved at the last minute from financial difficulties.

As soon as the siege of Paris ended and the armistice was signed, Zola was able to renew his contacts with the capital. He arranged with Louis Ulbach to write again for *La Cloche*. This time he was to report on the parliamentary proceedings in Bordeaux where the government was temporarily located. He also arranged with Émile Barlatier, an old friend of his father and editor of *Le Sémaphore de Marseille*, to do the same thing for that important Southern paper. This double collaboration lasted, in the case of *La Cloche*, till November, 1872, and in that of *Le Sémaphore de Marseille*, till May, 1877. For the former he wrote well over two hundred articles; for *Le Sémaphore*, a great many more.

If anyone wishes to know how a decent, patriotic Frenchman felt at the end of February, 1871 when the peace conditions imposed by Prussia became known, he needs only to read Zola's report.

> All my life, [he wrote], I shall remember this terrible hour. The galleries were filled with anxiety. You know the terms: the surrender of Alsace except Belfort, the cession of Metz and part of Lorraine, five billion francs to be paid in three years, the occupation of a section of Paris . . .
> The whole chamber was stupefied with grief. Angry mutterings ran through the galleries. The reading of the treaty was completed in deathly silence. From that moment on, the Assembly seemed almost crazed . . .
> When I left the Chamber, night was falling, a large crowd was standing there in the twilight, disquieted, yet eager for the bad news. I felt as if I were emerging from a burial vault and were passing through a people in mourning who had just conducted funeral services for their native land. There were no loud outcries, but the amount of the indemnity, the names of Metz and Strasbourg were being uttered in sadness and in grief. Ah, the sun has set tonight and Bordeaux has put on vestments of mourning.[3]

The tone is not only faithful to the sentiments of the time, but is a harbinger of some of the best pages of *La Débâcle*.

On March 14, 1871, Zola returned to Paris. Four days later the insurrection broke out, and the civil war of the Commune was on. One can follow the ghastly events in Zola's reports, now called *Lettres de Versailles*, either in *La Cloche* or, when that paper was temporarily suppressed, in *Le Sémaphore de Marseille*. Zola himself was independent, refusing to make common cause with either side; but he was more and more shocked by the ferocity with which the men of Versailles suppressed the Commune. When the fighting was all over, he was among the first to call for amnesty and reconciliation.

During the following months he continued his political reporting. In 1872, *La Cloche* ceased publication. For a brief time he wrote for *Le Corsaire*. His article entitled "Le Lendemain de la crise"—reprinted later with modifications as a short story called "Le Chômage"—contained such a violent attack on certain prominent members of parliament for their indifference to the problem of unemployment that the paper was promptly suppressed. When it reappeared, Zola's name was no longer among its collaborators.

In 1873 and after, his articles were limited to *Le Sémaphore de Marseille*. There, he wrote about the artistic and literary life of Paris, describing also such events as the visit of the Shah of Persia to the French capital, the laying of the cornerstone of the Sacred Heart Church (1875), the running of the Grand-Prix at Longchamp (1876), and so forth. A number of these Parisian *Letters* foreshadow scenes or themes in his novels.

I La Fortune des Rougon

In the meantime, the publication of *La Fortune des Rougon* in serial form, begun on June 28, 1870, was interrupted on August 10 by the gravity of events. Seven months later, *Le Siècle* resumed publication of the novel. As luck would have it, this coincided with the outbreak of the Paris insurrection, the last instalments appearing from March 18 to March 21. Because of national absorption in these dreadful occurrences, the impact of the serial on newspaper readers must have been slight, and the experience frustrating to the author. He could only hope for better results for the forthcoming volume. It finally came off the press in October, 1871 and included an introductory preface in which Zola announced his intention to "explain how a family conducts itself in a given society," how it "gives birth to a score of individuals who seem at first glance profoundly unlike one another" but "when analyzed are seen to be intimately linked to each other." He added, echoing Hippolyte Taine: "Heredity, like the phenomenon of weight, has its laws." He proposed to show how this Rougon-Macquart family is determined physiologically and environmentally, driven by the desires and appetites which in this modern age affect all classes of society from top to bottom. The first volume, *The Rise of the Rougons*, might well bear, he states, its scientific title: *The Origins*. The whole series is intended to "tell the story of the Second Empire [. . .] from the ambush of the coup d'état to the betrayal of Sedan."

Just because this novel is the first of the cycle and can, indeed, be viewed as an account of the origins of the family, one needs to linger over it for a moment. The narrative is linked to Louis-Napoleon's coup d'état on Dec. 2, 1851, the first step on the road to the establishment of the Second Empire. Zola relates the defeat of republican resistance, in Plassans and the surrounding area,[4] to the coup d'état, and the consequent triumph of the conservative groups, a triumph in which Pierre Rougon and his wife, prompted and guided by a son in Paris, play a shrewd part and thereby lay the foundation of their fortune. At the same time, as stated earlier, the novel introduces the ancestress of this family, Adélaïde Fouque, a neurotic, hysterical woman, subject to cataleptic seizures. Before the action of the novel begins, she had married in 1786 a gardener by the name of Rougon who became the father of Pierre the next year, and died unexpectedly in 1788. Taking then as lover a smuggler by the name of Macquart whom she never bothered to marry, Adélaïde gave birth to two illegitimate children, Antoine in 1789 and Ursule in 1791. Pierre, in 1810, married Félicité Puech who presented him with five offspring: Eugène, Pascal, Aristide, Sidonie, and Marthe. Ursule Macquart became in 1810 the wife of a certain Mouret. Three children, François, Hélène, and Silvère, were born to them. Antoine Macquart finally took as wife in 1826 Joséphine Gavaudan. They soon became the parents of Lisa, Gervaise, and Jean. These descendants of Adélaïde produced children in their turn who grace or sometimes disgrace the pages of the novels. In *La Fortune des Rougon* Zola introduces only the first and second generation of Adélaïde's descendants, and naturally concentrates on a limited number of these.

The pages devoted to genealogy were doubtless necessary but they make rather arid reading and retard the action of the book. Its fine qualities reside elsewhere: in the skilful evocation of Plassans with its class structure and layout; in the description of the Rougons' yellow salon and the machinations of its mistress, Félicité; in the beautiful, touching account of the idyllic love of Silvère and Miette and their tragic death; in the stirring narrative of the march of the republican insurgents, ill-armed, ill-led, outnumbered, and consequently doomed to defeat; in the hilarious comedy produced by Rougon's capture of a handful of republicans in Plassans while, unknown to him and his followers, the issue is being decided elsewhere, for the main body of the insurgents is crushed by Louis-Napoleon's troops at Orchères only a few kilometers away. Comedy reaches an even greater intensity in Chapter VI when Plassans undergoes three days of panic and is "saved" by Rougon who would have fled in terror without the guiding hand of his wife to restrain and direct him. These comic episodes are recounted in part with open cynicism, but also in a mock-heroic manner which satirizes without mercy or restraint these self-seeking, essentially pusillanimous, bourgeois Bonapartists.

The love idyll and the republican revolt are closely connected from the very first chapter. On a cold, moonlit evening of December, 1851, Silvère and Miette meet in an abandoned cemetery, from which most of the tombs have been removed—a convenient spot adjacent to the farm where Miette is employed, chosen by Zola not only for that reason but also because it permits him to link this pair with the idea of death from the start of his narrative. Silvère, with all the ardor of his seventeen years, announces his imminent departure for the war; and the pair set forth on a farewell walk, enveloped in the ample cloak which Miette, like other girls of Provence, frequently wore. Their moonlight stroll takes them past the houses at the end of town into the country. "Their hearts," writes Zola, "were sad, the happiness they felt at their physical closeness had all the painful emotion of a last farewell, and it seemed to them that they would never exhaust the bitter sweetness of this silence which gently cushioned their steps." They descended the road a long way down to the river, in a darkness mitigated only by the "clear, cold moon." The play of light and shade in this description constitutes one of its charms, as does the innocent love of this very youthful pair. But soon the silence of this moonlit night is broken, and moments later "a black mass appeared at the turn of the road; the *Marseillaise*, sung with avenging fury, burst forth in formidable tones." The insurgents, some three thousand strong, are on their way. The rest of the chapter is devoted to their march, and a genuinely epic touch is visible, forerunner of some of the best pages of later masterpieces. Silvère and Miette join in this march, and the chapter ends with Miette carrying the insurgents' flag, her cloak turned inside out so that its red lining is uppermost. In the brilliant moonlight, she appears to be a Virgin Liberty of flesh and blood.

The linking of the two themes continues in later chapters. Silvère and Miette are with the insurgents as they enter Plassans and momentarily take possession of the town. They are with them as the column leaves to continue its liberating and heroic march. Soon after, fatigue overcomes the girl. She and Silvère drop out; they rest by the roadside, lying innocently in each other's arms.

Death not only threatens them as it does whenever men and women go to war, but it seems to reside in their hearts beside their love. For after their first real kiss here in the semidarkness, a feeling of despair seizes them, and Silvère says, "It is better to die." And Miette repeats a moment later: "It is better to die." Zola adds:

At this desire for death, they embraced more closely. Miette expected to die with Silvère; [. . .] she felt that he would carry her joyfully with him into the earth. They would love each other there more freely than in the sunlight. Aunt Dide would die too and would come to join them. It was a kind of rapid presentiment, a strangely voluptuous wish that heaven, through the desolate voices of the tocsin [ringing in the distance], promised them to satisfy soon. To die! To die! the bells repeated this word with increasing fury, and the lovers yielded to these appeals from the shadows; they felt they were having a foretaste of their last sleep, in this somnolence created by the warmth of their limbs and the burning sensation of their lips which had just met again.

This extraordinary union of love and death is a theme that will haunt Zola the rest of his life and recur in many of his novels.

At this point, Zola indulges in a flashback which tells us the past history of Miette and her early friendship with Silvère. It is a perfectly charming narrative, written with sensitivity and poetic feeling. They first met at what is called in the French text the "puits mitoyen," a well located on the line separating Aunt Dide's property and the Jas-Meiffren where Miette was employed. The wall, which ran along this line, divided the well too. Unless they climbed the wall, the only way they could see each other was by looking at their image in the water below. Zola devotes several pages of his flashback to this delightful narrative. He relates the little "dramas and comedies of which the well was an accomplice." The episode lasted a month and contributed not a little to their growing friendship. Later, they met at night in the abandoned cemetery now used as a lumberyard, and later still, they went for walks in the darkness wrapped in her Provençal cloak. Silvère even taught her to swim in the waters of the Viorne. These innocent meetings went on for two years. "Their idyll continued through the icy rains of December and the hot nights of July, without ever descending to the shameful level of commonplace love affairs; it retained the exquisite charm of a Greek tale, its ardent purity, all its naïve, timid stirrings of the flesh experiencing desire and still unaware."

The flashback comes to an end when Miette awakes. Taking a short cut, they rejoin the ranks of the insurgents who have just entered Orchères. The rest of the chapter is devoted to the war, if one may dignify it by that name, to the brief, pathetic "battle" in which Miette is killed in the first volley, the insurgents who do not manage to escape are massacred, and Silvère is taken prisoner. He will be shot at the end of the book by a gendarme whom he had inadvertently injured earlier in the narrative.

La Fortune des Rougon is, then, a combination of several elements. It relates the defeat of popular resistance to tyranny and, in doing so, introduces here and there an epic note. It depicts in poetic terms a tragic love idyll. It includes pages of social satire which verge on uproarious comedy. It combines social and family chronicle. Except for the excessive genealogical information, all is done with skill. It is noteworthy that much takes place at night, and that Zola makes full use of the moonlight to produce varying effects. Sometimes the play of light and shadow creates sheer beauty. Sometimes it lends a bit of mystery or even hallucination to a scene. Admirable esthetic impressions result from the use of white and black in this book. Scarcely less important are yellow and red. Yellow is the color of the Rougons' salon. It is suggestive of envy, and more specifically of gold, not the gold that symbolizes perfection, but the gold that corrupts; at the end of the book when the *salon jaune* triumphs by the most dubious means, the connotation of corruption is clear. Red is represented not only by Miette's cloak but also by the blood that is spilled. On the blood of the insurgents killed by the troops, on the blood of the victims of the ambush arranged by Rougon, on the blood of Miette and Silvère, the latter slaughtered with the knowledge and consent of Aristide Rougon, is founded not only the success of the Rougons, but, in a larger sense, the edifice of the Second Empire. Born in blood, the Second Empire will die in blood. Zola does not here forecast its bloody end, but he clearly marks the quality of its beginning. All this is presented with vigor, frequently with eloquence in which effective metaphors often find their place. Little wonder that Flaubert, to whom Zola sent a copy, wrote him: "You have a rare talent."

Is *La Fortune des Rougon* a Naturalistic novel? Since it relies to a considerable extent on documentation and observation, and since it emphasizes environment and heredity, the answer must be in the affirmative. For his documentation, Zola made use of Eugène Tenot's *La Province en décembre 1851, étude historique.* For his description of Plassans and the surrounding country, the fifteen years he spent in Aix-en-Provence as boy and young man furnished him with all the material he needed. As for the question of heredity, Dr. Lucas' book must obviously be invoked.[5] The analysis of Adélaïde and her two children by Macquart derives in great part from that source. Zola even uses, in describing Ursule, a little of Lucas' jargon. And in spite of appearances, Silvère, too, partakes of this fatal heredity, for Zola attributes his ardor and his enthusiasms to nerves. He is, after all, the grandson of hysterical Adélaïde. In the novel, Dr. Pascal Rougon puts it succinctly, after listening to the boy's fervor: "Hysteria or enthusiasm, shameful madness or sublime folly. Always these devilish nerves!" But although the book is a Naturalistic novel, depending somewhat on formula, it bears the imprint of individual genius; it is a creation, the product of a temperament, not a mere assemblage. It deserves greater success than it had in 1871 or has achieved since. In 1871 the moment was not propitious, for the anxieties of the hour were still too great. In later years it has been overshadowed by the acknowledged masterpieces of the cycle.

II   La Curée

Zola's next volume, *La Curée,* has been overshadowed also, though for better reasons. The subject was one he had included in the first list of novels drawn up in 1869 for Lacroix, and he had begun to write it before *La Fortune des Rougon* appeared in book form. His journalistic articles in *La Tribune* and *La Cloche* testify to his interest in the speculation that was rampant during the early years of the Second Empire, a speculation that resulted in large part from the rebuilding of Paris under the aegis of Baron Haussmann.[6] But he was concerned also with the moral corruption which existed alongside the financial manipulations of the period. His book, as he put it in the preface to the first edition, introduces into this family chronicle the theme of "gold and flesh." He went on to state that his purpose was to show the "premature exhaustion of a race which has lived too fast and which results in the hybrid creature, the man-woman, of societies that have gone to rot," to depict the "mad speculation of an era embodied in an unscrupulous temperament," and to portray the "nervous disintegration of a woman whose native appetites are unleashed by an environment of luxury and shame." These three "social monstrosities," as Zola accurately dubs them, are incorporated in the three main characters: Aristide Rougon, called Saccard in the novel, the unscrupulous money-mad speculator of the Second Empire; Maxime, his effeminate and vicious son; Renée, his wife, the unbalanced and idle woman of the world of fashion and luxury. In addition to speculation and corruption, incest between son and stepmother is one of the themes of this book, which Zola hoped would be a "work of art and science" as well as a chapter of social history.

The serial publication of this book in *La Cloche* in 1871 caused even more trouble than *Madeleine Férat* had done a few years before. The authorities became alarmed and intervened; and as a result Zola requested Ulbach to discontinue publication. The volume itself appeared, unexpurgated, in February, 1872. The incest of Renée and Maxime undoubtedly shocked much of the reading public, particularly the scenes in Saccard's hothouse, for here the incest is deliberate and viciously enjoyed. The sensuality of the scenes is reinforced by the colors and perfumes of the exotic flowers surrounding the guilty pair. Zola's description goes far beyond the demands of realism. The flowers and Renée herself become, under Zola's pen, "flowers of evil" which Baudelaire might have appreciated and even envied, had he still been alive to read these pages.

Saccard's speculations are on the grand scale, depicted by Zola with almost an epic touch. Through the influence of his brother, Eugène Rougon, he obtains the post of "commissaire-voyer," which is somewhat equivalent to that of a highway commissioner in American municipal government. Unscrupulously using information thus acquired, and skilfully hiding behind straw men who act as buyers for him, he purchases properties at a low figure and sells them at a large profit. Sometimes they are properties slated to be razed for Haussmann's new boulevards; sometimes they are properties the value of which would increase after the construction of a new boulevard. In a short time, Saccard acquires a large fortune. The rush for spoils, the dash of the hunting pack on the carcass of the fallen animal—*la curée*, in other words—is admirably suggested by the narrative of Saccard's self-enrichment. It is a precarious fortune, however, based on speculations which do not inevitably succeed; and, as time goes on, Saccard's whole financial edifice becomes more and more fragile. It causes him— and this is one of Zola's striking inventions—to accept the relations of his son and wife whom he has accidentally discovered in a compromising posture. His need for her signature to a real estate deed is so great that the infamy of incest seems less important. To such depths do speculation and corruption lead. At the end of the book his financial situation is not only precarious but obviously close to disintegration.

Aided chiefly by documents, Zola has evoked with intuitive skill the money-mad atmosphere of the Second Empire. It is a very considerable achievement. One has the impression, however, that he was even more interested in Renée than in Saccard. Fully aware that he was writing a new *Phædra*,[7] he gave increasing importance to that aspect of his novel. Yet as a treatment of incest, it is not in the class of its illustrious predecessors in Greece, Rome, and France, for Maxime is an ignoble, degenerate creature not to be compared to Hippolytus, and Renée arouses no such compassion as Phædra inspires—not even in her death, unaccompanied by any genuine remorse. Doubtless Zola's tale is more moral than a modern treatment of the theme, Thomas Mann's short story, "The Blood of the Walsungs." In Mann's narrative, the consanguinity makes the incest more shocking than in Zola's book, and Mann's conclusion is cynical in the extreme.

As a picture of social corruption, *La Curée* is a powerful novel, even though one may feel that the Second Empire was not quite as black as Zola implies. As a portrayal of moral corruption, it is equally powerful, and the descriptions of the greenhouse with the scenes that occur in it are quite extraordinary. More than *La Fortune des Rougon*, it is one of those "excessive" books which Zola planned to write. It is a Naturalistic novel, for in addition to the *tableau de mœurs*, heredity plays a role. To be sure, it is emphasized more in the case of Maxime than in that of Saccard who seems impelled rather by the temptations that surround him than by some inherited trait. Zola had to remind himself "not to forget the matter of heredity,"[8] and the "hybrid creature," Maxime, is the result. But the novel goes beyond the limit of Naturalism and enters the realm of symbol and fantasy. The greenhouse is more than a collection of exotic plants; it is a symbol of decadence.

Saccard's manipulations are more than a series of financial operations; they finally become symbolic of speculative fury. However much Zola intended to reproduce reality, his temperament carried him beyond its confines.

III   Le Ventre de Paris

If this be true of the first two novels of the cycle, it is even truer of the third. Not that *Le Ventre de Paris* is lacking in careful observation and documentation.[9] On the contrary, Zola, faithful to his principles, not only read the relevant pages in Maxime Du Camp's *Paris, ses organes, ses fonctions et sa vie,* but visited the New Central Markets—the Nouvelles Halles centrales—notebook in hand and jotted down much of what he observed. He also linked the volume with his family chronicle through the person of Lisa Quenu, one of the children of Antoine Macquart. Married to a pork-butcher, she runs a prosperous shop with him in the quarter of Les Halles. She does not seem to have inherited any of the hysterical or degenerate features of her Macquart forebears but rather takes after her hard-working mother, Joséphine Gavaudan.

Nor is the social chronicle neglected. Florent, the half brother of Quenu, is a character who not only wins the reader's sympathy but represents the republican opposition to the Empire. Using again the method of the flashback, Zola tells us of Florent's arrest in 1851 by Louis-Napoleon's police, of his deportation to Devil's Island, French Guiana, of his subsequent escape and return to France. The opening chapter of the book shows him in starving condition, picked up by Mme François, a market-gardener, and carried into Paris on a load of carrots and turnips. Later he becomes the leader of a conspiracy against the government. If Zola intended this political plot to be taken seriously by the reader, he was not very successful, for it is inadequately developed. It serves chiefly as a means of contrasting the idealistic, naïve, ineffectual republican with the self-satisfied, materialistic bourgeois; for Lisa Quenu, who is middle class to her finger tips, finally betrays Florent to the imperial authorities.

This contrast helps also to underline one of the principal themes of the book, the war between the fat and the thin. Florent, emaciated by hunger, never puts on flesh in the course of the novel. He remains "as thin as a dry branch." Lisa Quenu, on the contrary, is well fed, plump, ample-bosomed. Quenu is even fatter than she.

They both, writes Zola, "reeked with health; they were superb, square-set, sleek; they looked at him with the astonishment of the very fat gripped by a vague foreboding when confronted by a thin human being." The title of the book naturally contributes to this antithesis, for depending on whether one's belly is habitually full or empty, one belongs to the fat or the thin. The latter are doomed to defeat; doomed, in a sense, to be "eaten" by their corpulent, well-nourished opposites. The idea is stressed throughout the narrative. In the fourth chapter, for example, the reader is told that the war of the fat and the thin goes back to the first recorded murder, for Cain was surely a fat man and Abel a thin one. Nearly all the characters of the novel are placed in their appropriate category. In the end, Florent, the thinnest of all, is "eaten" by the fat respectable people of the middle class. "What scoundrels respectable people are!" is the final sentence of the book.[10] Zola's concept of deadly conflict between the fat and the thin really cuts across class lines. Lisa Quenu and her husband may be authentic bourgeois, but it is difficult to view some of the characters whom Zola puts in the category of the fat as genuine representatives of the middle class. They may have enough to eat; but they seem, in other respects, closer to uneducated manual workers than to white-collar small-scale businessmen and women. In the author's theory of warfare between the two groups there is a certain degree of realism, though not as much as he thought; his method of presentation, however, is indubitably symbolical.

The New Central Markets were built in great part during the Second Empire, and the action of the novel appropriately takes place from June, 1858 to 1859. The Markets furnish, said Zola in the *Ébauche*, "the artistic side" of the novel with the "gigantic still lifes provided by the eight pavilions and the avalanche of food dumped every morning into the very heart of Paris." The New Markets represent an early use of iron framework in France. These girders rising high in the air and allowing a well-lighted interior because of glass panes aroused great interest. Partly to emphasize this aspect of the Markets, Zola introduced into his novel another member of the Macquart tribe, the young painter, Claude Lantier, who seems to be a kind of combination of the Dutch painter Jongkind and Paul Cézanne. Through the eyes of Lantier, who wants to treat modern subjects and would rather paint a pile of cabbage or a ragged beggar than a medieval castle, and through the eyes of Florent, the idealist, the Markets appear as a "monstrous flowering of metal whose stems, mounting spindle-shaped, and whose branches, twisting and crossing, covered a whole world with the light, graceful foliage of a century-old wood." Obviously, the Markets stimulated Zola's imagination significantly. In another passage he beholds them—through his character Florent—at daybreak:

Florent beheld the great markets emerging from the shadow of night, from the dream world where he had seen them, stretching out into the distance their palatial structure now visible to the eye. [. . .] they piled up their geometrical forms, and when the interior lights were extinguished, when the square, uniform shapes were bathed in the early light, they looked like a great modern machine, like a steam engine, a boiler destined to swallow up a whole people, a gigantic metal belly, bolted, riveted, made of wood, glass, and cast iron, endowed with the elegance and power of a mechanical motor functioning there, with the heat of its furnace, the deafening noise, the furious motion of its wheels.

The passage occurs in the opening chapter and significantly includes the word "belly" (*ventre*) which will appear again and again throughout the book. Furthermore, the Markets are transformed here into a kind of living creature, a monster, with an existence and personality of its own. This type of phenomenon will be found in some of Zola's later novels, presented in even more dramatic fashion.

Along with the pavilions themselves, Zola depicts the swarming, teeming life of the area, the incessant activity of the rue Montmartre, for example, with its interminable lines of wagons, its continual flood of people, its numerous shop windows, its shapes and colors.

In addition to the Halles and the life of the streets, the descriptions of food are fascinating, and, for many readers, of greater interest than the plot, which is slight and relatively simple. A description such as the making of blood-pudding sausage in Chapter III is essentially Naturalistic. One, like that of the fruit display of La Sarriette in Chapter V might resemble too much a catalogue-list, had Zola not taken the pains to qualify the fruit with some picturesque epithet. Or the piles of salt-water fish in Chapter III; here, again, a long list is relieved by various qualifications; dogfish, for example, are described as being "horrible, with their round heads, their widely slit mouths, like those of Chinese idols"; they are, in a word, "monsters designed to guard with their barks the treasures of marine grottoes." And the whole lot, suddenly illuminated by the sun, becomes a thing of beauty. "A shaft of sunlight, falling from a pane high above, lighted up the precious colors tenderly washed by the waves, blended and rendered iridescent in the flesh-tones of the shell-fish, the opal of the whitings, the mother-of-pearl of the mackerels, the gold of the mullets, the spangled gown of the herrings, the silver-service effects of the salmon." This goes beyond mere realism and becomes, especially in the original French, which is inevitably a little spoiled by translation, a form of poetry. So does the famous symphony of the cheeses where Zola combines color, smell, and sound in an extraordinary synesthetic impression.

Le Ventre de Paris is an original book, written, as the British critic Angus Wilson has said, on three levels: "social, moral, and sensuous." [11] It may be called Zola's first successful attempt at impressionism; and it is, at this date of 1873, the book in which Zola most closely approximated the "artistic style," the "écriture artiste," practiced by the Goncourts. At the same time, it has defects. The political plot is more comic than tragic. Very likely Zola intended this, though it leads the reader to think a little less well of Florent than he otherwise might; and one wonders whether Zola really wished to belittle a man for whom he obviously had sympathy and liking. The conspiracy may be "over-involved," as Mr. Wilson claims; but from another point of view it is poorly developed. The idyll of Marjolin and Cadine raises questions. It is quite different from that of Silvère and Miette. The new pair have little, if any, distinction of character and are linked by no perceptible ideal. When Marjolin is transformed by a blow on the head, as he unsuccessfully tries to rape Lisa Quenu, into mere animated flesh, devoid of intelligence, he becomes merely a kind of pathetic monster who inspires neither fear, nor anger, nor even interest. The whole episode involving Marjolin and Cadine "leads nowhere," if Mr. Wilson may be quoted again, and hardly justifies its existence. The critics of 1873 were less perceptive than those of the twentieth century, most of whom, in spite of reservations, see genuine merits in *Le Ventre de Paris*. Zola's contemporaries, with a few exceptions like Louis Desprez, Guy de Maupassant, and

J. K. Huysmans, were severe. The novel was published by Charpentier, who took over Zola's contract; Lacroix was bankrupt. Fortunately for the new publisher, the book sold a little better than its predecessors but was far from the great success that Zola was hoping for. Frustration still beset him.

In 1873, the Archbishop of Paris requested authorization to build a church on Montmartre, on a site overlooking Paris. A bill was introduced into the National Assembly in June, declaring the construction of such a church to be a matter of public utility. If passed, it would give the Archbishop the right of expropriation. This project led to a bitter quarrel in the Assembly and the press, for some of the more extreme conservatives wanted to include in the text of the bill the statement that the church would be dedicated to the Sacred Heart of Jesus and that it would be built in the hope that it would bring to France and to the capital "divine mercy and protection." The moderates wisely withdrew from the text any mention of the Sacred Heart and omitted any allusion to the mercy of God. Thus watered down, the bill was easily passed, for the conservative majority was large. Zola, writing for *Le Sémaphore de Marseille*, undoubtedly followed the debates and reported them briefly in his "Lettres parisiennes," but he does not seem to have had a great deal to say on the subject at this time. The construction of the church got under way a year or two later. It was still unfinished when Zola was working on his trilogy, *Lourdes, Rome,* and *Paris.* As will be shown in another chapter, it is not without significance for the last volume of that little series.

This year also saw the production at the Théâtre de la Renaissance of *Thérèse Raquin,* dramatized by Zola himself. Not all the critics were quite as severe as Sarcey, who wrote in *Le Temps:* "Thérèse Raquin is Lady Macbeth reduced to the dimensions of a shop-keeper [. . .] Everyone breathed a sigh of relief at the final curtain." To which Flaubert retorted: "The idiot goes to the theater to be amused." Other critics had a few words of praise, particularly for the wedding-night scene. In general, the play was considered inferior to the novel. It enjoyed only a brief run during the summer season, in spite of the presence of Marie Laurent, a well-known actress, in the role of Mme Raquin.

La Conquête de Plassans

Meanwhile, Zola had begun work on his next novel, *La Conquête de Plassans*, which returns, as the title indicates, to the provinces, and which introduces a character from each side of his unusual family: François Mouret, the son of Ursule Mouret (née Macquart), and his wife Marthe, the daughter of Pierre and Félicité Rougon.

For a long time Zola had been interested in the subject of insanity. In June, 1868 he had published in *L'Événement illustré*[12] a hair-raising tale in which a perfectly sane man is incarcerated on false evidence by his wife and her lover in an insane asylum. Later, when the repentant wife goes to liberate her husband, she discovers that he has become really insane. Religious mania also interested Zola. Excessive piety could lead to the unhealthy domination of a person, particularly a woman, by a father-confessor. It could even lead to a form of madness. *La Conquête de Plassans* treats these themes, for François Mouret, thought to be crazy, is shut up in *Les Tulettes*, the asylum which already holds his mad grandmother, Adélaïde Fouque. There he actually becomes insane. And his wife, Marthe, is not only dominated by her father-confessor, but has succumbed to the religious mania to which her unstable nature has made her susceptible.

This father-confessor to whom Zola gives the name Faujas introduces another theme into the novel. He is the type of ambitious, scheming, calculating, political priest who is devoid of sensuality,[13] for, as he says, "only chaste men are strong." It is he who fulfills the title of the book, for one first beholds his conquest of Mouret's house, which he enters with his mother merely as a tenant of the second floor; and then one witnesses his conquest of the town itself, to say nothing of his successful maneuvering for ecclesiastical preferment. Plassans, legitimist till now, elects a bonapartist deputy, in great part through his machinations. In the end, Faujas, his mother, his sister, and her husband perish; Mouret, escaping from the asylum, sets fire to his former dwelling and is killed with his victims in the flames, while not far away his wife dies in her mother's arms. The denouement is even more hair-raising than that of the newspaper tale of 1868.

The political and ecclesiastical intrigues are well told, and the picture of provincial society is well drawn. This aspect of the novel should not be overlooked, especially since Zola intended it to be "provincial France under the Empire." [14] In 1874, however, the book was little appreciated. There was something like a conspiracy of silence in the Paris press, for almost no attention was paid to it. About the only favorable comment came from Jules Claretie in *L'Illustration* (Oct. 31). In private letters Flaubert gave it praise, and the following year Brunetière admitted in the *Revue des Deux Mondes* that the scene of the fire was depicted with "gripping and lugubrious truth." Later still, Anatole France called attention to its truthful portrayal of small-town life. But these kind words did not help much. The book sold poorly and has remained the least read of Zola's series. It was, however, thanks to Turgenev, published serially in Russian in a St. Petersburg newspaper.[15]

IV *Literary Friendships*

Zola had met Turgenev at Flaubert's, probably at one of the latter's Sunday receptions, for the author of *Madame Bovary* welcomed his literary and artistic friends on that day. Zola and Flaubert had been friends since about 1871, though the younger man had come to Flaubert's attention earlier through the flattering article on *L'Éducation sentimentale*, which he had written for *La Tribune* in 1869. In it Zola had called Flaubert "a poet changed into a naturalist," and "a realist who draws from reality extraordinary concerts." After the war, when Flaubert acquired his apartment in the rue Murillo, the two began to see each other frequently.

Daudet had presumably been an acquaintance of Zola's since the mid-1860's, when they both wrote for *L'Événement*. The two were Southerners, which constituted something of a tie; nevertheless, their temperaments were different. Ultimately they were destined to clash, though not to the point of a complete break; but at this period they were in literary alliance. Before the year ended, Daudet was to publish his first realistic novel, *Fromont jeune et Risler aîné*, which Zola praised in an article published somewhat later as a work in which "the breath of modern life" is strongly felt.

Goncourt, Alexis, and a little later Céard, Huysmans, and young Maupassant were other writers of whom Zola saw a good deal. For some time he had been receiving his friends on Thursday evenings, and, of course, saw them at Flaubert's or elsewhere. In this year, 1874, five of them began to meet once a month (except in the summer season) for a dinner which they called the "Dinner of the Hissed Authors." Flaubert's play, *Le Candidat*, had suffered the ignominy of being hissed, as had Goncourt's *Henriette Maréchal* in 1865, and Daudet's *L'Arlésienne* in 1872. Success had not been the lot of Zola's *Thérèse Raquin*, and late in 1874 his *Héritiers Rabourdin*, a remake of Ben Jonson's *Volpone*, failed even more markedly. Turgenev justified his presence at the dinners on the grounds that he had been hissed in Russia. The five dined in various Parisian restaurants, starting with the Café Riche. References to these repasts with occasional echoes of the conversation, sometimes bawdy, sometimes brilliant, occur in the pages of Goncourt's *Journal* and in those of Daudet's *Trente ans de Paris*. Zola himself has given an account of these dinners in the article on Flaubert in *Les Romanciers naturalistes*.

This same year witnessed the publication of Zola's *Nouveaux contes à Ninon*. Many of them were scarcely short stories (*contes*) in the strict sense of the term, for they were more like sketches than fictional narratives of human beings at grips with life. Several, entitled "Souvenirs," were frankly autobiographical. Others were doubtless based on some personal experience or observation. This first edition included only eleven titles. Three more were added in 1885. All had been published in various newspapers and periodicals from 1865 to 1873.[16] One finds in them, particularly in those added to the second edition, an expression of Zola's anticlericalism and his humanitarian sympathies.[17] Above all, they reveal themes, tendencies, and devices which reappear, usually in a more perfected form, in *Les Rougon-Macquart*.[18]

V   La Faute de l'abbé Mouret

Meanwhile Zola was at work on *La Faute de l'abbé Mouret*. Its central subject and part of the planning antedate *La Conquête de Plassans*, but the final stages belong to 1874. Thanks again to Turgenev, the new novel appeared during February and March, 1875, in *Vestnik Evropy* (*The European Messenger*), edited by Michael Stassulevitch in St. Petersburg. Shortly after, it was put on sale in Paris.

In only a very limited sense can *La Faute de l'abbé Mouret* be considered a Naturalistic novel. The hero, Serge Mouret, a de-

scendant of psychopaths, fulfils his heredity by giving himself
over to mysticism, which Zola undoubtedly viewed as a kind of
neurosis. The picture of the village of Les Artaud, with its avaricious peasants whose only passion is for their plots of land with
which "they would fornicate" and with its girls who never marry
till pregnant, is painted in naturalistic lines and colors; but the
rest of the novel is essentially symbolic. The Second Empire is of
no consequence; no political questions arise in these pages. The
action could take place at almost any time and at almost any
place.

The central subject is that of the priest who falls in love. In a
larger sense it is the old conflict between paganism and Christianity, between nature and religion, between freedom and discipline.
But the conflict is curiously obscured, though by no means eliminated, by the device of having Serge Mouret fall in love with Albine only when in a state of amnesia brought on by a cerebral
fever. His fall occurs in Le Paradou, a Provençal garden of Eden.[19]
It is the walled park of a large estate near Les Artaud to which
Dr. Pascal Rougon takes his nephew on learning that the young
priest is seriously ill. There, Serge is welcomed by Jeanbernat, the
atheistic caretaker, a kind of "guardian angel," and nursed gradually to health by Albine, the caretaker's sixteen-year-old niece.
The girl is a child of nature who plays the role of Eve as Serge
plays the part of Adam. The analogy with the Biblical story is
deliberate and intended; of that Zola's work-sheets leave no possible doubt. While the serpent is lacking, expressly omitted, the
Tree of Life is present. In the shelter of that tree, tempted by
natural desire, the pair succumb.[20] Another character in the book
is Brother Archangias, vulgar, farcical at times, but austere, even
sadistic in his austerity, who views all women as temptresses and
agents of the Devil needing no serpent to encourage them. He
drives them from their refuge even as the Lord God drove the
first man and first woman from their garden of delight. Archangias appears just as Serge is recovering his memory. "Leave her,"
he cries, "touch her not, for she is the beginning of hell. In the
name of God, come forth from that garden!" As Serge unresist-
ingly nears the breach in the wall, Archangias drags him forth
from Le Paradou. In making Archangias such an unpleasant
figure Zola reveals his own sympathies.

Had Serge been in full possession of his faculties when he was

ÉMILE ZOLA

tempted and fell, the conflict between nature and religion would
have been much more clear-cut. As it is, there are mitigating circumstances. In spite of these, the young man suffers at the end all
the pangs of guilty conscience. In one sense, the Christian sense,
the fruits of love are anguish and death—anguish for the priest,
anguish and death for Albine; in another sense, non-Christian,
these are the fruits of Serge's final *rejection* of love and life. Zola's
own interpretation is clearly the latter. Serge remains in the grip
of Catholic discipline. A good many years will elapse before Zola
portrays in *Les Trois Villes* a priest who loses his faith, deliberately leaves the church, and marries without fear and without regret. In this book, as more than one critic has pointed out, the
only truly happy soul is the mentally retarded sister of Serge
Mouret, Désirée, who lives in a world devoid of intelligence and
tragedy, close to her beloved animals.

As in *Le Ventre de Paris*, we find in this novel extraordinary
descriptive passages. Some, to be sure, smack of the catalogue,
but many are impressive. One characteristic, appropriate to the
book, is the abundance of sex metaphors and similes. When the
young priest looked from his window one evening, in the first part
of the narrative, he beheld an arresting spectacle, for "by night,
this burning countryside assumed a strange, passionate posture. It
slept, like some woman with her legs flung apart, twisted, her
dress in indecent disorder, while heavy, warm sighs and powerful
odors arose from her sweating body. It was as if some mighty
Cybele had fallen there on her back, her bosom thrust upward,
her belly lighted by the moon, drunk with the ardor of the sun,
and still dreaming of impregnation." Little wonder that the peasants of Les Artaud are said to fornicate with the earth.

Such comparisons occur with greater frequency in descriptions
of Le Paradou. After Serge gets on his feet, Albine takes him to a
grotto, once perhaps a classical masterpiece, now almost hidden
from sight beneath the onslaught of the foliage and the flowers. It
had come to resemble, in Zola's words, "a verdant mass of locks
and tresses, studded with flowers, straying in wild dishevelment,
suggestive of some giant girl swooning with desire, her head
thrown back in a spasm of passion, her magnificent hair streaming, spread out like a sea of perfumes." And when Serge and Albine finally unite in the act of love, we are told that

it was the garden that willed their transgression. [. . .] It was the tempter, schooling them to love through its multitudinous voices. From the earth arose the scent of flowers a-swoon, a continuous whisper, relating the nuptials of roses, the voluptuous embraces of violets [. . .] [From the orchards, the meadows, the woods, the rocks, the animals came similar sensations.] From the most secret recesses, from the pools of sunlight, from the patches of shadow, an animal odor mounted, all the universe in heat. The whole of this swarming life shuddered in travail. Beneath each leaf, an insect was conceiving, in every tuft of grass, a family was growing; flies in the air, clinging together, could not wait to settle. The specks of invisible life that infest matter, the atoms of matter themselves, loved, mated, made the soil heave with sensuality, turned the park into one great orgy.[21]

In this situation, under these influences, the union of Serge and Albine is almost foreordained, and when accomplished, nature is led to sing a hymn of joy, for "it was a victory won by the animals, the plants, all matter which had desired the entry of these two children into the eternity of life. The park applauded thunderously." Such descriptions obviously go far beyond the limits of Naturalism. They take us into the symbolical and from there into the mythical.

The theme or myth of a virgin forest or an abandoned park returned to a state of nature, in which a young man meets the girl of his conscious or unconscious dreams, is found in Zola's short stories, in *Simplice* and *Un bain*. Viewed in conjunction with *La Faute de l'abbé Mouret*, they testify to the appeal that this theme had for Zola.[22] But in the novel, the concept is developed on a much greater scale and with deeper significance. It becomes a veritable myth of fecundity. The forest or garden is pulsating with life. A profusion of reproduction surrounds the young man and young woman who cannot then escape its influence. Even outside the garden Serge Mouret had been made conscious of the phenomenon, for the task of the peasants is to fecundate the earth and to people it. Once in the garden everything speaks of the life-force, and the Tree above all represents it. "So strong was its sap that it burst through the very bark, bathing the tree with an effluence of fecundation, making it the symbol of earth's virility." In yielding to it, the lovers are only fulfilling their human destiny.

The idea recurs in the third part of the book, in the section where Serge Mouret, torn now by a conscious conflict between desire and discipline, sees in a hallucinating vision all nature attacking the church and causing its downfall. In this vision the Tree takes on gigantic proportions and helps burst the church asunder. In Le Paradou it had authorized the union of man and woman; here, too, it seems to free them for the role that nature intended them to play. The sexual act in other volumes of *Les Rougon-Macquart* may be represented as dangerous, as a loss of energy and a defeat of man's will, but in this novel it is viewed as a manifestation of the vital force of nature. Its denial is synonymous with sterility. Its fulfilment is a promise of fecundity without which the universe is doomed to extinction. Such is the theme which this extraordinary novel develops with great power and a good deal of poetry.

The critics' silence with regard to Zola's novels was now broken. Barbey d'Aurevilly exploded with rage in *Le Constitutionnel*. Articles in *La Revue de France* and *La Revue bleue* were equally denunciatory. Brunetière in *La Revue des Deux Mondes* was naturally unfavorable though he admitted that there were "charming things in the narrative of the love of Serge and Albine." Flaubert mingled praise and blame, finding genius in some parts, but thinking the Paradou episode a failure. Maupassant wrote an enthusiastic letter in which he expressed unreserved admiration. Perhaps best of all for Zola, even though he was still being paid a monthly stipend, was the fact that the novel sold better than the others; this meant that he was reaching a wider audience. There were four printings in 1875; it was a modest *succès de scandale*.

VI Son Excellence Eugène Rougon

The Second Empire, and with it politics, returned to Zola's saga in his next novel, *Son Excellence Eugène Rougon*, published serially in *Le Siècle* from January 25 to March 11, 1876, and in book form by Charpentier a few days later.

The political novel was not unknown before Zola. Balzac, Vigny, Stendhal, Flaubert, and Hugo had contributed to it in one way or another. In the broadest sense, *La Fortune des Rougon* can be called political, and certainly *La Curée*, *Le Ventre de Paris*, and *La Conquête de Plassans* have affiliations with the genre. Like some of their predecessors, they are sociopolitical; what direct political activity they contain remains peripheral or fragmentary. In *Son Excellence Eugène Rougon,* political activity and the careers of politicians are central to the narrative. Parliamentary debates and procedures are depicted. A government minister who falls from power, then schemes to recover it, is an essential part of the picture. Above all, what is called "machine politics," with its rush for spoils (*la curée* again), forms the core and substance of the narrative. In these respects *Son Excellence Eugène Rougon* sets a literary precedent.[23]

Zola's journalistic career must have helped him to some extent in the preparation of his novel, although his work-sheets fail to indicate that fact. His connection with *La Tribune, Le Rappel,* and *La Cloche* from 1868 to 1870 had given him information and insight concerning the political battles of the last years of the Empire. After the war his reporting of the sessions of parliament for *La Cloche* and *Le Sémaphore de Marseille* increased his knowledge and understanding of political maneuvering. For a short time, as has been seen, he was secretary to a member of the government at Bordeaux. All this background could scarcely avoid being of value. It is, therefore, evident that direct observation of the political scene underlies the composition of *Son Excellence Eugène Rougon.* In addition, documentation was extremely important. Most useful were Ernest Hamel's *Histoire illustrée du Second Empire,* three vols., 1872–74, and Paul Dhormoys' *La Cour à Compiègne. Confidences d'un valet de chambre,* 1866.[24] From conversations with Flaubert, Goncourt, and other friends, Zola also gleaned some useful facts and impressions.

The book contains a savage satire of the *régime,* in which petty politics, personal ambition, lack of genuine statesmanship, and harsh repression of the opposition are the dominant factors. Napoleon III is presented briefly, but does not play a major role in the narrative. Except for a few moments, as when he reacts violently to Orsini's attempt on his life and pushes a highly repressive security law through a servile Assembly, he is shown as dull and indecisive. Zola concentrates rather on Eugène Rougon, whose heredity is less important in this novel than his representative and symbolic function. Scholars have shown that he is a composite figure, a combination of characteristics taken from Eugène Rouher who was a well-known politician of the Second Empire, General Espinasse who was appointed Minister of the Interior after the Orsini outrage, and Persigny, Baroche, and Billault, all ministers at one time or another. In one of Rougon's speeches Zola even attributes to him a remark made by Jules Favre, a republican opponent. Zola himself is reflected in the man, though not to the extent that some critics have maintained. Something of Zola's determination, will, and strength have gone into him, but Zola was far from being the unscrupulous person that Rougon is shown to be. Rougon symbolizes the practical politician, surrounded and served by his pals, his "gang"; in a word, his machine.

Space does not permit a discussion of all the characters of the novel, of Marsay, for instance, who is clearly modeled on the Duc de Morny, the bastard half brother of Napoleon III. But a word must be said about Clorinde Balbi, undoubtedly suggested to the novelist by the Countess de Castiglione, a famous beauty of the Second Empire, the proud possessor of a bosom of "royal beauty," as it was commonly described at the time. She arrived in Paris in 1855, became a social sensation, and, attracting the Emperor's attention, became his mistress for a brief period. Clorinde Balbi is physically as well endowed as her prototype. She possesses other characteristics which recall "la Castiglione" and before the end of the novel becomes, like her, Napoleon's mistress. Her relations with Eugène Rougon constitute one of the intriguing features of the book, for Rougon is essentially a chaste man, doubtless believing, as did Faujas, that only the chaste are strong. Not that he is incapable of lust; on two occasions in the novel he tries to possess Clorinde. Still, he is far more interested in power than in sex. He refuses to marry Clorinde when she sets that as a price for her favors, arranges a marriage of convenience for her with Delestang, one of his machine, and marries a colorless woman, Véronique Beulin-d'Orchère. While Clorinde and Rougon are in alliance politically as long as she thinks it to her advantage, there is conflict between them on the sexual level, and when she concludes that the right moment has come, she betrays him by persuading the Emperor to name her husband to Rougon's post. This warfare provides some of the dramatic interest of the novel and reveals something of Zola's attitudes toward sex; for when we compare several of these early novels, we discover that the author was both attracted and repelled by it. A certain puritanism exists alongside a pagan acceptance of nature.

When Zola was planning this novel, he forecast that it would become a "broad page" of social and human history.[25] Unfortunately, Zola let himself become too enmeshed in the net of petty machine politics and governmental corruption. No grandeur lifts the book above that level; no really great issue inspires its pages; no splendid character emerges from its chapters. Nevertheless, its satire is effective. If Zola's purpose was to discredit the imperial *régime* of Napoleon III, he was eminently successful.

VII *Conclusions*

The first six novels of the *Rougon-Macquart* are a significant accomplishment. They represent first of all an impressive amount of sheer labor: one substantial volume a year, and this in addition to newspaper articles, not only in *Le Sémaphore de Marseille*, but also in *Vestnik Evropy*—since March, 1875, Zola had been contributing a monthly letter on literary and artistic topics to this St. Petersburg publication. Whatever might be said of Zola he could not be accused of indolence. These novels further represent a literary achievement of considerable magnitude. Zola's style is not yet fully developed. In some of his descriptions—the food displays in *Le Ventre de Paris*, the exotic plants in the conservatory of *La Curée*, the trees and flowers of Le Paradou—there is abuse of mere enumeration. Certain adjectives—*adorable, exquisite, deranged* (*détraqué*), for example—are overemployed. On the other hand, many passages are robust and many are colorful, indeed poetic. An epic note audible in *La Fortune des Rougon* is full of promise for the future. In that novel Zola also showed that he was not devoid of the comic spirit. His capacity for satire is a striking characteristic of nearly all of them.

Although the number of characters created is not yet on the Balzacian scale, it is nevertheless considerable, for well over a hundred different human beings cross the pages of these novels, representing varied types and activities placed in varied environments. Paris and the provinces are depicted. Businessmen, politicians, priests, peasants, society women, middle-class women, adolescents of both sexes, domestic servants—all these appear. Many of the characters presented are thoroughly unpleasant. In particular, the three principals of *La Curée* are persons for whom the reader can have neither liking nor sympathy. And in general, Zola's characters, like most people in real life, are motivated by self-interest. Some rise above it. Silvère and Miette give their lives for the Republic; and all the insurgents singing the *Marseillaise* on their way to defend the cause of liberty testify to the existence of political idealism. The fact that they are doomed to defeat does not detract from their spirit and courage. Florent too, in *Le Ventre de Paris*, is on the side of the angels. However ineffectual he is, one prefers him to the practical bourgeois who surround him. Dr. Pascal Rougon is devoted to his profession and unselfish in its practice. Serge Mouret is perhaps, in Zola's view, misguided, but there is no question of his basic attachment to truth and honor. Albine may be amoral, but, except possibly in the narrowest sense of the word, is certainly not immoral. Genuine love motivates her as it motivates the youthful pair in *La Fortune des Rougon*. The universe depicted in these novels is admittedly a materialistic universe from which God is largely absent, but it is not entirely devoid of idealism.

In spite of an achievement that few of his contemporaries were equaling, Zola had not yet won the success of which he dreamed. His friends recognized his merits, though Goncourt was beginning to be jealous.[26] The critics in general, however, and above all the great reading public had not yet been conquered. But, in the words of the old cliché, it is darkest before the dawn. Within a year Zola would no longer be able to complain of lack of recognition.

CHAPTER 5

Success

L'Assommoir

THE uproar caused by the publication of *L'Assommoir* was extraordinary and seems today almost incredible. In the first place, the novel's appearance in Yves Guyot's paper, *Le Bien public,* was suspended in June, 1876, at the end of the sixth chapter. This was not, as people suspected, for reasons of morality, but rather because this liberal organ was distressed by the unflattering picture of the working class that was being presented to its readers. Catulle Mendès then offered to make room for it in *La République des lettres,* where chapters VII to XIII appeared from July to early January, 1877. In September, 1876, a violent attack on the novel was made in *Le Figaro* where Albert Millaud declared that what Zola was writing was not realism but pornography. Zola replied in a letter published in *Le Figaro* on September 7 that it was hardly proper to judge the book before it had all appeared and went on to say that his intentions were perfectly decent. Millaud at once made another assault. This time *Le Figaro* failed to publish Zola's reply in which he stated that he was "no maker of idylls" and that a social evil can be effectively attacked only with "a red hot iron," *un fer rouge.* In *Le Gaulois,* a critic by the name of Fourcauld took up the cudgels against the book. "The novelist," he wrote, "does not spare us a single drunkard's vomiting." [1]

The novel appeared in book form at the end of January, 1877. Its text differed rather markedly from that of the serial version, for Zola re-established passages that had been suppressed by Guyot or Mendès and cut out others that he now considered unnecessary. The battle of words was at once resumed. Pontmartin, Pons, Scherer, Houssaye, and Ranc all condemned the work. Pons was particularly violent. "Revolting scenes, ignoble sentiments, deliberate obscenities," he exclaimed in his *Coups de plumes indépendants.* A writer in *Le Télégraphe* accused Zola of plagiarizing

Denis Poulot's *Le Sublime*. But others struck a different note. Albert Wolff—in *Le Figaro*, of all places—Georges Brunet, Anatole France praised the vigor and the realism of Zola's creation. Most of his friends rallied to his support—privately, if not publicly. Whereas Edmond de Goncourt found it difficult to conceal his jealousy and Flaubert was not enchanted by the subject, though he thought many pages powerful, Paul Bourget, Maupassant, Huysmans, and Mallarmé viewed the novel as an extraordinary achievement.[2] And now, partly because of this battle of words, the public rushed to the bookstores. Thirty-eight printings were made in 1877, twelve more in 1878. By the end of 1881 ninety-one editions[3] had come off the press. Zola's success was assured. Charpentier, setting an admirable example for all succeeding publishers, tore up the contract which entitled him to Zola's novels for a flat monthly sum and put him on a royalty basis.

It will be remembered that Zola had intended from the beginning to include a novel on the working class in his *Rougon-Macquart*. No one, he thought, had yet portrayed the workers truthfully. This view was far from wrong. Most of Zola's predecessors had been either uninterested in the proletariat or merely sentimental about them. In all of the *Comédie humaine* there is scarcely a genuine representative of the working class, for one does not customarily put domestic servants and peasants in that category. George Sand sentimentalized about the workers, and idealized them. In truth, in her novels they are artisans and peasants rather than authentic proletarians. Victor Hugo, in *Les Misérables*, came nearer to reality in his humanitarian concern for the underprivileged, but the workaday world in which a man earns his bread by the sweat of his brow is only suggested, not carefully and minutely described. Hugo, be it said to his credit, was aware of the problem of unemployment; yet in this epic he discussed it only briefly, and his solution was hardly radical. In 1865, Edmond and Jules de Goncourt, in the preface to *Germinie Lacerteux*, proclaimed the right of the lower classes, *les basses classes*, to a major role in the novel. The protagonist chosen for that novel was a domestic servant, not a factory worker. Its grim realism, doubtless encouraged Zola in his own projects. He was encouraged, too, by the modernity of some of the subjects treated by the painters. From 1869 to 1877 such pictures as Manet's

"Laundry," Monet's "Railroad Bridge at Argenteuil" and his "Saint-Lazare Railroad Station," Degas' "Ironing-women," Renoir's "Main Boulevards" and "The Dance at the Moulin de la Galette" made their appearance. In his art criticism, Zola had railed at neo-classical and sentimental canvasses, giving his approval to Courbet, Manet, Pissarro, Jongkind, and Monet. "Their works are alive," he wrote in his *Salon* of 1868, "because they have taken them from life and have painted them with all the love they feel for modern subjects." In *Le Ventre de Paris* he created a painter who espoused these principles.

Alphonse Daudet perhaps came closer to depicting the working class than any predecessor or contemporary of Zola. In *Fromont jeune et Risler aîné* (1874) he included a realistic description of a drab section of Paris in which Sidonie Chèbe had been brought up, and in *Jack*, published serially in 1875 and in book form early in 1876, he introduced a metallurgical factory. Neither book can properly be called a proletarian novel. The former is essentially a tale of adultery leading to disaster and death. The hero of *Jack* is forced by circumstance into a working-class career. He is far from typical of the modern proletarian.

Consequently, Zola was inaugurating something new when he composed *L'Assommoir*. Although it does not give us a picture of the factory worker, it contains a far more realistic picture of the Parisian working class and their milieu than anything published before 1877.

For one thing, Zola knew from personal experience what he was writing about. In the period before he found work with Hachette & Cie he had known hunger and had inhabited delapidated quarters. It is not impossible, as M. Mitterand states, that "the first idea of a working-class novel germinated in Zola's mind at the beginning of his residence in Paris, during these years 1859 to 1862, when he lived in destitution, without influential acquaintances, in direct contact with the poor." [4] One of his uncles, Adolphe Aubert, had been a house-painter, then a concierge. His wife was a seamstress. They had one daughter named Anna, a girl who apparently gave them some trouble and may have contributed her name, if not more, to the heroine's daughter in Zola's novel. This very modest family was essentially working class. Zola's wife, Gabrielle-Alexandrine, was of very humble origin. These connections and his own experience from 1859 to 1862 surely gave Zola knowledge of conditions at the bottom of the social scale and insight into working-class characteristics.

The proletariat, moreover, was beginning to impress itself, much more than in Balzac's day, on everyone's consciousness. The Workers' International was founded in London in 1864, and a French section was established the following year. From 1866 to 1870 strikes occurred, in some of which the International played a part. A few were successful; more were suppressed, often with brutality. The proletariat was becoming more than a fact; it was rapidly becoming a force. Paris, in particular, was made aware of the problem. The transformation of the capital under Baron Haussmann had the partial result of driving the working population from the center of the city to the periphery, thereby setting up two cities in Paris, one rich and one poor. Anthime Corbon, a former member of the working class, called attention to that situation in 1863, adding that the wealthy were literally surrounded by the poor. Zola was no less conscious of this phenomenon than Corbon.[5]

Certain newspaper articles written by Zola from 1868 to 1872 reveal his preoccupation, and even forecast certain aspects of L'Assommoir. His comments on Jules Simon's L'Ouvrière in La Tribune, June 28, 1868; his advice to the Queen of Mohély in the same paper on July 12, 1868, to visit a working-class quarter; his remarks on the effects of Haussmann's activities on the working class (La Tribune, Oct. 18, 1868); and his article on unemployment in Le Corsaire, which was mentioned in a previous chapter, tell the same story, that he was acutely conscious of the problem of poverty. An article in La Tribune, Oct. 10, 1869, republished under the title "Mon voisin Jacques" in the Nouveaux contes à Ninon, and a sketch, "Le Forgeron" ("The Blacksmith"), which first appeared in the Almanach des travailleurs in 1874, are a preview of two characters of L'Assommoir, Bazouge and Goujet. It is apparent that while Zola was writing his early novels he had by no means forgotten his project for the working class. Indeed, he clipped useful documents during those years. One item thus preserved told of the death of a small child, killed when the drunken father falls and lets the child drop. Zola added laconically: "Episode for the novel on the working class." Another more extensive clipping was Sarcey's article in Le Gaulois, Feb. 8, 1870, which portrayed the Parisian worker as "lively, jocular, and improvident." Shortly after that Zola drew up a half-page of notes which he entitled "Working-class novel—the Batignolles novel." It forecast a book dealing with a laundress.[6]

The Commune of 1871 led the bourgeoisie to fear the working class and its leaders. For this reason Zola may have thought the moment unpropitious and therefore delayed executing his project. Four years later tempers had cooled sufficiently for him to feel safe in going ahead with it. During the summer at Saint-Aubin-sur-mer, on the coast of Normandy, he laid the foundations and erected, as he told Charpentier in a letter dated August 14, the scaffolding of a novel which he hoped would be extraordinary. At the end of September he declared himself "delighted" with the plan of his work. "It is very simple and energetic. I think that the life of the working class has never been tackled with this degree of frankness and honesty." Early October saw him back in the capital. On the 20th he wrote to Alexis: "The day after my arrival I had to take the field for my novel, look for a likely quarter, visit workmen. I had an extraordinary zest for work. On the 10th I started simultaneously my novel and a big study on Flaubert for Russia. And since the tenth, I've been working nine hours a day."[7] He went on to say that he was pleased with his study on Flaubert and still more pleased with the first chapter of his novel.

I *The Characters and the* tableau de mœurs

L'Assommoir was the most human and compassionate book that he had so far written. Far from being a vilification of the working class, as some hostile critics of the period claimed, it revealed profound sympathy for their lot. Its central character engages one's interest as much as any grand heroine of classical or romantic literature. Her problems and her situation are different, her character simple, her education slight; but her appeal is genuine, her fate moving. Here was proof, indeed, that the so-called lower classes have a right to a central place in literature. Furthermore, the *tableau de mœurs,* the picture of working-class living conditions, was not only novel, but truthfully and artistically done. It gave balance and support to the career of the heroine. Zola realized that this picture was as essential as the narrative of the heroine's life. He had originally thought of entitling the novel "The Simple Life of Gervaise Macquart," with emphasis on the modesty of her ambitions; but soon after in the *Ébauche*, he saw that this was inadequate. "I can save myself," he wrote, "from this platitude of the plot only by the enormity and the truth of my working-class pictures." [8] *L'Assommoir* is then a combination of two things, a life and a neighborhood, merged into an organic unity.

The word *assommoir* comes from the verb *assommer* which means to club or to fell by a blow. The noun therefore refers to the instrument used, and may be translated literally as a club or a cudgel, possibly even a sledge hammer. It was applied by the workers of Paris in their picturesque language to a cheap saloon, and in Zola's novel it designates the one owned by old man Colombe, located at the corner of the rue des Poissonniers and the boulevard de Rochechouart in the heart of a working-class quarter. Vizetelly, in his bowdlerized translation, entitled the novel *The Dram-Shop*. The most recent and best version in English, that of Mr. A. H. Townsend, has wisely retained the French title.

Colombe's *Assommoir* contained its own distilling apparatus which was, as Zola puts it, "the main feature of the establishment," a machine "which the customers could watch functioning, long-necked still-pots, copper worms disappearing underground, a devil's kitchen alluring to drink-sodden working-men in search of pleasant dreams." [9] A few pages farther on in this chapter, the big copper-red still is again described. From the huge retort "a thin stream of liquid alcohol was trickling. The great still, with its oddly shaped receptacles and its endless coils of piping, seemed to be in a peevish mood; not a single gay plume of steam was coming forth. A barely audible breathing could be heard within it, a subdued subterranean snorting. It seemed as though some deed of darkness was being performed in broad daylight by a grim toiler that was mighty but voiceless." The sinister touch is evident—not to be forgotten by the reader. We have here one of those mechanical monsters of Zola, taking on a life of its own, affecting the lives of others. Yet it is not constantly recalled; for several chapters it is allowed to remain dormant in the reader's memory. Later, in a critical moment, it reappears like some evil beast, some fantastic apparition casting on the wall behind it shadows in the shape of "figures with tails, monsters opening wide their jaws as if to swallow up the world."

The book's title is not explained in this fashion to the reader until the second chapter where the drinking establishment is seen for the first time. Meanwhile, in the opening chapter, the acquaintance has been made of Gervaise Macquart, who is sitting by the window of her miserable room in the Hotel Boncœur, looking down into the street below, waiting for the return of her man, Auguste Lantier. Readers of the series had learned something about her in the first novel, *La Fortune des Rougon*. She is the daughter of the old reprobate, Antoine Macquart, and his hard-working wife, Joséphine. Back in Plassans she had unwisely given herself to Lantier, a worker in the hatmaking trade and thereby acquired two illegitimate children, Claude and Étienne. She is now twenty-two, "tall and slim, with fine features which were already beginning to reflect the strain of her hard life." She is afflicted with a "limp in her right leg, scarcely noticeable except when she is tired." Lantier finally returns, a quarrel ensues, and the chapter ends with his abandonment of Gervaise.

The other aspect of the novel, the *tableau de mœurs*, is not forgotten in this first chapter. It is found in the evocation of the quarter viewed through the eyes of Gervaise as she waits by the window. The hotel itself is a "ramshackle three-story structure painted the color of wine dregs up to the third floor, with weatherbeaten shutters." To the right, in the direction of the Boulevard de Rochechouart, she could see "groups of butchers standing in their blood-stained aprons before the slaughterhouses." To the left, following a long, ribbon-like avenue, her eyes "came to rest upon the white mass, almost directly opposite, of the Lariboisière Hospital, then under construction." As daylight increased and the city awakened, she witnessed "the constant stream of men, horses, and carts flooding down from the heights of Montmartre and La Chapelle, pouring between the two squat tollhouses." This glimpse of the quarter is brief, but effective. As Gervaise herself vaguely realizes at the end of the chapter, it sets the geographical and sociological limits of the life she is to lead.

Another contribution to the *tableau de mœurs* in this opening chapter is the famous, indeed notorious, scene in the wash-house culminating in the fight between Gervaise and Virginie, the sister of the girl with whom Gervaise suspects Lantier of having spent the night. The interior of the wash-house—the pallid daylight, bluish haze, heavy humidity, the odor of soap and the whiffs of chlorine, the lines of women scrubbing with their brushes and

ÉMILE ZOLA

pounding with their paddles, the steam engine shrouded in a
white mist, "puffing and snorting ceaselessly"—all that is rendered
vividly. And the fight in which Virginie is thoroughly trounced is
remarkable. It imparts to this chapter that "excessive" touch with
which Zola wanted to endow all his novels and which he certainly
succeeded in imparting to this one.

Gervaise marries a roofer by the name of Coupeau, glimpsed in
the first chapter, but viewed more carefully in the second. He appears to be one of the type of Parisian workmen described by
Sarcey as "lively, jocular, and improvident." With him Gervaise
begins the upward climb which lasts through several chapters. It
is in the midst of her prosperity that the episode occurs which, as
more than one critic has seen,[10] constitutes a turning point in her
fortunes. She is now the mistress of her own shop, and although
her husband has been the victim of an occupational hazard,
breaking his leg in a fall from a roof, and has become indolent
and taken to excessive drinking of wine during a prolonged conva-
lescence, things look rosy to her. One hot June afternoon finds her
sorting out dirty, smelly clothes in her establishment. "Sitting on
the edge of a stool, bent double, stretching her hands to right and
left with slow, easy gestures, she seemed to be gradually intoxi-
cated by this stench of humanity, smiling vaguely, dreaming. It
may be that her indolence first came to her then, from the suffo-
cating odor of the old clothes poisoning the air around her." Coupeau enters the shop, obviously having had a drink too many.
Stumbling over the laundry, he insists on embracing her. "She let
herself go," writes Zola, "made groggy by the slight dizziness
which the pile of laundry gave her, feeling no repugnance for his
wine-steeped breath. And the loud kiss they exchanged, full on
the mouth, in the midst of this dirty laundry, was like a first
downward plunge in the slow decay of their lives." The author's
intention is unmistakable. Pliable at a moment when she should
have been strong, Gervaise's weakness matches Coupeau's.
Though their pace is different, they have both started on the road
to ruin.

Gervaise's weakness toward Coupeau, and later toward Lantier,
is equaled by another frailty, her love of food. At a time when she
could ill afford it, she celebrates her birthday with a gargantuan
feast washed down with quantities of wine. The preparations, the
meal itself with fourteen people at the table, the uproar at the end

when everyone is stuffed with food and drink—all that occupies the whole of Chapter VII. It is one of the famous descriptions of the book. More naturalistic in this case than impressionistic, essentially a *tableau de mœurs*, it is a concrete example of a side of Gervaise's character which contributes to her decline. Money seemed to melt away. "One trouble," explains the author, "was that yielding to her appetite, she was growing fatter and seemed not to have the strength to worry about the future."

Other descriptions and other characters contribute to the *tableau de mœurs*. The chapter devoted to Gervaise's wedding is as famous as that on the birthday celebration. It stands comparison with Flaubert's picture of Emma's wedding in *Madame Bovary*. The latter is a country event, Gervaise's a city affair; but both are masterpieces of realism, and both contain a touch of humor. Zola's text does not match the stylistic beauty of Flaubert's, but his canvas is on a larger scale. It includes, not only the scene at the mayor's office and at the church, the wedding dinner at the Moulin d'Argent, but also an incredible visit to the Louvre where the whole group passes rapidly from one room to another with only an occasional glimmer of appreciation, though Zola himself manages to indicate by an appropriately placed adjective his own reactions. The group finally loses its way in the myriad of rooms and would have been locked in for the night, had a guard not led them to the exit. The whole episode has its hilarious side, but it has its touching aspect, too, for these people, limited by their education and experience, confront a world they cannot possibly comprehend. Zola skilfully combines in this episode the comic and the pathetic.

One of the characters of the novel is a smith by the name of Goujet. In the midst of the workers who drink too much, he is the skilful, honest, faithful manual worker who remains sober. Through him the reader has a glimpse of another social problem, technological unemployment, for Goujet is in great danger of seeing his work mechanized. Indeed, before the book ends, the process has begun. This is not, however, the chief reason for his presence in the novel. He is in love with Gervaise, respectfully, silently, touchingly. Although it offsets a little the brutality that piles up overwhelmingly in the novel, Zola himself questioned just how realistic this love was. Writing about his book in *La Vie littéraire* he said: "I fear that I lied somewhat with Goujet, for I have given him feelings that do not belong to his environment." However that may be, Goujet also furnishes Zola with an opportunity to depict the trade of the ironsmith. The sixth chapter evokes the interior of the shop where he works. Zola activates his description by a dramatic contest between Goujet and another smith picturesquely called Bec-Salé (Salt-Mouth), Goujet's nickname being Gueule d'or (Golden Mouth). Each forges a forty-millimeter bolt. Rather amusingly, Zola goes to the dance for his metaphors and similes.[11] As Bec-Salé swings his hammer Dédèle, the latter is described as "doing a big *entrechat*, toes in the air like one of the dancers at the Élysée-Montmartre showing her underthings" but the smith becomes exhausted by his efforts and botches the job with his last two blows. Gervaise, who was looking on, "could see plainly how the last two heel-taps of dancing Dédèle had marked the bolthead," giving it a lopsided appearance. Then it was Goujet's turn. "His style," writes Zola, "was classical, correct, balanced, graceful. In his hands Fifine was not doing a dance-hall fling, kicking her pins higher than her skirts; instead she rose and fell in cadence, like a noble lady with a serious countenance leading an old-fashioned minuet." When he finished, "the bolthead was neat and polished, without a seam, a veritable jewel of craftsmanship, round as a billiard ball cast in a mold." The whole passage contains some of the fanciful artistry that we observed in *Le Ventre de Paris* and *La Faute de l'abbé Mouret*.

A moment later, Goujet took Gervaise into another shed where machines were at work. There she could see

the mechanical chisels which chewed up iron bars, cutting off a piece with each bite of the teeth, spitting out the pieces to the rear one by one; the bolt-and-rivet machines, big and complicated, forging a bolthead with each pressure of their powerful screws; the trimming machines, with iron flywheels and balls of cast iron which beat furiously on each piece produced to remove loose metal; the tapping machines, operated by women, which put threads on bolts and nuts, with their steel gears grinding and shining in a bath of oil.

Above them, making a sound "like a great rustling of wings," were "leather belts, long ribbons that hung from the roof in a gigantic spider web, each strip ceaselessly revolving. The steam engine that drove them was hidden in a corner behind a low brick wall, and so the belts appeared to be running by themselves, bringing movement out of the depths of the darkness with their ceaseless gliding, smooth and uninterrupted as the flight of a night bird." These are the machines which threaten Goujet with unemployment. Something, of course, is lost even in Mr. Townsend's good translation which, nevertheless, may suggest the power of the original.

The big tenement in the rue de la Goutte d'or in which Gervaise and Coupeau live after she acquires her own shop, and which houses the Lorilleux couple who are small-scale goldsmiths, Mme Gaudron, a wool carder, Mlle Clémence, a clothes presser, Monsieur Madinier, a maker of cardboard boxes, the Bijard family with its drunken, brutal father, old Bru, a former house-painter, and a good many others including, naturally, Monsieur and Madame Boche, the concierges—this tenement plays a part in the novel similar to that of the big markets in *Le Ventre de Paris:* "Squared off like a chunk of crudely mixed mortar rotting and crumbling under the rain, the huge rough cube of the building was silhouetted against the bright sky high above the neighboring roofs, with its unplastered, mud-colored side walls as bare as the dreary blankness of prison walls, except for rows of roughly jutting stones suggesting jaws full of snaggy, decayed teeth yawning vacantly." This drab building not only fixes the locale of much of the action and contributes to the *tableau de mœurs*, but seems, like the Markets in the earlier novel and like Colombe's distillery, to have a life of its own. As Gervaise gazed on it, she was "surprised by this immensity, feeling as though she were within a living organism, in the very heart of a teeming city. She was impressed by this structure as though she were seeing some human giant." It also contributes markedly to the vertical effect which Zola uses in the novel.[12] When Gervaise, at the end of the chapter, looks at it again from below, she is impressed by the building's height and its crushing weight: "It seemed to have grown larger under the moonless sky. The gray walls, as though cleansed of their leprous discoloration and washed over by darkness, stretched wide and rose high, and they seemed even more bare and thin, stripped now of the rags that had hung in the sun to dry. [. . .] All this made Gervaise feel that the building was bearing down upon her, threatening to crush her, striking a chill through her body." On the other hand, looking from the top floor down, one senses an abyss below. Ironically, when Gervaise loses her

ÉMILE ZOLA

shop on the ground floor and has to rent a squalid room at the top
of the tenement house, her upward move is indicative of failure
and decline. Later, she is expelled from this room and allowed to
occupy old Bru's cubbyhole *under* the stairs; this downward step
has its customary significance of defeat. Gervaise's career has this
up-and-down characteristic. The first four or five chapters chronicle her rise; the remainder, her fall. If one were to diagram the
narrative, an appropriate figure would be a triangle, almost isosce-
les. The decline of Gervaise is somewhat longer than the ascent,
though if Chapter XI, largely devoted to her daughter Nana, be
overlooked, it is scarcely more protracted.

Coupeau shares to some extent in this evolution. A successful
worker in the first part of the book where he has no upward
climb, his physical fall heralds his moral decay. Zola pays more
attention in this case to the downfall than to the earlier stage of
success. Two reasons explain this fact. Coupeau's decay is one of
the causes of Gervaise's defeat and needs to be emphasized on
that account. The other reason is sociological. Through Coupeau,
the book becomes in some degree a study of alcoholism in the
Paris slums. When Coupeau turns from wine to spirits, the critical
step has been taken. It occurs at the end of Chapter VI when he
comes home "dead drunk, white-faced, teeth clenched, nose
pinched in." The rotgut of Colombe's *Assommoir* could be de-
tected "in the poisoned blood that had marked his skin with blem-
ishes." From this point on Coupeau marches inevitably to his
death in a raving attack of delirium tremens. Zola documented
himself very carefully on this subject.[13] His description makes
Charles Jackson's pages on the same theme in *The Lost Weekend,*
good though they are, appear pallid and diluted.

The third principal character in the book, Auguste Lantier, does
not participate in Gervaise's rise to prosperity, but takes an active
part in her decline. In Chapter VI Virginie reports his return to
the quarter, and in the next chapter Gervaise herself glimpses
him. This arrangement underlines the ominous quality of his return which soon takes place, for in Chapter VIII he is brought
home by Coupeau, and shortly after invited to share a room in
their flat. A *ménage à trois*, in which Gervaise shares her favors
with both men, inevitably follows. She is quite literally their prey
and is particularly the prey of Lantier, who lives on her earnings
without contributing a cent to her support. As soon as her com-

plete ruin is manifest, he seeks a new victim and finds one in Virginie. This man is surely one of the worst "rotters" known to literature.

Death hovers over the pages of *L'Assommoir*. Although it is not linked with love as in the case of Silvère and Miette in *La Fortune des Rougon*, its presence is frequently felt. Merely hinted at in the first chapter, it is evoked more significantly at the end of the wedding dinner through the person of the undertaker Bazouge with his drunken, ominous prophecy. It enters the narrative directly with the death of Mme Bijard and her little girl.[14] It strikes home with the demise of Coupeau's mother. Then, when Gervaise finds herself living next door to Bazouge and at the same time sees herself powerless to halt her downward plunge, death becomes almost an obsession, attracting and repelling her in turn. It mercifully takes Coupeau, and at long last lays its cold hand on Gervaise herself. This simple woman whose modest ambition was "to have a steady job, always enough to eat, a fairly clean corner to sleep in, [. . .] not to be beaten, and to die in her own bed in her own home," is unable to realize even this humble aim. She dies at forty-one, as Zola had planned, slowly, horribly, "exhausted by work and poverty," [15] in that foul cubbyhole where old man Bru had met his end. Bazouge comes for her, drunk as usual. "When he took hold of Gervaise with his big dirty hands, he felt a bit of tenderness, and gently lifted this woman who had long yearned for his attentions. Then laying her down in the coffin with fatherly care, he babbled between hiccups: 'Well, there you are; listen carefully. It's me, Bibi-the Gay One, called the ladies' comforter. There, now you're happy. Go to sleep, my beauty.'" These final words of the novel, devoid of any high-flown rhetoric, underline the totality of Gervaise's defeat.

II *The Style*

The style of *L'Assommoir* has been the subject of a good many comments from the time of its appearance to the present day.[16] That Zola was early preoccupied with the question is clear from a letter he wrote to Alexis in September, 1875, in which he said that the style would be "difficult to discover." His solution was to combine the literary and the popular, but in using the popular, he went much further than he or anyone had ever done.

Like many of his contemporaries, Zola escaped from the rigidity of classical sentence construction. He had begun that process as early as *Thérèse Raquin*, and it is completed in *L'Assommoir*. Subject and verb are frequently separated, sometimes by a participial, prepositional, or adjectival phrase, sometimes by a simple adverb. Object and verb are also often disjoined. Verbal nouns, those ending in *-ment*, the equivalent of the participial noun in English, often help to activate the sentence. The stylistic trick of placing an adverb at the end of a sentence and setting it off with a comma, already used by Hugo and Flaubert, is fairly common, though by no means abused. The sensual is rendered as vividly as possible by an appropriate adjective or verb. The two-part or three-part periodic sentence, which Zola had long utilized, reappears in *L'Assommoir*. The so-called creative *and*, which was mentioned in connection with *Thérèse Raquin*, is again found, though less frequently than before. In short, the sentence structure has become extraordinarily flexible.

The greatest stylistic novelty in *L'Assommoir* is the working-class vocabulary that Zola introduced. He found much of it in Denis Poulot's *Le Sublime*, and Alfred Delvau's *Dictionnaire de la langue verte*. When accused of plagiarizing the former, he admitted that he had found it useful. He obviously viewed it as a document, not much different from an encyclopedia or a dictionary. He probably should have mentioned it in his preface, though it is really a borderline case. Certainly, had he not made use of this book, his novel would have been less picturesque and less accurate. The manual workers of Paris did not talk like members of the French Academy or even like educated bourgeois. In addition to the novel's title, the nicknames of some of the characters, and a few other details, Zola found in *Le Sublime* such words or expressions as *pisser à l'anglaise* (to take French leave), *béquiller* (to eat), *canon* (glass of wine), *cheulard* (drunkard), *rouchie* (whore), *singe* (boss), and many others. ·

Whether the source is *Le Sublime*, or Delvau's dictionary, or just ordinary slang with which Zola was familiar, one finds popular vocabulary throughout the book, in direct discourse, naturally enough, but also in free indirect discourse (called in French, *le discours indirect libre*). Among many examples, one of the best occurs in Chapter XII, the paragraph beginning in the French: *Que d'embêtements! A quoi bon se mettre dans tous ses états et se turlupiner la cervelle? Si elle avait pu pioncer au moins! Mais sa pétaudière de cambuse lui trottait par la tête.* In English: "What a lot of annoying things! What was the use of getting into a stew and beating her brains out? If only she could take a snooze! But she couldn't get out of her mind this noisy dump they lived in." The whole paragraph is in the same style and produces an extraordinary effect of vividness and the substance of life itself.

Conclusion

L'Assommoir can legitimately be called a masterpiece, surpassing everything that Zola had hitherto written. Not linked too closely to the Second Empire, although a few allusions place the book in time and occasional remarks are made on politics, it transcends the immediate moment and has greater universality than the preceding volumes of the series. The story of Gervaise Macquart could have occurred in previous decades or in following ones. Although the twentieth century has made such a fate somewhat less likely, a perfect social order has not yet been achieved. The book is, therefore, not without its appeal today. Violently attacked, as has been seen, in 1876–77, a few people nevertheless saw its power and its grandeur. Two of Zola's friends, Paul Bourget and Stéphane Mallarmé, wrote him that he had found a new manner, a new ideal, something genuinely modern. The deceptively simple construction, the depiction of the everyday life of ordinary people, the unfolding of a tragedy, the evocation of an environment unfamiliar to many, but none the less real, the compassion underlying the narrative, the obviously noble purpose of arousing the sympathetic indignation of the reader to the end that some social action would ensue, all this made and still makes *L'Assommoir* a memorable book. Before 1877 Zola had been known to a few as a promising writer. After 1877 he was recognized as one of the literary giants of the nineteenth century.

CHAPTER 6

The Battle of Naturalism

From Une page d'amour (*1878*) *to* La Joie de vivre (*1884*)

L'ASSOMMOIR made Zola a rich man. It enabled him to take a long vacation at L'Estaque on the Mediterranean in the summer of 1877; and it permitted him to move to a more luxurious apartment at 23 rue de Boulogne (now rue Ballu) as well as to look for a country home which he soon found at Médan on the Seine, not a great way from Paris. The "vacation" was largely spent in writing a new novel, one that had not been previously planned for *Les Rougon-Macquart*. After *L'Assommoir*, he decided that something markedly different was needed, something calmer, and something upper class. *Une page d'amour* was the result, published in book form in the late spring of 1878, more or less simultaneously with a play, *Le Bouton de rose*, which was a complete failure. The novel was moderately successful, but it was not, from any point of view, in the class of *L'Assommoir*. Zola tried his hand, as he stated in his *Ébauche*, at an analysis of what the Romantics would have called a grand passion and what a French classicist would have conceived of as a conflict between love and duty. Hélène Grandjean, née Mouret, the sister of Silvère and the aunt of Abbé Serge Mouret, is the widowed heroine of the book. She seems not to have inherited any of the unpleasant characteristics of her Macquart ancestry; but she is, of course, a carrier, and she has passed on to her young daughter Jeanne some of the family neuroses. The unfortunate child has also inherited pulmonary weaknesses from her father, who has died of tuberculosis. The mother falls in love with a married man, Doctor Henri Deberle. After the briefest liaison in the history of literature, the two are separated by the death of the youngster. Hélène then marries another man, and they retire to Marseilles.

Most critics, with the exception of Henri Guillemin, who has recently given the book his accolade,[1] feel that Zola's portrayal of the unhappy lovelorn pair does not achieve greatness. They concede, however, that the neurotic jealousy of Jeanne, who senses that her mother is in love with the doctor, is skilfully done and that the book also includes scenes and techniques of considerable originality. One is the double rendezvous. Hélène Grandjean becomes Dr. Deberle's mistress on the same afternoon and in the same apartment where Mme Deberle was about to succumb to the wiles of a young stockbroker by the name of Malignon. Warned by Hélène of the imminent arrival of the Doctor, who had been informed of the assignation by an anonymous letter written in fact by Hélène, they precipitately depart. Minutes later, Hélène opens the door to the Doctor, and the inevitable happens. This arrangement inspired Flaubert to enthusiasm. "The double scene of the rendez-vous is. SUBLIME," he wrote Zola. Sublime or not, the scene is well written and very effective.

Another arrangement, less dramatic, to be sure, also awakened interest. Zola wrote the book in five parts, each one divided into five chapters. The last chapter of each part is devoted to a view of Paris. Except in the fourth part where Jeanne is at the window on a rainy afternoon, the city is seen through the eyes of Hélène. The descriptions vary with the season, the weather, and the time of day. They match the mood of the observer. Flaubert thought less well of these chapters, but others, notably Mallarmé and Cézanne, found them worthy of praise.

I *The Polemicist*

These five or six years from 1877 on were filled with incredible activity. Zola not only wrote much dramatic criticism during this period, but concerned himself with the dramatization of some of his own novels. In 1877, while "vacationing" at L'Estaque and working on *Une page d'amour,* he took time to help William Busnach and Octave Gastineau on the scenario of *L'Assommoir,* which opened at the Ambigu on Jan. 18, 1879 and had a run of three hundred performances.[2] In 1879–80, in addition to composing and publishing a long novel, *Nana,* he brought out *Le Roman expérimental.* He wrote several short stories at this time and shortly after. He penned an adaptation of *La Curée* for the stage; entitled *Renée,* it was not performed for several years. He assisted Busnach with the scenario of *Nana* and to some extent with the dialogue.[3] During these years critical articles poured from his pen. Appearing in various Parisian newspapers or in *Vestnik Ev-*

ropy, they were promptly republished in volume form.[4] In 1880–81 he accepted an offer from *Le Figaro* to do a series of articles on any subjects he chose. They were collected in *Une campagne* (1882). He also wrote a number of prefaces. And, from 1882 to 1884, he published a new novel every year. One of them, *Pot-Bouille,* was promptly dramatized by Busnach with Zola's assistance.

Many of the critical articles were part of Zola's contribution to the battle of Naturalism which began with the publication of *L'Assommoir* and was waged by Zola and his friends, particularly the younger ones, against the traditionalists headed by Ferdinand Brunetière. If there was an official founding of the Naturalist movement, it doubtless occurred at the dinner offered by Zola's young disciples at the Restaurant Trapp on April 16, 1877. Edmond de Goncourt reported it briefly in his *Journal:* "This evening Huysmans, Céard, Hennique, Paul Alexis, Octave Mirbeau, Guy de Maupassant, the young men of realism or naturalism, acclaimed us, Flaubert, Zola, and myself, as the three masters of modern literature, in the course of an exceptionally gay, cordial dinner. This is the new literary army taking shape." The menu consisted of Bovary soup, salmon-trout *à la fille Élisa,* chicken stuffed with truffles *à la Saint-Antoine,* artichokes *au cœur simple,* parfait *naturaliste,* Coupeau wines, and *Assommoir* liqueurs.[5] Flaubert, who undoubtedly enjoyed the occasion, was nevertheless hostile to schools and -isms in general. Goncourt, more and more jealous of Zola's success, tended to go his own way. It was soon apparent that Zola was the real leader of Naturalism. While he always insisted that Naturalism was not a clique or a coterie but rather a concept or a phase of literature, he rarely failed to reply to attacks; he wrote unremittingly in support of works and authors he viewed with favor, and he denounced the old-fashioned, the sentimental—everything, in a word, that was not, in his eyes, true to life. He admired Hugo's genius but severely criticized much of his work. Sardou he called a mere amuser. Dumas *fils* would be a good Naturalist if he did not moralize so much; Augier suffered from a similar defect. At the same time, Zola's articles show that even if no coterie existed, he supported, whenever he could, promising writers on the Naturalist side.

Of the five young men who were the principal hosts at the dinner of April 16, several—Huysmans in particular—had already published. For most of them, however, a volume of short stories entitled *Les Soirées de Médan* (1880) constituted a veritable launching. The story of this collection has often been told. It was first thought of one evening at Zola's Paris apartment where Alexis, Céard, Hennique, Maupassant, and Huysmans frequently went after dining together. On this occasion, they were reminiscing about the Franco-Prussian War. Hennique suggested that each one write a story connected with the war and that the narratives be published together in one volume. The idea was accepted, and, according to Céard, the title was chosen to render homage to the hospitality the group had enjoyed at Zola's country house where he now lived eight months a year and where he received his friends as freely as in Paris. For this collection Maupassant wrote "Boule de suif"; Huysmans contributed "Sac au dos"; Céard, "La Saignée"; Hennique, "L'Affaire du Grand 7"; Alexis, Après la bataille"; and Zola, "L'Attaque du moulin." The book created something of a sensation, and, if nothing else, revealed the great talent of Guy de Maupassant. Of this collection, the two stories most read today are his and Zola's.

While *Les Soirées de Médan* mark a date to be remembered in the history of French Naturalism, a much more important event of 1880 for any serious student of the movement was the publication of *Nana*.

II Nana

If the destructive power of love was apparent in *Une page d'amour*, it is even more strikingly evident in this new novel, which created as great a sensation as *L'Assommoir* and sold even better. This is scarcely surprising in view of the subject, for what Zola was really treating here was not love but sex. An immense gulf separates Hélène Grandjean from his new heroine, Anna Coupeau. The former, like any normal person, was capable of experiencing sexual desire which, in her case, was never completely isolated from the appeal of personality. She was a woman of taste and refinement. Nana, on the other hand, is a harlot, and in the course of the novel, she becomes "a force of nature, a ferment of destruction, without willing it herself, corrupting and disorganizing Paris between her snowy thighs." [6]

This aggrandizement of the prostitute suggests that Zola treated a traditional theme in a new and personal way. The fallen woman, the victim of masculine perfidy, the fatal beauty drawing men irresistibly under her sway, the prostitute "with a heart of gold," the calculating demimondaine—all existed in French literature before Zola put pen to paper. L'abbé Prévost's Manon Lescaut, Hugo's Marion de Lorme and Fantine, Balzac's Mme Marneffe, Murger's Mimi, Dumas' Marguerite Gautier and Suzanne d'Ange, and Goncourt's Élisa come to mind. They frequently had their counterparts, sometimes their models in real life. Under the Second Empire, the demimondaine flourished. Blanche d'Antigny, Anna Deslions, and Cora Pearl, for example, were topflight courtesans with a wide reputation. Yet none of them had a career equal in significance to that of Zola's Nana.

In earlier works, in *La Confession de Claude* and in *Madeleine Férat,* Zola had touched on the theme. His heroines, as we have seen, were not demimondaines. Laurence, in the *Confession,* was a fallen girl, a prostitute, whom an idealistic young man sought vainly to rehabilitate; Madeleine, a young woman whose one misstep had fatal consequences. While Madeleine, it will be recalled, was viewed by the old housekeeper as a Fatal Woman, she was far from being one. The accusation was quite unjust. In 1869, when Zola submitted his first list of novels to Albert Lacroix, he included one on the demimonde, or, as he put it, "le monde galant." By 1879, with new experience and knowledge of the world as it is, he was ready to treat this subject and to give it greater import than had any of his predecessors.

His knowledge, however, did not include firsthand acquaintance with the demimonde. Before his liaison with the girl who became his wife, he was too poor, as well as too timid, to try to frequent it. Since then, he had led—in contrast to many of his contemporaries—a remarkably chaste existence. Furthermore, he maintained that the writer needed a placid, uneventful marriage as "the very prerequisite of good work, of regular, solid output." "The chaste writer," he also said, "can be immediately recognized by the fierce virility of his touch. He is filled with desires as he writes, and these desires prompt the outbursts in his great masterpieces." [7] In consequence, before writing even the *Ébauche* to *Nana,* Zola had to document himself on the demimonde. In this extremity, he appealed to his friends, Edmond Laporte, Ludovic Halévy, and Henri Céard, for information. They furnished him with many facts about the demimonde in general, and about certain demimondaines in particular.[8]

The *Ébauche* contains, as it does frequently, a central character and a general idea. Nana, already known to Zola's readers from *L'Assommoir* where her first seventeen years were reported, is to be the protagonist. She is "the true prostitute" ("la vraie fille"), a fitting descendant of the Macquart line, but a good-natured girl ("bonne fille"). She is the embodiment of sex appeal. The more general subject is that of the "pack after a bitch who is not in heat and laughs at those who pursue her." The book is to be "the poem of male desires." This thought leads Zola to plan on a *tableau de mœurs* and a biting satire of Second Empire society. The latter will be accomplished in part by the portrayal of Nana's principal victim, Count Muffat de Beuville, chamberlain to the Empress, and Muffat's wife Sabine. A host of other characters contributes to the *tableau de mœurs* and many of them to the narrative of Nana's career.

In the opening chapter, Nana is presented in the title role of *La Blonde Vénus*, a musical play of the type being produced by Offenbach and Halévy. Zola had a poor opinion of Offenbach's music,[9] but this type of play had been all the rage in Paris in the 1860's. In spite of the fact that Nana can neither sing nor act, she succeeds in not alienating the audience in the first two acts and then captures it in the third when she appears virtually naked, covered merely with a flimsy gauze which revealed "her rounded shoulders, her Amazon's breasts with their pink nipples stiff and rigid like spears, her broad hips swaying voluptuously, her plump blonde's thighs." The audience, largely masculine, was stilled: "No one was laughing now. The men's faces were serious as they leaned forward, their nostrils pinched, their mouths dry and taut. [. . .] All of a sudden, in the good-natured girl, the woman appeared, disturbing, bringing with her the contagious madness of her sex, opening up the unknown depths of desire. Nana was smiling, but with the determined smile of a devourer of men."

The symbolic significance of Nana is clearly suggested in these lines; she is not only "Venus arising from the waves with no veil save her tresses"; she is also the Fatal Woman, the "femme lubrique," the "ferment de destruction." And the audience, which includes several of Nana's future lovers, is obviously titillated.

What is more, it is not merely this fictitious audience that is responsive to her appeal. Was not perhaps Zola himself "filled with desires" as he wrote, and did not these desires "prompt" such an outburst? It seems highly probable, for the puritan streak in his character is to be explained by the combination of attraction and aversion to sex. His whole work reveals that he was both fascinated and repelled by the erotic.

Although the theater continues to furnish important incidents and motifs to the novel, Nana's personal life is followed more closely after this performance than her theatrical career. She is still not above making a quick franc by running to an assignation arranged by the procuress Mme Tricon, but she soon becomes the mistress of the wealthy banker Steiner who keeps her in luxury. He buys a country house for her where she good-naturedly lets herself be persuaded by the longing of young Georges Hugon who is scarcely more than a schoolboy. She then seduces Count Muffat but quickly breaks with both him and Steiner to take up with Fontan, a low comedian, who treats her with contempt and brutality. She has a Lesbian affair with Satin, a young prostitute of about her own age. Then she again accepts Muffat who keeps her even more luxuriously than Steiner ever did. She is the modern decadent, untroubled by convention or by conscience.

The combination of attraction and aversion to sex that existed in Zola explains in good part Count Muffat. Present at the first performance of *La Blonde Vénus*, he falls little by little under Nana's spell. A puritanical background accounts for his resistance. His childhood had been filled with the reading of pious books warning him of the wiles of the devil and the weaknesses of the flesh. His marriage was devoid of passion. Suddenly the attraction of the flesh was revealed to him. By the end of the first chapter, as Nana left the theater in the company of a foreign prince, he gave up the struggle.

Then, with brain on fire, Muffat decided to walk home. The struggle within him had wholly ceased. A flood of new life was drowning out the ideas and beliefs he had harbored for forty years. While he strode the boulevards, the last carriages deafened him with Nana's name; the street-lights set a nude body dancing before his eyes, evoking the supple arms, the white shoulders of Nana; and he felt that he belonged to her, that he would have abjured everything, sold everything, to possess her for a single hour that very night. Youth was awakening at last, a greedy, adolescent puberty, flaming suddenly in his cold, Catholic make-up and in the dignity acquired in his mature age.

From this point on his fall is rapid. He soon possesses her, though it would be more accurate to say that she possesses him, for she merely sells herself to the man and obviously cares nothing for him. Indeed, within three months she is treating him with contempt and has so little regard for his feelings that she informs him of his wife's infidelity. Here, Zola creates one of the few poignant moments of the book. His description of Muffat's despair, as he roams the streets of Paris in the moonlight, which gives way to darkness and to rain, and as he stands under the lighted window of Fauchery's apartment watching a shadow drama in which his wife is one of the principals, inspires a momentary sympathy and pity for the Count. But when his downfall goes even further, it is difficult for the reader to sympathize. Nana so bewitches him that he is not only impoverished but is completely degraded by her. Before their liaison is ended, she even treats him like an animal, sometimes making him act the part of a bear, sometimes that of a dog[10] or a horse. Once she demands that he wear his chamberlain's uniform of which she then makes fun, and completes the process of degradation by kicking him in the behind, making him take off the costume and walk and spit on it. Zola goes to such extremes that he turns Muffat into an unbelievable figure, for while it is not unknown for men idealistically chaste in their youth to become sensual in their middle age,[11] it is not credible that a man of Muffat's background, education, and standing should so completely degrade himself. Only when he discovers his doddering, senile father-in-law in bed with Nana does he finally break with her. In the last part of the book he ceases to be a convincing character.

Space does not permit full analysis of this novel even though other characters and scenes deserve attention. Of the latter, only two can be briefly discussed.[12] The first is the description of the Grand-Prix at Longchamp. It had been the subject of one of Zola's "chroniques" in *Le Sémaphore de Marseille,* but he did not content himself with referring to that text, now three years old. He went to the track on June 8, 1879, armed with notebook and pencil, and took copious notes. The result in the novel is an extraordinarily colorful, vivid description of the grounds, the track, the spectators, the race itself. It is linked to the central action of the book, for Nana is there in person, and a horse named for her is not only entered in the race but wins it in a photo-finish. The enthusiasm aroused by this victory is tremendous. Nana, surrounded by an excited crowd, experiences a veritable apotheosis. She appears, as Zola put it, to be "Queen Venus enthroned amid cheering, delirious subjects."

The other scene is that in which Nana's corpse just after her death is the central figure. The chapter was qualified by Flaubert as *michelangelesque*. This woman who had recently been so chic, so successful in her fashion, a "marquise" in the ancient profession of streetwalkers and courtesans, an aristocrat of vice, who had owned a luxurious house in a stylish quarter of Paris and spent two hundred thousand francs a year, ruining many a man in the process, lies dead of smallpox in a hotel room, while outside, war having been declared, patriotic crowds surge along the boulevard shouting "On to Berlin! On to Berlin!" Zola's description of her corpse on the very last page is deliberately revolting. The single phrase, "Venus was rotting," will perhaps give some idea of the rest. At the conclusion of his frightful picture, "On to Berlin" is heard once more. The combination of her death and the outbreak of the fatal Franco-Prussian War completes the satire. The country is being led to a great debacle by a ruling class as corrupt as the harlot at whose rise it had connived, a harlot, who, coming from working-class origins, had taken, in a sense, class vengeance upon them. As in many of Zola's novels, the end coincides with a great catastrophe or one that is obviously approaching.

Nana is Zola's most notorious novel. Is it also, as Mr. Turnell maintains, one of his most successful and ingenious? Judged as a symbolic novel, the answer is yes. Flaubert was enthusiastic. "Nana," he wrote to the author, "turns into myth without ceasing to be a woman." And he wrote to Charpentier: "What a book! It's tremendous! and friend Zola is a man of genius. Let everyone realize it." [13] When viewed from other points of view than the symbolical, the book raises doubts. Not only does Muffat cease to be a credible character, but the social group chosen by Zola for his canvas, though numerous, is limited. This group is vividly depicted, but it is not a thoroughly representative microcosm of French society. From this realistic point of view, *Nana* seems less successful. It remains, nevertheless, an extraordinary production.

one of those "excessive" books Zola intended to write, a clear proof of his exceptional genius.[14]

The remaining three novels to be reviewed in this chapter, *Pot-Bouille*, *Au bonheur des dames*, and *La Joie de vivre*, cannot be classified as major productions, though Zola prepared them with his customary care and zeal. Certainly they are not in the class of *L'Assommoir*, nor even in that of *Nana*.

Pot-Bouille

One of the articles Zola wrote for *Le Figaro* in 1881 was entitled "L'Adultère dans la bourgeoisie." Its central idea was the following: "If in the working class, environment and upbringing push girls into prostitution, in the middle class they lead them to adultery." The article went on to suggest that the middle-class marriage market is a cause of evil. Mothers teach their daughters how to catch a young man by the skilful use of sexual attraction. "It's a veritable course in decent prostitution." The resulting marriages are without genuine affection.

The same idea underlies *Pot-Bouille*.[15] Zola intended to show that morally the bourgeoisie was inferior to the working class. A large modern apartment house in the rue de Choiseul, inhabited by a number of middle-class families, is placed in comparison with the tenement house in the rue de la Goutte d'or where Gervaise came to her dreadful end. *Pot-Bouille* is a kind of middle-class *Assommoir*, though it is far from being as good a book. To be sure, it contains a devastating satire of the bourgeoisie; but the middle class was not quite as bad as Zola portrayed it. Moreover, he committed the error of overdoing sexual irregularity. One fornication or adultery follows so closely on another that the reader is surfeited and ends by being incredulous.

Octave Mouret, one of the principal characters in *Pot-Bouille*, is obviously a promising young businessman; but his sexual habits resemble those of an alley cat. Campardon is perhaps a good architect, but he does not hesitate to introduce his mistress into his own household, aided by his wife's tolerance. The other characters are mostly on the same level. One of them, Trublot, a skirt-chaser par excellence, so pleased Paul Alexis that he adopted the name when he became a columnist for a Paris paper. Monsieur Josserand is the only character who touches the reader. At the end of the second chapter there is a moving moment when, exploited by his family for whom he works himself to the bone, insulted by his wife who is a monster of selfishness, he finds himself alone and returns to his after-hours work by which he gains a few additional francs for his wife and children. "Tears that he did not feel fell on the papers before him in the solemn silence of the house where everyone now slept." He is ultimately so harassed by his family, particularly by his wife, that he dies. He seems deserving of a better fate.

Of the many scenes which upset conservative critics in 1882 when *Pot-Bouille* appeared, the description of the birth of an illegitimate baby to one of the maids in the apartment house caused possibly the greatest uproar. Adèle gives birth to this child, alone, unattended, in her room at the top of the building. If Zola had never witnessed a birth, he must have documented himself fairly well, for his account is clinical and reasonably accurate. Dr. Martineau, who wrote a book on *Le Roman scientifique d'Émile Zola,* found only one minor error in it. It is not, of course, agreeable reading. Zola later justified it by saying that descriptions of death abound in literature, so why not birth? It was a legitimate question.

In his preliminary notes Zola wrote that he intended to link his novel with historical events, and he chose for that purpose the Roman question and the elections of 1863. When he came to compose the novel, this intention, admittedly secondary, was largely though not completely overlooked. This is a pity, for had Zola put greater stress on politics, he could have reinforced the impression of bourgeois irresponsibility and reactionary stolidity that he sought to create. Additional material on this subject would also have broken the monotony of the tiresome seductions and adulteries which fill far too many pages. To be sure, Zola writes about them with a kind of emotional revulsion which is sensed by the perceptive reader. The book is not salacious; it does not incite to lust, nor does it use what are called in English "four-letter words." For the devotee of certain twentieth-century novels this will perhaps be a matter of astonishment, though, doubtless, not regret.

III   Au bonheur des dames

After this book, Zola must have decided that his series needed a little "sweetness and light." *Au bonheur des dames* was the result. The title, which means literally "At the ladies' good fortune," is the name of a department store in Paris, run by Octave Mouret, the young businessman of *Pot-Bouille*. Before the end of that novel, he married his employer, Mme Hédouin. When she conveniently died, Mouret became the sole owner of the establishment. The new novel relates his successful transformation of this store into an extremely large enterprise which ruins, through its greater resources and its resulting ability to undercut its competitors' prices, all the little shops in the neighborhood.

The subject had been in Zola's mind ever since 1871. In the revised list of novels he drew up at that time there is one on "big business (dry goods)—Octave Mouret." He was aware of the development of Parisian department stores like the Louvre and the Bon Marché, and saw in their growth and success a significant feature of urban civilization. As usual, he took careful notes on these two establishments, and many of the details were incorporated into his book, which is consequently in part a piece of commercial and social history presented in the form of fiction.

The novel has a Horatio Alger tinge, for the central female character is a poor but honest and virtuous working girl, Denise Baudu, who, after great trials and tribulations, marries at the end of the novel her wealthy employer, Octave Mouret.[16] At the same time, Zola being Zola, the novel is not all sweetness and light. Sex in its less pleasing aspects is by no means absent. The vicious bickerings, jealousies, slanders, and intrigues of the store's employees are not concealed. The crushing defeat of the little shop owners in the vicinity is complete and even heart-rending. Zola was quite unable to avoid sex and disaster even though he told himself in the *Ébauche* that this novel should contain a "complete change of philosophy" and be "without pessimism," that it must not let "the stupidity and melancholy of life be its conclusion," but rather that it should reveal "the continual labor" that is life's characteristic, as well as "the power and gayety" that accompany its birth. "In a word," Zola added, the novel must "march with the century, must express the century, which is a century of action and conquest, of efforts in all directions."[17] This the novel does to a marked extent, and although it is not one of the best volumes of *Les Rougon-Macquart*, it is the first concentrated study of a modern economic or industrial phenomenon in the series. *L'Assommoir* was more sociological than economic. *Au bonheur des dames* forecasts books like *Germinal, L'Argent,* and *La Bête humaine.*

The reader of *Au bonheur des dames,* a reasonably optimistic book, would not suspect that its author was possessed by fear of death. Yet such is the case. He had revealed this fear in a short story, "La Mort d'Olivier Bécaille," published in Russia in 1879. Its hero was so haunted by the prospect of death that the very thought made him shudder at night and quake even by day. That this is a reflection, though perhaps an exaggerated one, of Zola's own feelings seems fairly clear.[18]

The following year, 1880, three deaths brought grief to Zola. The first, that of Edmond Duranty, the novelist, and a friend since the early 1860's, occurred on April 10. Flaubert died on May 8, and Zola was profoundly affected.[19] Then, on October 17, the death of his mother provided the worst blow of all. His fear of death, genuine enough before 1880, now became morbid.

IV   La Joie de vivre

This is manifest in *La Joie de vivre,* first begun in 1880, but put aside, according to Paul Alexis,[20] because the subject was too painful. Three years later Zola returned to it. The subject is more complex than the above lines might suggest, for it deals with much more than the phenomenon of death. The principal male character, Lazare Chanteau, is a failure, a man incapable of perseverance, who undertakes one project after another, and is unsuccessful in all. He has a morbid fear of death, particularly after the demise of his mother. Like Olivier Bécaille and like Zola himself, the very thought makes him shudder. In spite of this resemblance to the author, one cannot see here a complete self-portrait, for Lazare Chanteau obviously has none of the determination, drive, and persistence that were among Zola's prominent traits. The principal female character is almost the moral antithesis of Lazare. She is Pauline Quenu, the daughter of the couple prominent in *Le Ventre de Paris.* A descendant of the Macquart line, she has somehow escaped all the undesirable qualities of her forebears. Zola intended, as he wrote in his *Ébauche,* to show her "full of the joy of life, dominating all catastrophes, rising up every time, and raising up the others (more or less)." [21] This intention is carried out. Pauline is the personification of goodness, gayety, and optimism. She is, moreover, a reflection of a trait in Zola himself, for while he was deeply conscious of the painfulness of life, "la douleur de vivre," he also strongly experienced the joy of existence, "la joie d'être." [22] A third character is Lazare's father, in whose house Pauline comes to live. If any human being should long for death, it is this man, who suffers excruciatingly from gout. Yet, at the end of the book, when his malady has become chronic and he is in constant agony, he cries out, on learning that their servant has committed suicide: "How stupid to kill oneself." It is, therefore, apparent that the title of the novel has a double significance. That it is partly ironical is confirmed by a letter that Zola wrote later to a Dutch acquaintance in which he stated that he had first thought of calling it *Le Mal de vivre* but that the irony of *La Joie de vivre* seemed to him preferable.[23] Yet the title is also to be taken literally. The novel gives a positive, affirmative answer to the age-old question: is life, even when accompanied by suffering and tribulation, worth living?

For some critics, *La Joie de vivre* is Zola's best psychological novel. Lazare's terror of death is successfully portrayed, as well as his weaknesses and insecurities and his essential selfishness. The conflict in Pauline is also well done. She falls in love with Lazare, becomes engaged to him, and is about to marry him when she discovers that he is interested in another girl. After a long conflict with herself, which Zola analyzes quite skilfully, she gives him up and urges him to marry the other. Pauline is, indeed, a model of virtue and goodness. In fact, one's chief reservation about the book is that she is almost too good to be true.[24]

V *Conclusions*

In retrospect, it is apparent that none of the novels discussed in this chapter is equal in scope and stature to *L'Assommoir*. *Nana* comes closest to achieving such distinction. Its symbolic and satiric values are very high, its literary achievements notable. The trouble is that its characters fail as human beings to touch the reader, as Gervaise indubitably does. To the fate of Nana's victims one is quite indifferent. A momentary pity for Count Muffat is quickly dissipated by the spectacle of his further follies. In general, the reader feels that Nana's dupes are deservedly victimized. Then Nana herself inspires no sympathy, to say nothing of admiration. Her final destruction causes no regret, whereas the decline of Gervaise with its inevitable denouement of death is a very moving spectacle, particularly as the reader's sympathy had been won by the chronicle of her initial, laborious success. While Nana may be the product of society, she makes no effort to escape from her lot. On the contrary, she seems quite satisfied. For this harlot, therefore, compassion is scarcely indicated. The reader may be amused or interested, intellectually persuaded that Zola's satire was justified. He is not stirred to the depths of his soul. Compassion, of course, is not the only touchstone by which great literature may be identified, but when it exists together with excellence of form, the value of a work is surely enhanced.

The other novels reviewed in this chapter also fail, for one reason or another, to move the reader as *L'Assommoir* does; the only possible exception is *La Joie de vivre* where the issue of the joy or joylessness of life is made to seem important. If this book is not more effective, it is because Pauline is incredibly virtuous, and because Lazare and his father are not sufficiently distinguished. On the moral level, Lazare is clearly an inferior human being. The father suffers physically, and, to the extent that any physical pain arouses compassion, the reader can sympathize with him. But Chanteau's mind and character have little distinction; sympathy for him remains, therefore, superficial. *La Joie de vivre* has been called a "magnificent failure." As a chronicle of human failure and human neuroses, it contains, in fact, many powerful pages.

All five novels reveal genuine and, frequently, extraordinary talent. They tended in the 1880's to confirm the opinion, widespread after *L'Assommoir*, that Zola was one of the leading novelists of his time.

CHAPTER 7

The Top of the Ladder

Germinal

WITH *L'Assommoir* Zola had by no means exhausted the subject of the working class. His notes, preserved in the Bibliothèque Nationale, indicate that since 1871 he had intended to write a second novel on this social group. It was to be "particularly political," treating the worker in revolt and involving the Commune with its tragic end.[1] As time went on, his plans were modified. This second novel, involving the Commune, was never composed as such. That unhappy event found its place ultimately in *La Débâcle*, which deals with the great events of 1870–71.

Nevertheless, a second book on the working class was desirable. As laundresses and roofers had existed before the Industrial Revolution, the novelty of *L'Assommoir* was less in the trades depicted than in the picture of living and laboring conditions in an urban working-class environment. The representation of a big industry in which scores of workers toiled for a given company and were dependent on that company for their bread would be something quite different and even more significant. *Au bonheur des dames* evoked a commercial establishment organized on a large scale. While this was a modern phenomenon, it placed before the reading public men and women who did not feel themselves to be proletarian. Although they possessed neither special skills, nor land, nor tools, and were, therefore, pretty much at the mercy of their employer, they were "white-collar" workers. The real proletarian was to be found in the textile factories and metallurgical foundries, in the shops and locomotives of the rapidly developing railroads, and in the mines.

Moreover, the Second Empire, especially in its later years, was shaken by a number of violent conflicts in some of these industries. Encouraged by the 1864 "law on coalitions," which abolished penalties against nonviolent organizing, but which was not really as liberal as many people thought, the workers went on strike in the textile factories of Roubaix, in the metallurgical foundries of Le Creusot, and in the mines of La Ricamarie and Aubin, where blood was spilled. As stated in an earlier chapter, some strikes were aided by the International, founded in 1864. The conflict between capital and labor rapidly took on the aspect of a class struggle, greatly alarmed the bourgeoisie, and assumed an importance which a socially minded novelist like Émile Zola could scarcely ignore.

Nevertheless in mid-January, 1884, if Edmond de Goncourt is to be credited, Zola had not fully made up his mind just what subject he would next treat. He was thinking of a book on the peasantry, according to the famous *Journal*, which goes on to state that a novel on the railroads appeared to be in abeyance, and that the man of Médan tended to favor "a strike in the mining country with a bourgeois having his throat slit on the first page." A trial would follow in which "a serious and thorough study of the social problem would be introduced." [2] It seems likely that before the month was over, Zola had come to a decision and had begun the composition of his *Ébauche*.

Was he influenced in this decision by other events than those just recorded? It is possible that Daudet's *Jack* and three second-rate novels, Hector Malot's *Sans famille*, which devoted several chapters to work in the mines; Maurice Talmeyr's *Le Grisou*, also inspired by the mining industry; and Yves Guyot's *Scènes de l'enfer social—La famille Pichot*, which told not only of a mining accident, but of a strike and its repression, may have whetted his interest. A painting by Alfred Roll, entitled *La Grève des mineurs*, exhibited at the Salon of 1880, may also have stimulated his imagination.

Then, as he pondered the problem, recent political events undoubtedly intrigued him. The discussion of socialism had been enlivened in 1881–82 by a serious split in the French socialist party. In those years, the majority rejected the Marxist doctrine of social revolution in favor of a policy of gradualism. In 1883 they took the title of "Federation of Socialist Workers." The minority, opposing this heresy, founded the Labor Party (*Parti ouvrier*) under the leadership of Jules Guesde and continued to preach the need for revolution. During these and preceding years, nihilist agitation was going on. The terrorist campaign in Russia, culminating in the assassination of Alexander II in March, 1881, filled the press of Western Europe. The influx of Russian political refugees and agitators, including men like Bakunin, Kropotkin, and Lavrov, did not go unobserved in the French capital. Zola met some of them through Turgenev with whom he must have discussed the subject of anarchism and nihilism. He devoted to the Russian question one of the articles he wrote in 1881 for *Le Figaro*. Entitled "La République en Russie," it treated among other matters the nihilists' recruitment and their aims. A book narrating a strike could obviously be enriched by introducing into its pages these intellectual currents of the century.

Zola had penned about half of his *Ébauche* when a strike broke out on February 21 in the mines of Anzin in northern France. One of the most serious conflicts of this period, it was to last fifty-six days and create much bitterness. From Zola's point of view it was almost providential. He promptly left Paris for the scene of action. There, he sought out Alfred Giard, whom he had met in 1883. Giard was a liberal-minded Deputy from the constituency of Valenciennes, and he permitted Zola to pose as his secretary. Thanks to that stratagem, the novelist was able to attend workers' meetings that otherwise would not have been open to him. He stayed a week or two in the area, interviewing the miners, visiting their villages and the cafés they frequented. He met Émile Basly, the leader of the strikers. After carefully viewing the miners' side, he got permission from the director of the Anzin mines to inspect their establishments. Guided by one of the company's engineers, he even descended into one of the pits, which he thoroughly explored. In later years, an old mine inspector said that he had never heard a man ask so many questions. Then, returning to Paris, Zola resumed work on his *Ébauche*, the tone and temper of which were modified by his observations, for some of the more sensational melodrama he had had in mind was dropped. Not that all melodrama was eliminated; far from it. But his imagination was now tethered to a realistic experience, so that it is doubtful whether the finished novel would seem quite as authentic or be quite as moving had Zola never visited Anzin. At the same time as he resumed work on the *Ébauche*, he started, or perhaps continued, his labor of documentation, consulting technical works dealing with the mining industry, newspaper accounts of earlier strikes, particularly those at La Ricamarie and Aubin in 1869,[3] as well as books on socialism and the Workers' International. *Germi-*

nal was to be a heavily documented novel,[4] one of the most heavily documented of the *Rougon-Macquart.*

I *The Characters*

Even more than *L'Assommoir, Germinal* is a profoundly human, compassionate, and moving book. It shows a number of human beings engaged in an epic struggle against forces greater than themselves, a conflict in which they are doomed to defeat. The class struggle is predominant and in the course of the narrative it takes on the overwhelming quality of a cataclysm. Yet in defeat the miners do not appear as something negligible and insignificant. They have lost a battle, but their cause is still alive. At the end there is even a vision of hope for the future.

Both sides in this contest are carefully presented, for Zola, though obviously sympathizing with the workers, made a conscientious effort not to paint the owners of the mines too blackly. The latter are represented by three different characters. First appears Léon Grégoire who, with his wife and daughter, typifies the idle capitalist. He is a Montsou shareholder, living exclusively on dividends. Zola treats him with some irony, showing his profound and comical astonishment when he discovers that the miners can resent the fact that he and his family live comfortably on the proceeds of their work. There is irony, too, in Zola's presentation of their charities, for in a smug, holier-than-thou attitude, they give only food and clothing, never cash, which they believe would be consumed exclusively in drink. At the same time, the novelist indicates that the Grégoires are law-abiding, respectable people, who do not spend their money in riotous living. At the end, like almost everyone else in this novel, they suffer, for their daughter Cécile is killed in a scene that has symbolic significance.

Next, on the capitalist side, there is M. Deneulin, the owner of the Jean-Bart mine. Early in the planning stage Zola determined to include a small concern, run by an individual owner. Caught between two fires, the miners' demands and competition from a big trust, he is unable to do for his workers all that he might wish. His final defeat rings, says Zola, "the death-knell of small industrial enterprises," a phenomenon not limited to the nineteenth century, for it is a common occurrence in our own day.

Finally, on the owners' side, stands M. Hennebeau, the local manager of the Montsou mines. He is the paid representative of shareholders scattered, with the exception of Grégoire, over France and Europe. These absentee owners have no contact with the miners and no interest in their problems. Hennebeau takes his orders from a board of Directors sitting in Paris who rarely appear in the mining area. He is a decent fellow, with no personal desire to crush the workers, somewhat rigid, thoroughly upright, whose only weakness is his desire for his unfaithful and unworthy wife.

The workers' side is fully represented. Its principal character is Étienne Lantier, an offspring of the Macquart line, his mother being none other than Gervaise, the heroine of *L'Assommoir*. In Zola's genealogical tree, he is described as having a "heredity of drunkenness turning into homicidal mania," and during the planning stage that aspect of Étienne remained important in Zola's mind. Modifications of that conception soon crept in. By the time Zola came to write the novel, Étienne's alcoholism and homicidal tendencies played a relatively minor role. When he finally kills, it is almost as much in self-defense as through an irresistible, hereditary impulse. Meanwhile, his part in the action was magnified, for in the last part of the *Ébauche*, Zola decided to make him the leader of the strike and simultaneously a representative of one of the intellectual currents of the period. On almost the last page of the *Ébauche*, the novelist says that Étienne is an "authoritative collectivist"—in other words, a Marxist. Étienne comes from the outside and can view the working conditions in the mines with a fresh, though perhaps not wholly unprejudiced, eye. At times, he is Zola's mouthpiece.

Rasseneur, a former miner turned *cabaretier*, represents the reformist approach to labor problems. He is intended to be a *possibiliste*, typical of those who in the years 1881–83 broke away from the Marxist group in the French socialist movement. The growing rivalry between him and Étienne for leadership of the miners furnishes one of the dramatic actions of the novel.

A third intellectual attitude is exhibited by Souvarine, a Russian nihilist with a past of terroristic activity. A disciple of Bakunin, "the exterminator," his physical appearance was quite possibly modeled on Peter Kropotkin, one of the Russian anarchist-refugees in France. Like Bakunin, he believes in destruction by any means. Only when present society has been wiped out can a new world of justice and fraternity be built. He momentarily wins Étienne Lantier to some of his views, but Lantier, like a good

Frenchman, is too rational to accept very long the irrational folly of his Russian friend. Playing a passive role during the first six parts of the novel, Souvarine takes the spotlight in the seventh and last part when he sabotages the Voreux mine.

Among the ordinary workers represented in the novel, the foremost are the members of the Maheu family. The oldest is Vincent Maheu (called Bonnemort), who had been brutalized and stupefied by forty-five years spent underground. His stunted body, square hands, simian arms; his flat, livid features blotched with blue; his unsteady legs; and his dreadful cough and black spittle testify to the unhealthy life he has led. Instead of finding a little comfort and ease in his old age, he is forced to cling to a surface job he can barely accomplish in order to get a few more francs pension. His son, Toussaint, is now the real head of the family. The type of the good worker, he is conscientious and reliable; uneducated but not stupid. His wife Constance is similar in character, but with a tendency toward vehemence, which emerges little by little in the course of the narrative. She is, to be sure, somewhat animalistic as a result of the near starvation level at which she is forced to live. Of her many children, Alzire, Jeanlin, and Catherine are the most notable. Alzire is an eight-year-old humpback, a helpful, appealing little girl. Her life and death provide some of the kind of pathos furnished in L'Assommoir by Lalie Bijard. Jeanlin can be classified as a delinquent. Catherine, although a product of her environment, has undeniable charm. Going the way of most girls of this mining area who have sex relations before marriage, she becomes, more or less fatalistically, the mistress of Chaval; but her growing fondness for Étienne, whom she has met too late, is made manifest as the book proceeds. The rivalry between Chaval, a brute of a worker, selfish and treacherous, and Étienne Lantier over the girl provides some of the drama of the book. Moreover, Zola's tender analysis of the unspoken love of Catherine and Étienne offsets to some degree the brutality that inevitably occurs in the narrative. She dies in Étienne's arms, in one of those scenes where Zola combines love and death in intimate and inseparable union.

The Maheu family is clearly placed in symbolic opposition to the Grégoires. The latter, wealthy, comfortable, and well fed, with domestic servants at their beck and call, possessing an excellently furnished house with large grounds, have but one child.

The Maheus, with seven children, are so poor that they can barely get enough to eat. Their house, although neat, is so small that one bed has to serve night and day, Bonnemort taking the bed that Zacharie, the eldest son, has just vacated. They are compelled to ask for credit from the unscrupulous grocer Maigrat, who has close affiliations with the mining company, and are so greatly in debt that they are forced to the humiliation of asking charity from the Grégoire family. When, at the end of the book, Cécile Grégoire is strangled by Bonnemort, her death balances that of little Alzire, the hunchbacked daughter of the Maheus, who dies of starvation during the strike, and that of Toussaint Maheu, killed by a bullet in the clash that ultimately occurs between the strikers and the troops summoned to protect the mines. Cécile's death becomes a component of the social conflict, an almost inevitable part of the denouement. As Zola put it in one of his work-sheets, he wished to show this logical outcome, "cette résultante," of the Maheus versus the Grégoires.

Other figures complete the cast on the workers' side. Like Chaval, they are not admirable. The Levaque family is in marked contrast to the Maheus, for its members are slovenly and stupid. Pierron, a stool pigeon for the company, and his wife, who sleeps with the head foreman, command no respect. Her mother, La Brûlé, represents blind hatred of the capitalists. Mouque is a second Bonnemort, and his son, Mouquet, is a thoughtless young worker, destined, had he lived, to be as stupefied as his father.

Mouque's daughter, La Mouquette, deserves a special word. There is more than a touch of the Rabelaisian in her. Endowed by nature with enormous breasts and buttocks, which almost burst out of her clothing, she is crude in her language, shameless in her morals, but generally good-natured. Her large "derrière" is deliberately displayed to indicate her scorn or contempt. In the chapter on the clash with the soldiers, this gesture provokes "tempestuous laughter." But this girl, so gross in her appearance and manners, is capable of self-sacrifice. When the bullets fly, she saves Catherine's life at the cost of her own. A minor character, she nevertheless stays in one's memory.

None of these characters is analyzed in depth. This is due, at least in part, to the fact that most of them are simple people without subtlety. Furthermore, the group in this social narrative is more important than the individual. Zola indicates, as in the case of La Mouquette, their physical appearance fairly clearly, and emphasizes an essential trait of character. Some bodily feature and this trait are then stressed in the volume, so that by the end they are stamped on the reader's mind. Zola's method of presentation is specially well illustrated by one of the minor characters of the book, La Brûlé. She is first described as "an old witch with owl's eyes and a pinched mouth like a miser's purse" quarreling with another woman. On her next appearance she is dubbed an "old revolutionary," which is certainly not incompatible with her physical appearance. The third time, after a row with Pierron, she walks away "with her eagle nose, her flying white hair, her long skinny arms gesticulating furiously." In the night meeting of the miners in the forest, eerily lighted by the moon, La Brûlé is again the old witch. All this prepares the reader fully for the part she plays in the revolutionary march of the miners across the country-side, during which she is frequently in the lead and always violent. In the climax of this action, before Hennebeau's house, she appears as an avenging Fury, threatening to strip Cécile Grégoire, wreaking vengeance on the corpse of Maigrat, and carrying her booty on the end of a stick in a procession suggestive of bloody revolution. In the clash with the soldiers, she takes a characteristic part. Here too, her flying hair, her skinny frame, her furious gestures, and her violent insults suggest the evil witch of legendary fame. She is the one who begins the "battle of the bricks," and she is killed in the volley fired by the exasperated soldiers, brought down "stiff and crackling, like a bundle of dry faggots, stammering one last oath in the gurgling of blood." In these cases, Zola sometimes uses the word "witch," sometimes merely a connotative epithet. For the psychological trait, he sometimes uses the word "revolutionary," or again something connotative. In all of *Germinal* one finds no better example of Zola's skill in uniting the physical and the psychological, in suggesting the more than human, the supernatural, than in this portrait of a minor, but picturesque character.[5]

II   *Structure, Action, and* tableau de mœurs

The central action of *Germinal* is the great strike which breaks out in the Montsou mines in 1866. Although it is, of course, fictitious, it is at the same time a composite of the Anzin strike of 1884 and those at La Ricamarie and Aubin of 1869, with a few details from the 1870 conflicts at Le Creusot and Fourchambault, as well as from the disturbance at Montceau-les-Mines in 1882. Aided by his powerful imagination, which was essentially visual and epic, Zola welded all the details into an artistic whole.

The novel is divided into seven parts with a total of forty chapters, each chapter being only half as long as those in *L'Assommoir*. Not until the fourth part does the strike begin. Over a third of the novel is devoted to the preliminaries and testifies to the importance Zola attached to them. These first three parts relate Étienne's arrival in the mining area, his first day's work in the mine, and his growing role among the miners during the next eight months. They present the dramatis personae, give an admirably clear and detailed *tableau de mœurs,* and indicate the consequences of the living and working conditions on the miners, anemia being one result, promiscuity another. The terrible drabness of the miners' lives is scarcely relieved by the few pleasures they enjoy. This is made clear by the renowned chapter on the Montsou fair-day, which is a good example of Zola's Naturalistic art, realistic and picturesque. The chapter is enlivened by such things as a cock fight, a finch contest, and a row between a nailsmith and Catherine's brother Zacharie; it is climaxed by a lively dance at the Bon-Joyeux. Zola's capacity for evoking sound and motion is illustrated by this dance, for he shows couples responding to the music, giving a vision, almost a blur, of moving, sweating men and girls, swaying and swirling in a welter of sound. Those not dancing sit in another part of the establishment drinking beer, the mothers among them suckling their babies, "while the children who could already walk, gorged with beer and on all fours under the table, relieved themselves without shame." If the dance itself is a moving picture, with emphasis on sound and motion, the later paragraph succeeds in depicting the blonde flesh of the Flemish women, the flowing beer, and the semidrunken laughter which "kept mouths open, gaping to the ears." However much the miners and their women seem to enjoy all this, the reader cannot help concluding that even in their amusements the lot of these human beings is far from enviable. Can society do no more for them than this?

The politico-economic problem is posed in these preliminary parts. Indeed, the very first chapter evokes the spectacle of simple men a prey to a capitalistic ogre, "a sated and crouching god to whom they all gave their flesh and whom they had never seen."

Through Étienne Lantier this issue is defined more clearly still. In Part III, when he becomes a boarder at the Maheus', their evening conversations inevitably return to the great question. These passages show, in Auerbach's phrase, the "awakening" of the proletariat; Zola can be seen fashioning his work "out of the great problems of the age." [6] He was one of the few French novelists of the nineteenth century to do this, and in *Germinal* he picked on a problem germane not only to his day but to ours as well.

Strikes are rarely caused by theories and generalities. The Montsou strike is no exception. It was touched off by the Company's action in announcing a new system of remuneration. Seeking to reduce its operating costs because of the prevailing economic depression, it posted a notice to the effect that after a certain date the *boisage* (propping or tubbing) would be paid for separately and the compensation for each truckload of coal reduced by 20 per cent. The Company claimed that the reduction was balanced by the payment for the *boisage,* but the workers were convinced that in reality they were confronted by a lowering of an already intolerably low wage. That same evening, at Rasseneur's café, the strike was decided upon. "Rasseneur," writes Zola, "no longer opposed it, and Souvarine accepted it as a first step. Étienne summed up the situation in a word: if it definitely wanted the strike, the Company would have it."

The next three parts of the novel are devoted to the strike. On the first day, there is a confrontation between Hennebeau and a delegation of the miners. It takes place in Hennebeau's residence where the luxurious furnishings are in marked contrast to the miners' poverty. Maheu has been chosen as spokesman, and in a very effective scene this quiet, simple man somehow finds the words with which to state the workers' case. Since they are apparently condemned to starve anyway, he says that they "prefer to die doing nothing." Then, when Étienne intervenes, the opposition between him and Hennebeau takes on greater symbolic significance; Étienne introduces a revolutionary note while Hennebeau takes refuge in his Board of Directors and unwittingly conjures up that "sated and crouching god," that capitalistic ogre already glimpsed in the opening chapter.

As in the Anzin strike of 1884, discipline reigns at Montsou during the first weeks, and hopes ride high. But, little by little, hopes diminish as the few francs previously collected by Étienne for the emergency fund are spent. In the third week, he summons Pluchart, an organizer for the Workers' International, to their aid. At the end of a meeting at the Bon-Joyeux café, the miners vote en bloc to join the International. This turns out disappointingly, for the famous Association, so feared by the bourgeois, is able to send only four thousand francs, which last but three days. More threateningly than ever, starvation looms before the miners' families. In this extremity, Étienne calls a meeting in the nearby forest of Vandame.

It takes place on a cold January night under a rising moon and is one of the famous scenes of the book. Not only does it mark a decisive turn in the action, for the miners resolve to force all the pits in the area to shut down, including Deneulin's Jean-Bart, where Chaval and Catherine are still at work, but it establishes Étienne's supremacy, consecrates his victory over Rasseneur, and through his speech establishes the revolutionary aim of the strikers. It is, moreover, an admirable example of Zola's manipulation of a crowd and a wonderful illustration of his artistry in uniting the blackness of the earth, the lines of the trees, and the solid mass of humanity, illuminated at first only by the starry sky, then gradually by the cold, white light of the moon. Indeed, this luminary is used for theatrical effect, as Étienne, mounted on a tree stump, barely visible in the darkness, but soon spotlighted by the rising moon, seemingly takes on increased stature. The whole scene is enhanced by this play of light and shade. As the enthusiasm grows and turns to frenzy, the clearing is bathed by the moonlight "while the beeches, erect in their strength, with the delicate tracing of their branches, black against the white sky, neither saw nor heard the miserable beings in turmoil at their feet." And the chapter closes as "the tempest of these three thousand voices filled the sky, and died away in the pure brightness of the moon." Zola's exploitation of the moonlight in this chapter recalls that of *La Fortune des Rougon*. In the earlier novel, it lent charm and beauty to the midnight stroll of Silvère and Miette, and gave grandeur to the arrival of the marching insurgents. Here it casts a spell on the scene in the clearing, creating at times a hallucinatory effect, portentous of things to come.[7]

From this moment on, the action moves in a crescendo. With some interludes, parts V and VI are devoted to the violence that inevitably enters this strike as the miners seek to make it general.

Assembling before the Jean-Bart mine, they cut the cables, extinguish the boiler fires, and force Chaval, who emerges from the pit along with Catherine and the others, to join them. One then witnesses the march, turning at times into a headlong dash, of the miners and their women across the frozen plain from one pit to another, becoming ever more destructive. At one point, the engineer Négrel, Mme Hennebeau, Deneulin's daughters, and Cécile Grégoire glimpse the mob. They behold the mining women "with their disheveled hair, their naked skin showing through their rags" and hundreds of men, some of them carrying iron bars, "a compact mass which rolled along like a single block in confused, serried rank." "Their eyes were burning, and only the holes of black mouths singing the *Marseillaise* were distinguishable, the stanzas being lost in a jumbled roar, accompanied by the clang of sabots on the hard earth. Above their backs, amid the bristling iron bars, an axe passed by, carried erect, and this single axe, which was like a standard, showed in the clear air the sharp profile of a guillotine-blade." Against the crimson sunset, this spectacle seemed, indeed, "the red vision of the revolution, which would inevitably sweep them all away, on some bloody evening at the end of the century." From the miners, "a great cry arose, dominating the *Marseillaise:* 'Bread! bread! bread!'" This is another famous scene and needs to be read in its entirety and in the original French to be fully appreciated.

The miners' march comes to an end before Hennebeau's residence where a final bit of violence takes place. Cécile Grégoire, mauled by the women, is rescued, but Maigrat, the grocer, not so lucky, is killed in a fall and his body mutilated in savage vengeance. Finally, the gendarmes arrive, and an uneasy peace is restored.

After an interlude of relative quiet, violence recurs in the clash between the miners and the soldiers guarding the pits. In this chapter, the narration moves logically and implacably to its inevitable conclusion of death. Zola permits the events to unfold in chronological order, creating automatically their formidable impact. This device, which is essentially dramatic, is accompanied by another, used by Zola with great skill. It consists in weaving fact and fiction into a single, integral pattern. Events which occurred in the 1869 strikes at La Ricamarie and Aubin are introduced here. Words, gestures, and incidents, which Zola culled from the newspaper accounts of the time, find their appropriate place in the clash at Montsou. But, of course, he did not rely exclusively on source material. One finds a good example of his method in the climax of the clash. As at La Ricamarie, the soldiers in *Germinal* fire spontaneously before their commanding officer can issue the order. As at Aubin, the dead number fourteen. On the other hand, the persons killed are of Zola's choice and invention. La Mouquette's act of self-sacrifice had no counterpart in 1869. La Brûlé's activity and her death were not modeled on that of any specific woman in the earlier strikes. At the end, Zola brings to this scene Abbé Ranvier, the socialist priest, who calls down God's wrath on the assassins and the fire of heaven on the bourgeois guilty of "massacring the workers and the disinherited of the world." His source material provided no such incident as this.[8] Like the march of the miners in Part V, this battle between the workers and the soldiers is notable for the skilful manipulation of a mob. It, too, needs to be read in its entirety and in the original French.

The seventh and last part of *Germinal* is devoted to a great catastrophe, caused by the courageous but criminal sabotage of Souvarine. A number of reasons impelled Zola to compose this section. A large-scale mining accident was almost inevitably expected in a novel on the mines. The cave-in early in the novel, which resulted in the death of one man and broken legs for Jeanlin, was a small affair. Something more impressive was needed, and this disaster, partially inspired by a genuine accident which took place in the Marles pit in the Pas-de-Calais,[9] filled the need. By using sabotage rather than a natural accident, Zola was able to link the action to one of those intellectual currents which he was exploring. Throughout the first six parts, the anarchist Souvarine had played a relatively minor role. He could now come into his own, and show of what he was capable. Then, the idea of letting Chaval, Catherine, and Étienne be caught in the bottom of the mine, threatened by the rising waters, not only created a tense situation, but permitted a final solution of this triangle theme. It also gave Zola the opportunity to introduce a rescue operation which demonstrated the better, nobler side of human beings in a moment of crisis. Perhaps, above all, the introduction of a great catastrophe at the end was used by the novelist to reinforce, by its apocalyptic, nightmarish quality, the epic character of the book.

[125]

ÉMILE ZOLA

III *Artistry*

Action and characters are by no means all of *Germinal*. The
descriptive elements in this book are of major importance in any
evaluation of Zola's achievement. For example, there is Le Voreux
mine, the very name of which is suggestive of voracity. From the
first moment that Étienne Lantier beholds it on a black March
night pierced only by a few "dismal lanterns" and "three coal fires
burning in braziers," the mine appears as something monstrous
and fearful. "With its squat brick buildings, crammed together in
a hollow, and the chimney sticking up like a menacing horn, the
pit was evil-looking, a voracious beast crouching there to devour
the world." It swallows its daily ration of human flesh, "gulping
down men in mouthfuls of twenty or thirty." Throughout the book
it is presented in these terms, and when it is finally destroyed by
Souvarine's sabotage Zola depicts its demise in similar, anthropomorphic words:

The boiler-house broke apart and disappeared. Next the square tower
containing the gasping pump fell on its face like a man shot down. And
then a terrifying thing: they saw the engine, torn from its bed, wrestling
against death with limbs pulled from their joints. It moved, extended
its driving-rod, its gigantic knee, as though it meant to rise, but
smashed, swallowed up, it was dying. The only thing that remained
standing was the thirty-meter chimney, and that was swaying like a
ship's mast in a hurricane.[. . .] Suddenly, it plunged down, devoured
by the earth, like a great candle that had melted away. [. . .] It was
all over. The evil beast, crouching in its hollow, sated with human
flesh, had drawn its last long heavy breath.

The mine is clearly presented as being more than a material phenomenon. Like the markets in *Le Ventre de Paris*, it takes on a life
of its own, but here it is transformed into an evil force with which
human beings are compelled to struggle—an epic battle in which
neither side wins. Is it then, as some critics maintain, the chief
protagonist of the novel? Not quite, for men and women were all-
important in Zola's eyes and remained central to his narrative.

The animals which appear in *Germinal*, as in other volumes of
the *Rougon-Macquart*, contribute more than a sentimental touch
to the narrative. Zola introduces, for example, two horses, Bataille
and Trompette, who work underground, and uses them most

effectively in some of the dramatic situations. The corpse of
Trompette, brought to the surface just before the clash between
the miners and the troops, creates a grim, lugubrious prelude to
that ultimately tragic scene. At the end of the chapter the horse
still lies there, in eloquent juxtaposition to the human corpses the
clash has produced. The death of Bataille, in the great catastrophe
caused by Souvarine, contributes to the sentiment of terror created by these pages. This panic-stricken horse, galloping through
the tunnels of the mine, caught at last in a narrowing gallery and
the rising waters, and dying with a long, agonized cry, becomes
almost a symbol of apocalyptic doom.

The epic struggle in *Germinal* of men and women against
forces greater, more powerful than they is not only narrated in
terms of action but frequently suggested by appropriate images
and colors.[10] The opening chapter does this with great skill. The
pitch-black, starless night with a lone traveler advancing on a
road "that runs straight as a jetty through the blinding, swirling
sea of darkness"; the March wind "blowing in great gusts like a
storm at sea," a wind made icy "from sweeping over miles of
marshes and bare earth," seeming to "bring the death of labor and
scarcity which would kill countless men," wailing "like the cry of
weariness and hunger rising from the depths of night"—all this
contains the notion of storm and struggle and, with the emphasis
on black, sets the most important tone of the novel, for the blackness carries with it a presentiment, a foreboding, perhaps even a
prediction of disaster. Then, when the darkness is pierced by red,
by the flames of braziers and the flickering of the lanterns mentioned above, when Bonnemort and his horse appear against this
backdrop of reddish light, and Étienne is able to glimpse in the
distance, in "the dark unknown," furnaces and coke ovens with
their "sloping lines of crimson flames," when the capitalistic ogre
is evoked in this eerie darkness touched by red, the feeling of
terror and the notion of struggle are reinforced. If black is synonymous with gloom and disaster, the flames of this chapter are suggestive not only of conflict, but also of Hell, of the hell which will
be depicted in pages to come.

The storm image recurs, sometimes with the appropriate colors
of red and black, in later chapters of the book. It reappears in "the
roaring flood of strikers" sweeping across the plain in Part V.
Here, the picture is tinged with red by the brilliant, crimson sun-

set and the revolutionary singing of the *Marseillaise*. The image occurs, naturally, in the scene before the Voreux pit in Part VI, where "waves" of strikers swell the threatening group of men and women confronting the troops and finally a "downpour" of bricks hurled at the soldiers produces a volley of bullets with the red blood of the workers gushing forth. The storm image supports the apocalyptic description of the final catastrophe, when the waters flooding the mine roll implacably in seeming pursuit of the human beings caught underground. In this description black plays a major role, for after the few flickers of their lamps are extinguished, the total blackness in which Catherine and Étienne wait and try to hope is not the least of their ordeals. A remnant of the storm image in the final chapter of the book recalls the recent conflict: "Little red clouds, the last vapors of the night, were melting into the limpid blue." But the termination suggested by the disappearance of the clouds is only temporary. The last page, with emphasis once again on red and black, predicts a new contest in which truth and justice will awake and prevail, for the "fiery rays" of an April sun were causing the rebirth of nature, and in similar fashion "men were springing up, a black avenging host was slowly germinating in the furrows, thrusting upwards for the harvest of the coming century, and soon this germination would crack the earth asunder."

Although black and red are unquestionably the predominant tones of the book, white is frequently used. In the forest scene, the cold light of the rising moon, combined with the shadows and the surrounding darkness, was extraordinarily effective. Elsewhere, white plays varied roles. The whiteness of Bataille, looming up out of the darkness of the inundated mine, gives to that death scene a ghostly quality which enhances its horror. Then, one of the means by which Zola contrasts the Maheus and the Grégoires is by the opposition of two kinds of white. The anemic, pallid complexion of the mining family is contrasted with the healthy, fresh appearance of the well-fed, well-dressed bourgeois. Later on, white and black are used. In the scenes of violence in which Cécile Grégoire and Bonnemort figure, "the girl's white throat" fascinates the old miner; and when, in Part VII, he clasps her neck again, this time fatally, his features are "tattooed with coal" and a "black saliva" dribbles from his mouth. Here and there, white is used for other purposes. The white tablecloth in the Grégoires' dining room, the white and blue lacquered furniture in Cécile's bedroom, and her white dressing gown are obviously suggestive—along with the domestic servants, ample food, and so forth—of a certain economic level which the miners cannot attain. Père Quandieu, the old foreman stubbornly resisting the strikers threatening his pit (Chapter 4, Part V), is made more impressive by his white hair and goatee, miraculously unstained by coal. And, when the miners emerge from the blackness of their underground labors into the light of day, they can feel a measure of relief and experience a sentiment of escape in spite of the drabness of the surface area.

The novel's last page, predicting future conflict, brings at the same time an expression of hope, and here Zola introduces most effectively two appropriate colors: green and gold. "The April sun," he writes, "was now well up in the sky, shedding its glorious warming rays on the teeming earth. Life was springing from her fertile womb, buds were bursting into leaf, and the fields were quickening with fresh green grass. Everywhere seeds were swelling and lengthening, cracking open the plain in their upward thrust for warmth and light." Under a golden sunrise, the scene is filled with the verdure of spring, bearing with it a vision of new life and the promise of better things to come.

The colors and images of *Germinal* give it a distinction that the dismal landscape and the drab life of the miners could not. Sometimes the images are classical, sometimes not; but they are always appropriate and effective. They indicate that Zola, as has been seen in previous novels, is more than a realist; he is a poet, and a poet with a robust style, for he demonstrates in *Germinal* the kind of writing he had recently advised young novelists to adopt. He had told them to abandon the "artistic style," the "écriture artiste," advocated by Goncourt, in favor of a "strong, solid, simple, human style." [11] What he did in *Germinal* was perhaps not simple, but it can justifiably be called "strong, solid, and human." An elemental book, which deals with the problem of survival in a material universe, *Germinal* uses methods appropriate to that problem. The four elements, earth, air, fire, and water, play their respective and sometimes ambivalent roles. Men dig in the earth and run the risk of being crushed by the earth. At the same time, they are warmed by the coal from it bowels and nourished by its products. They breathe the good air; but the poisonous air which may occur in a mine, *le grisou* (fire-damp), is capable of destroying them. The wind that blows can be gentle, but on this dismal plain it is more a wind of famine or revolt; in the latter case it can lead to a better day. Fire flashes from the soldiers' guns, and it burns underground creating a worse hell in the Jean-Bart mine than the working conditions metaphorically create in Le Voreux. And as for water, its destructive power, when unleashed, is only too apparent in the great catastrophe at the end. The material universe with which these human beings have to cope can be and is an awesome thing.

The new life and new hope manifest in the final vision of the book, the concept of death followed by renewal—this is one of the major themes of Zola's work. In the action of this novel and in its symbolic title *Germinal,* one of the spring months of the calendar adopted by the French Revolution, that theme is clearly expressed. Taking on the aspect of a fertility myth, it helps to enhance the epic grandeur of the book. Furthermore, in spite of the pessimistic picture and narrative of much of the volume, this theme is essentially optimistic, suitable to the idea expressed or implied in *Le Roman expérimental* that the Naturalistic novelist seeks by his presentation of a given situation to arouse interest and inspire social action, thereby improving the lot of humanity. The title came to Zola quite suddenly, after he had hesitated over many others. At first, it seemed to him "too mystical, too symbolic." But it represented what he was looking for: "a revolutionary April, a flight of a decrepit, sick society into the springtime." [12] His intentions are made clear not only by these lines, but by a letter he wrote to Francis Magnard of *Le Figaro* in April, 1885. Answering the accusation that he had slandered the miners by depicting them as sexually immoral and besotted by drink, he replied: "My only desire was to show them [the miners] as our society fashions them, and to provoke so much pity, such a strong outcry for justice, that France will finally cease letting herself be devoured by the ambition of a handful of politicians, in order to attend to the health and material well-being of her children."

With *Germinal,* Zola reached the top of the ladder of success and achieved his greatest literary triumph. Powerful, extremely poetic in its way, compassionate, indignant, dominated, in spite of the conflict between workers and management, by a strong sentiment of human solidarity, it consecrated Zola's reputation not only in France but in Europe. Karl Bleibtreu in Germany doubtless expressed the view of many Europeans when he declared: "I do not believe any man so abandoned by God, so bare of all moral emotion, that he is not gripped and shaken by this immortal work." [13] To that opinion most twentieth-century Americans will subscribe.

CHAPTER 8

L'OEuvre *and* La Terre

L'*ŒUVRE* (1886) is neither an autobiography of Zola nor a novelized biography of Paul Cézanne, but both men have made an important contribution to it. Without relating his own career in detail from birth on, Zola nevertheless nostalgically returned to his youth, recalling the days when he tramped the hills of Provence with his friends, reviewing the difficulties they sought to overcome in Paris, evoking their struggles, enthusiasms, pleasures, successes, and defeats. *L'Œuvre* is a novel "into which," he said in a letter to Henry Céard, "my memories and my heart have overflowed." [1] As for Cézanne, his part in the narration is a complicated question.

Art and love are the two main themes, embodied in the two principal characters, Claude Lantier and Christine Hallegrain. The former, briefly seen in *Le Ventre de Paris,* is a son of Gervaise Macquart, and through him the book is linked to the Rougon-Macquart tribe. Issuing from a neurotic line, the gifted son of a commonplace mother and a scoundrelly father, his unfortunate heredity makes of him an incomplete genius, something like Frenhofer in Balzac's *Chef-d'œuvre inconnu.* "With Claude Lantier," Zola wrote in his *Ébauche,*

I want to depict the struggle of the artist with nature, the effort of creation in a work of art, the blood and tears that are shed in giving one's own flesh to create life, the endless battle with truth, the constant defeats, the wrestling with the Angel. In a word, I shall relate my own intimate life as a creative artist, the perpetual pangs of childbirth. But I shall enlarge the subject by a dramatic action, by never letting Claude be satisfied, unable to give birth to the genius within him, and by leading him to kill himself before his unachieved masterpiece. He shall not be impotent, but a creative artist with too wide an ambition, seeking to put all nature into one canvas, and he will die of it. [. . .]

The whole artistic drama will therefore lie in this struggle of the painter with nature.[2]

Claude Lantier, then, as a key sentence of this text indicates, is, in part, a reflection of Zola himself; obviously an important difference is that Zola succeeded in his own work, whereas Claude Lantier failed. To explain Claude Lantier more fully one needs to turn to certain painters of the period. Here, the *Ébauche* is again helpful, for Zola writes in another paragraph that his protagonist is "a Manet, a dramatized Cézanne, nearer to Cézanne." Something of the early Cézanne, the young man of the 1860's, does exist in Lantier. Like his prototype, Lantier has spent his youth in Provence, in and around Plassans, the fictional equivalent of Aix-en-Provence. Like Cézanne—and Zola—he has gone to school there and, as one of "the three inseparables," has shared the enthusiasms and the pleasures of that little group. Like the Aixois painter, he has settled in Paris, where he becomes a part of the youthful revolt against the standards of the École des Beaux-Arts. Moreover, the Cézanne of the 1860's had the instability and lack of self-confidence that exist in Lantier. Zola had not forgotten that he wrote to Baille in 1861: "Paul may have the genius of a great painter, he will never have the genius to become one. The slightest obstacle causes him despair."[3] The case for identifying Lantier with Cézanne is, therefore, neither wholly foolish nor unsubstantial. Cézanne, himself, apparently came to that conclusion, for he ceased to see his old friend after the publication of *L'Œuvre*.[4] Nevertheless, it would be an error to make a complete identification; Claude Lantier is by no means exclusively modeled on Cézanne. In addition to Manet and to Zola, traces of Monet, Jongkind, and André Gill may be found in Lantier's life or work.

The most obvious link between Lantier and Manet is the painting which Lantier in the novel and Manet in real life exhibited in 1863 at the famous Salon des Refusés, authorized by direct order of the Emperor Napoleon III. Lantier's, entitled "Plein-Air," is inspired by Manet's "Déjeuner sur l'herbe":

This picture, as yet unfinished, was characterized by superb vigor and the brilliance of its colors. Into a forest clearing with a solid background of greenery fell a stream of sunlight, broken only by the darkness of a path running off to the left with a bright spot of light in the far distance. Lying on the grass in the foreground, among the lush vegetation of June, was the naked figure of a woman. One arm was folded beneath her head, thus bringing her breasts into prominence; her eyes were closed and she was smiling into space as she basked in the golden sunlight. In the background, two other nude women, one dark and one fair, were laughing and tumbling each other on the grass, making two lovely patches of flesh-color against the green, while in the foreground, to make the necessary contrast, the artist had merely placed a man's figure. He wore a plain black velvet jacket, and was seated on the grass so that nothing could be seen but his back and his left hand upon which he was leaning.[5]

In Manet's painting, there are two men, neither of whom has his back to the onlooker, and two women, only one of whom is completely nude; she is seated, not lying down, but the idea of placing a naked woman in such a situation was clearly suggested to Zola by Manet's work. When Lantier's painting was completed and hung at the Salon, it had the same effect as Manet's: it provoked nothing but laughter and ridicule from the uncomprehending bourgeois.

The remaining artists of the above-mentioned group all lent something to the views or personality of Lantier. In addition to some biographical details,[6] Monet probably contributed his theories on color. He maintained, as does Lantier, that color varies according to the time of day and the intensity of the light. He had not yet produced his series of Cathedral paintings, but long before 1885, when Zola was writing *L'Œuvre*, he had rejected the notion that there were accepted colors for flesh, water, trees, or houses. What the artist sees in the light of the moment is what he should depict. When Claude Lantier says: "We need sunlight, open air, painting that is clear and fresh, things and people as they really are seen in the light," he is echoing the theories of Monet and other members of the Impressionist school. Then, the modernism of Jongkind possibly contributed something to Zola's painter, who is attracted to the life and movement of contemporary Paris, as was the Dutchman. Finally, André Gill, the illustrator of *L'Assommoir*, whose death occurred in the insane asylum of Charenton on May 2, 1885, just as Zola was about to begin writing the novel, possessed much of the instability that characterized Lantier. He had, moreover, an unhappy experience at the 1882 Salon similar to that which Lantier endured in the tenth chapter of *L'Œuvre*.[7] The result is that Claude Lantier must be viewed as a composite figure. No matter what Zola said in his *Ébauche*, in the finished novel Lantier does not appear to represent exclusively any one painter of the Second Empire.

The dramatic action of *L'Œuvre* is twofold. It lies first of all in Lantier's struggle to realize himself, to produce the masterpiece of which he dreams, and secondly, in the rivalry which ultimately develops between Christine Hallegrain, the lovely girl who becomes Claude's wife after being his mistress, and Art. The two themes are intimately linked, for the girl who finally consents to pose nude for "Plein-Air" is Christine. That part of the picture is, in reality, a great success. Claude's friends recognize it, particularly Bongrand, an older painter of genuine merit, who says to Claude: "I'd give ten years of my life to have painted that stunning gal of yours." But the general failure of the picture and particularly the public reaction to it is such as to depress Claude and lead Christine, in an explosion of sympathy and love, into Claude's bed, and then to send them both to Bennecourt where they spend four years in a kind of earthly paradise. This is a charming episode, but its episodic nature becomes increasingly apparent. They inevitably return to Paris where Claude's great ordeal really begins. Christine's begins as well, for when Claude, after three successive failures, decides to do something vast and settles on the upstream view of the river from the Pont des Saints-Pères (called today the Pont du Carrousel), her suffering, as he "struggles with nature," equals his. At the end, when Claude has been driven virtually insane by his project, she rebels, seeing in the symbolic naked woman he placed in the center of this picture an enemy to her hopes, her tranquillity, her very life. "It's this painting, *your* painting! It's killing me, it has poisoned my life. [. . .] Ten years of neglect and repression; ten years of meaning nothing to you, of feeling more and more rejected, and reduced to the role of a mere servant, seeing this other creature, this thief, come between us, seeing her take you triumphantly and insultingly from me [. . .]. And now she is your wife, isn't she? It is not I but she who sleeps with you, the damned trollop!"

The woman of the picture has become a kind of Fatal Woman, devourer of this man, if not of men in general; to combat her,

Christine herself plays the role of a Fatal Woman, seducing her husband in a highly sensual scene. The whole passage, culminating in Claude's seduction, followed by his suicide, is one of those extraordinary compositions of Zola's that go beyond the limits of objective, realistic art. The chapter ends, however, with a bit of somber realism. Calling on his memories of Duranty's funeral, Zola has depicted Claude's in simple and moving terms.

Other characters in *L'Œuvre* can be identified in varying degree. Dubuche, the architect, is one of "the three inseparables" of Lantier's youth, and must, therefore, be partially inspired by Baptistin Baille. Here, as in the case of Cézanne, the identification is by no means complete, for Baille's career is not paralleled by Dubuche's. Jory, the journalist, owes something to Paul Alexis; Fagerolles, to Maupassant and Gervex;[8] and Mahoudeau to the sculptor, Philippe Solari, one of Zola's schoolboy friends. Bongrand, according to Zola's preliminary notes, is "a stylish Manet, a Flaubert, rather." The most complete and indubitable identification of all is that of Lantier's faithful friend, Sandoz, with Zola himself. Sandoz is a novelist, a Naturalistic novelist, and through him Zola defines the essence of his novels which embrace:

the new study of physiological man, the all-important role of environment, the perpetual act of creation to be found in nature; in short, life itself, all life from one end of the animal kingdom to the other, universal life without heights or depths, beauty or ugliness; the audacities of language he wished to introduce, the conviction that everything should be expressed, that abominable words are often as necessary as red-hot irons, that a language may be enriched by dipping into such necessities; and finally, the sexual act, the origin and everlasting achievement of the world itself, brought out of the hiding place of shame, where it is usually relegated, and reinstated in its glory, in the full light of day.[9]

There is obviously intellectual kinship between Lantier and Sandoz, hardly surprising since both reflect the views of their creator.

L'Œuvre is certainly not the most important novel nor the best of the Rougon-Macquart series, but it is, in many ways, an absorbing book. Those interested in the early life of Zola and in the history of French Impressionism should find it fascinating. The first half of the book with its reminiscences, its romantic treatment of the boy-meets-girl theme, and its description of the prolonged honeymoon at Bennecourt is delightfully written. One senses, to be sure, that tragedy is in the offing, and tragedy inevitably arrives. Here, as in other novels of the series, Zola's sympathy with and understanding of human frailty is manifest on almost every page. The final remark of Sandoz, as he and Bongrand leave the cemetery where Claude's body has been lowered into the grave, is Zola's answer to the problem of human tribulations. "And now, back to work" (*allons travailler*), says Sandoz, "still blinded by his tears." Work is the supreme refuge and consolation of the strong.

Zola finished writing this novel in February, 1886, and turned immediately to other projects. He had collaborated with Busnach on a stage adaptation of *Germinal* which had been scheduled to appear late in 1885. The government censors, however, forbade the performance because of the "socialistic tendency of the work." It was finally produced in April, 1888, but has never been published. Meanwhile, Zola helped Busnach on the adaptation of *Le Ventre de Paris* which opened at the Théâtre de Paris on February 18, 1887. Both plays were more melodramatic than the novels from which they were drawn. Zola explained in an interview with Gaston Calmette that he and Busnach were experimenting, that they were writing "*mixed* plays, in which there are things of which I disapprove, conventions I condemn, but in which there are tableaux I like and would willingly sign, if I were alone." [10] These plays did not consume all of Zola's time. The rest was largely devoted to the planning, composition, and publication of *La Terre,* the novel on the peasantry which he had planned to write for the last four or five years.

La Terre

As was the case concerning the proletarian novels, Zola felt that his predecessors had not treated country life with the necessary realism and scope. George Sand's peasants were too idealized. Balzac's were closer to reality but were introduced in an episodic rather than a central fashion. Maupassant, like Balzac, saw their cupidity and avarice, but did not treat them on a large scale. Furthermore, as Zola himself put it in 1876: "None of our novelists, up to the present moment, has dared relate the true dramas of the village, because none of them has felt himself to be in possession of the truth." [11]

The fact is that before 1887 the only book which presented the peasantry with what Zola considered adequate realism was his own novel, *La Faute de l'abbé Mouret*. Readers will remember that the inhabitants of Les Artaud were exceedingly avaricious, sexually uninhibited, and fanatical in their passion for land. The tableau Zola gives of peasant life in *La Terre* is on a much larger scale and covers more aspects of country life, but is not essentially different. The same land-hunger, self-interest, and sexuality are present. In the earlier novel, attention was focused on Abbé Serge Mouret. In *La Terre*, what was subsidiary in 1875 becomes primordial.

Before writing this novel, Zola indulged in his customary planning. He spent a few days visiting La Beauce, the principal wheat-raising section of France. He interviewed Jules Guesde, the leader of the "Parti Ouvrier," to learn the socialist position on the agricultural problem. Friends and acquaintances provided him with information. He consulted various books, such as Eugène Bonnemère's *Histoire des paysans* and Abbé Roux's *Pensées*. This whole question has been exhaustively treated by Professor Guy Robert in "*La Terre*" *d'Émile Zola*, published in 1952. Those interested in the genesis of the novel will find all the necessary information in that notable volume.

The central theme of this novel is indicated in its title, *La Terre*. "I want to write the living poem of the land" were the first words of Zola's *Ébauche*. The book opens with a Millet-like scene in which Jean Macquart is pictured sowing wheat. He moves slowly forward, scattering the seed "with a long, sweeping movement of his arm," his body swaying to and fro, his heavy shoes sinking "into the rich soil and catching it up. Behind him a harrow to bury the grain followed slowly along, drawn by two horses." And the chapter ends as it began: "Jean sowed till night-fall. [. . .] He came and went with long rhythmical strides over the ploughed land; and the grain in his seed-bag dwindled, and the seed behind him fertilized the ground." Zola succeeds in this chapter in evoking what Victor Hugo called "le geste auguste du semeur." And he does it on a large scale, for other parcels of land are being sown; other men are trudging over the land scattering the seed with the same "obstinate gesture," a gesture of men at war with the immensity of the soil, intent on conquering its vastness, determined to win the struggle for life.

This vision of La Beauce is repeated, with appropriate variations, throughout the novel. At the end of the first part, Jean

L'Œuvre *and* La Terre

Macquart sees it under a light cover of snow: "the sky was clear and keen, dotted with stars—a wide, frosty sky, from which a bluish radiance fell with the purity of crystal, and the infinite expanse of La Beauce unfolded itself before him, white, flat, and motionless like a sea of ice." In Part III the growing crop is described: "the yellowish green of the wheat, the blue-green of the oats, the grayish green of the rye, fields extending to infinity, spread out in all directions, between the red patches of crimson clover." In August, the crop has matured. It has become "a sea of flaming gold [. . .] a sea whose fiery swell is stirred into movement by the slightest breath of wind." Part V opens with a description of the fertilizing of the land, bringing with it "the upward thrust of coming spring." "Decaying matter was returning to the common womb, death was on its way to re-create life." In the very last sentence of the book, La Beauce is again seen through the eyes of Jean Macquart: "He was leaving, when, for the last time, he let his gaze stray [. . .] to the endless tillage of La Beauce which the sowers, with their monotonous gesture, were filling with seed. Men might die, but seed was being sown, and the bread of life was springing from the earth."

In most of these passages, which are longer than indicated here, the accent is on fertility and life. Birth-growth-decay-death-rebirth, this process is the central concept on which the novel is based. Although the land nourishes, it is a harsh mother. Drought and disaster may wreak havoc. In Part II a hailstorm causes terrible damage. In Part III, a prolonged drought threatens the wheatfields. The battle of the peasants with nature is not easily won; yet their passion for the land is genuine and abiding. The old peasant of the book, Fouan, "had loved the land like a woman who kills and for whom one commits murder." When his son Buteau comes into possession of enough land, the young man is filled with satisfaction: "never had he plowed so deeply; it belonged to him, he wanted to penetrate it, fertilize it to the womb." Hourdequin, though more bourgeois than peasant, acquires the same passion, not only because he sees in the land "the common mother," but because he has fallen in love with it, has married it, and wants to impregnate it as he would a woman. In *La Faute de l'abbé Mouret*, sexual images and comparisons were frequent; the same can be said of *La Terre*.

Other features of country life appear in this novel. In addition to the sowing and harvesting, Zola depicts a social evening by the fire (in French, *la veillée*), a market scene, a "bal forain" (a traveling carnival), the insemination of a cow, and the birth of a calf, simultaneously, as it happens, with that of a child. These last incidents aroused a storm of criticism. The scene of insemination occurs in the opening chapter where a fourteen-year-old girl by the name of Françoise Mouche is leading a cow to a nearby farm which owns the bull. On the way, she has trouble with the frisky cow who begins to run and drags her along the ground. Jean Macquart comes to her aid. The little episode has the advantage of introducing the pair to each other, and is, therefore, a preliminary to later action in the novel. The actual scene of the cow's impregnation in which the girl has to assist the bull is depicted with a realism which shocked many contemporary readers. They were equally shocked by the scene depicting the birth of a calf to Buteau's cow while his wife is producing a baby only a few feet away. The realism here is even more uninhibited. But, in Zola's view, these things are a part of nature. As Victor Hugo once put it: "Everything in nature belongs to art." Zola doubtless surpassed him in applying that theory, but his pages are less shocking to twentieth-century readers than to those of 1887. It is noteworthy that in the scene of insemination neither Françoise nor Jean Macquart, who is with her, displays the slightest embarrassment. Moreover, these particular scenes contribute to the fertility theme and the life-cycle concept which animate the novel.

I *Action and Characters*

The dramatic action of *La Terre* is twofold. The first involves possession of land; the second, possession of a woman. Louis Fouan, seventy years old, in good health except for his legs, which no longer enable him to follow a plow or carry out the multiple farm chores entailing their use, decides to deed over his property to his two sons, Buteau and Hyacinthe, and his daughter, Fanny Delhomme, on condition they pay him a stipulated income which they soon fail to do. One of the principal themes of the book, therefore, is the ingratitude of children; another is the progressive decline of the old man, who is ultimately murdered by one of them. The drama involving possession of land is completed by the maneuvers of Buteau; after the death of his uncle, old Mouche, he takes his share of his father's land, marries Lise Mouche, to whom he has already given a child, and is thus enabled to work a respectably large piece of property which includes not only the land Lise has inherited but her sister's as well. He then seeks by the most ignoble means to prevent Françoise's marriage to Jean Macquart in order to avoid losing her share. Failing to do this, he hopes somehow to recover the lost property, as well as the house which has fallen to Françoise's lot. Murder brings about the desired result.

The second dramatic action centers on Françoise Mouche, who becomes an object of rivalry between Buteau and Jean Macquart, and an object of jealousy and hatred to her sister. It is linked to the first by Buteau's desire to own her land. He therefore seeks to possess her, by force if not by consent, even in his wife's presence, ultimately going so far as to enlist his wife's aid in the rape of her sister. Jean Macquart, on the other hand, has no ignoble motives. After first thinking that he wants to marry Lise, he realizes that it is the younger sister in whom he is really interested. Their marriage finally takes place, to the discomfiture of Buteau. Unfortunately, the feelings of Françoise and Jean are not identical. While he has genuine affection for her, she is unable to respond to it. As Zola shows quite skilfully, she is really attracted to her unworthy brother-in-law. It is one of those situations in human life which inevitably lead to some sort of tragedy, in this case, the tragedy of death. Zola handles it well.

Apart from the semilyrical passages on the fertility and the beauty of the earth, the best pages of the book are those depicting old Fouan's calvary. The second chapter of the fifth part has undeniably tragic grandeur. It opens with the old man out-of-doors on a damp, cold autumn afternoon, having just been thrown out of Buteau's house after a violent quarrel. His wandering then begins. Without a cent in his pocket, he dares not enter a café. Crossing the bridge, he finds himself before his daughter Fanny's house. Better to die of hunger, he thinks, than to ask asylum there after their earlier quarrel. His legs carry him almost mechanically to Hyacinthe's hovel, called Le Château; but the sharp laughter of La Trouille, ringing out suddenly, seems to paralyze him. She had sought to rob him when he lived with them. His fear of this girl, his granddaughter, drives him off. "For a long time he wandered at random. Night had fallen, the icy wind lashed him [. . .] Between two squalls a shower fell, sharp and stinging. Drenched, he walked on, soaked again by the rain." Finding himself before the ancestral house of the Fouans, now occupied by Françoise and Jean, he realizes he cannot take refuge with them; for from there, too, he has been driven away. Returning to Buteau's, he is wretched enough to enter; but again, on hearing Buteau say: "He's too fond of his belly not to come back when he's hungry," pride keeps him away. Later, he knocks at his sister's door and receives only mockery. His wandering continues. After twenty-four hours, hunger and cold send him back to Buteau's, where, surrendering, he eats and falls asleep. The rest of the chapter relates his growing solitude. His son finally ignores him. His grandson Jules, is, for a time, his only friend, but ultimately that solace goes. "He had no longer even this urchin to talk to, he buried himself in absolute silence; his solitude was widened and increased. Never a word on any subject to anyone." The old man's calvary is depicted on an epic scale, comparable to that of Père Goriot or King Lear. In these pages, Zola has successfully competed with Balzac and Shakespeare.

Other subjects contribute to this substantial novel. Agricultural problems were not confined to the small holdings of peasants; large properties had their full share. To illustrate this, Zola introduced La Borderie, a farm of about five hundred acres, and its owner, Alexandre Hourdequin. It is being run on a larger scale, with some mechanization and modern fertilization, yet Hourdequin has almost as much difficulty in dealing with depressed agricultural prices as do the peasants. The exploitation of this big farm provides one of the interesting contrasts of the book. The pages devoted to La Borderie are also the occasion for more sex; Hourdequin is under the spell of Jacqueline Cognet, one of his female workers. She is his mistress, but does not reserve her favors for him alone. Their relations prepare a part of the denouement, which includes not only the death of Françoise and Louis Fouan, but also the death of Hourdequin and the burning of his farm buildings. With the Franco-Prussian War looming ahead and virtually announced, these tragedies make one of those great catastrophic endings which characterize so many of the *Rougon-Macquart*.

II *Comedy in* La Terre

La Terre contains a noteworthy vein of Voltairian and Rabelaisian comedy. The first is illustrated by the irony in which Zola indulges at the expense of the ex-brothel keepers, M. and Mme Charles Badeuil, known rather as M. and Mme Charles. They have made a fortune with a house at Chartres and have retired, turning the place over to their daughter and son-in-law, Hector Vaucogne. In their retirement they have become ultra-respectable and highly moral. In the last chapter of Part III, M. Charles is anxiously interrogating his wife about their old establishment which she has just visited:

M. Charles was overheard questioning Madame Charles, without waiting to be alone with her, so anxious was he to hear how things were going at Chartres. It was a passion with him still; he was always thinking of this house, so energetically founded years ago, so regretted since their retirement. The news was not good. To be sure, their daughter Estelle was energetic and intelligent; but decidedly, their son-in-law Vaucogne, that flabby, spineless Achilles, did not back her up. He spent his days smoking his pipe; he let everything spoil and go to pieces [. . .] At each fresh ravage she reported, M. Charles gave a sigh; his arms hung down, his pallor increased. One last grievance, which she whispered in a lower voice, finished him off.

"Then, he goes himself with the girl in Number 5, a big, heavy girl . . ."

"What's that you say?"

"Oh, I'm sure of it, I've seen them."

M. Charles, trembling, clenched his fists, in a movement of exasperated indignation.

"The wretched fellow! To wear out his personnel! To squander his establishment! Oh, it's the end of everything."

The irony may not be very subtle, but it is irony rather than broad Rabelaisianism.

The latter is evident in the episode of the drunken donkey, in the warnings given by the pet geese of La Trouille to inform her of her father's arrival at inopportune moments, and above all in the noisy accomplishments of this same father, Hyacinthe Fouan. A word about this last character is necessary. He is known to the whole countryside by the name of Jésus-Christ—so-called because of his appearance, not for any Christlike qualities. He is, in fact, an idler and a drunkard who lives by poaching. Endowed by nature with extraordinary flatulence, he has made a talent of it, and convulses people by the blasts, resembling gunshots, which he can produce at will. Whether readers will find this funny depends on their sense of humor. If it is of the Rabelaisian type, they will be amused; if it is like Queen Victoria's, they obviously will not.

III *Other Matters and Conclusions*

Other characters people the pages of this book, and other topics are introduced. Fouan's older sister, La Grande, and her pathetic grandchildren, Palmyre and Hilarion, are not unimportant. The old woman, as indicated in the scene of Fouan's wandering, is as hard as nails, concerned only with acquiring money and keeping it. She is also malicious; when she helps Françoise, it is not through kindness, but to make trouble; she knows it will enrage Buteau and Lise. Her grandchildren are the victims of her selfishness. Isolated and unhappy, they have fallen into an incestuous relationship. The boy, mentally retarded, is a kind of monster. The poor girl, abandoned by her grandmother, dies from hunger and overwork while laboring on Buteau's land for a derisory wage. In the midst of the harvest, she is found "stretched out, with her face turned upwards to the sky, her arms in the form of a cross as though crucified on the earth which had used her up so quickly by its hard labor, and was killing her." The boy, taken in by his grandmother, who treats him like a beast of burden, is finally killed by her in a terrible scene of attempted rape.

Through the priest Abbé Godard, the tavern-keeper Lengaigne, Hyacinthe's friend Leroi (called Canon), the schoolmaster Lequeu, and a few others, Zola introduces the subjects of religion and politics. The peasants have their superstitions, but are essentially irreligious. In regard to politics, most of them are indifferent. Two elections occur: in the first, Chédeville, a former Orleanist turned Imperialist, is elected; in the second, he is defeated by Rochefontaine, an industrialist named as the official candidate by the government. Zola does not really develop either of these topics in any substantial way; they remain subsidiary to the rest. While planning the book, he wrote Van Santen Kolff: "Every time nowadays that I undertake a study, I run up against socialism." [12] *Germinal* may be a socialist novel, but certainly *La Terre* is not. Perhaps he was annoyed rather than won by Guesde's attitude in their interview.[13] Whatever the reason, he is less radical than in the earlier novel. Nowhere in *La Terre* is the institution of private property questioned. It is suggested that large farms can be more efficient than small; yet, at the end of the book, the small holdings are surviving in spite of all difficulties.

Although religious and political questions are less developed than they might have been, *La Terre* is conceived and written on a grand scale. The style is similar in many respects, always allowing for the difference of subject, to that of *L'Assommoir* and *Germinal*.[14] This novel undeniably has a touch of greatness. If it is inferior to *L'Assommoir* and *Germinal*, this is perhaps because of its excessive sordidness and its lesser humanity. It lacks, too, the compassion which marks the others. The only character who wins and keeps the reader's esteem from beginning to end is Jean Macquart, who cannot really be considered the hero of the novel. He is an "outsider" who remains an outsider even to Françoise, whom he marries and genuinely loves. Deep friendship, loyalty, honor, and love are virtually unknown to the inhabitants of this God-forsaken village. But the vision of La Beauce, the hymn to the earth, and the struggle of men, however selfish and mean of spirit they may be, to wring a living from the soil are unforgettable. One's final conclusion must be that *La Terre* is a violent, "excessive," poetic, sordid, sometimes moving, sometimes comical, and, in the last analysis, exasperating book.

It produced an uproar even more than had *L'Assommoir*. On August 18, 1887, while the novel was still appearing serially in the *Gil Blas*, *Le Figaro* published the "Manifeste des Cinq," signed by P. Bonnetain, J. R. Rosny, Lucien Descaves, P. Margueritte, and G. Guiches. Written by Bonnetain and Rosny, it condemned Zola for "betraying his program," and denounced *La Terre* in particular. In this novel, "the master has descended to the very depths of degradation." Whether Goncourt and Daudet inspired these young men to write their manifesto, as has been charged, is doubtful. One suspects that they were probably not displeased by it.

Anatole France, who was anything but prudish, denounced *La Terre* in one of his critical articles. Sarcey and Brunetière also criticized it with severity. A few writers gave it praise. Praised or blamed, lauded or assailed, *La Terre* sold well.

CHAPTER 9

Jeanne Rozerot

Finis to the Rougon-Macquart

AFTER *L'Assommoir* Zola became a substantial man in more than one sense. Indulging his appetite, he put on flesh until in the 1880's he weighed two hundred pounds and had a waistline of nearly forty-five inches. Alarmed, he managed to reduce somewhat. In December, 1887, he tipped the scales at 176 pounds. This was much better, but the next year, unsatisfied, he went on a more rigorous diet, and in a few months took off thirty pounds more.

The incentive was undoubtedly Jeanne Rozerot, a young seamstress whom Mme Zola had engaged, and to whom Émile Zola was soon greatly attracted. She was twenty years old, good-looking, with gorgeous black hair, and a modest demeanor. Late in 1888 she became Zola's mistress; he set her up in an apartment at 66, rue Saint-Lazare. The extraordinary thing is that he began the kind of affair he had never viewed with approval and about which he had written, as in *Pot-Bouille*, with emotional revulsion.

The question naturally arises as to why Zola did not divorce his wife and marry the girl. It would have been the forthright thing to do, and divorce had been legalized by the Third Republic in 1884. Although Zola prided himself on his forthrightness, he doubtless felt morally bound to Alexandrine who had shared two decades of his life, including the lean years of his youth. He could not honorably walk out.

Three years later, in 1891, Alexandrine was informed by an anonymous letter of her husband's liaison; her fury was extreme. Although Zola then pretended to give up his mistress, it was impossible for him to do so. Not only were his affections genuinely engaged, but he now had two children by her, a daughter and a son.[1] He had wanted children very much; their birth fulfilled a deep-seated desire. His association with Jeanne Rozerot had become something fine and beautiful, something that many a legally married couple could envy.

At one moment in this unfortumate situation, Mme Zola was on the point of leaving her husband, not for the unselfish purpose of freeing him so that he could be happy with Jeanne, but rather as an expression of her anger or her grief. The domestic crisis did not, however, result in a separation; Zola and his wife continued to live together. After a time, he was able to visit Jeanne and his children freely and openly instead of clandestinely. Much later, Mme Zola displayed magnanimity, not only by making the children's acquaintance and treating them with kindness, but above all by taking, after her husband's death, the necessary legal steps which permitted them to bear their father's name. A by-product of this affair was the break between the Zolas and Henry Céard, who had acted as Zola's go-between and served as godfather to Denise, the first-born. Céard apparently grew weary of his activities in this triangular situation.[2]

Meanwhile, Zola had produced three novels: *Le Rêve* (1888), *La Bête humaine* (1890) and *L'Argent* (1891). The first is a kind of fairy tale, which need not be discussed at length. After *La Terre,* something mild was in order. What was needed, it was said, was a new *Paul et Virginie.* "Let us then do another *Paul et Virginie,*" wrote Zola in his *Ébauche.* The book he produced, however, was not an exotic tale like that of Bernardin de Saint-Pierre, but a novel in which a decent upbringing by respectable foster-parents overcomes the bad heredity of the Rougon-Macquart family, a novel in which a young girl dreams of a prince charming, meets and marries him, only to die at the threshold of the cathedral after the wedding ceremony. It is the least interesting and the weakest novel of the *Rougon-Macquart.*[3]

I La Bête humaine

La Bête humaine is much more typical of Zola's genius. It is, in fact, his most pessimistic, his blackest, his most nightmarish book. Its subject is threefold: the railroads, the judicial system, and human passion in its most elemental aspect.

In France, as elsewhere, the railroad system in the nineteenth century had a phenomenal growth. This accomplishment and activity of modern man was worthy of treatment and had long been planned by Zola as a subject. He chose for the theater of action the line from Paris to Le Havre and documented himself in his customary way,[4] obtaining permission to make a trip on a loco-motive, as he had sought and received authorization to descend into a mine pit when planning *Germinal*. The line plays an active role in the narrative and is seen by Zola as a living thing, "un être," a "large body, a giant creature lying on the earth, its head in Paris, its vertebrae stretched along the line, its limbs widening out with the branch-lines, its feet and hands in Le Havre and the other towns it served."[5] The multiple, feverish activity of this railroad line is admirably evoked by Zola. Then, too, as might be expected, he bestows symbolic value on a particular locomotive, partially expressed in anthropomorphic terms. La Lison is "one of those express engines with double, coupled axles, presenting a powerful stylish appearance with its big, light wheels linked by arms of steel, its wide breastplate, its long, powerful loins, all this logic and this certainty which constitute the sovereign beauty of metal creatures, precision in strength. [. . .] She was gentle, obedient, smooth-starting, regular and even in her gait, thanks to her good vaporization."[6] Everything in this description, which is longer than the text given here, is suggestive both of technical excellence and of human traits. The engine is frequently described in the novel in feminine terms, and in some of the passages there is a suggestion of the erotic. The locomotive becomes a symbol of the forces of passion which reside in men. At the end of the book, the locomotive and the train represent France itself rushing to disaster—a catastrophic conclusion, as in so many of the *Rougon-Macquart*.

From the point of view of this symbolism, it is appropriate that the crime which provides much of the action of the book should take place on a train and that it should be a crime of passion. Roubaud, an employee of the railroad, discovers that his wife Séverine had been seduced during her adolescence by Grand-morin, a retired magistrate and a Director of the Western Rail-road. On learning this as well as the fact that Grandmorin is seek-ing to continue sexual relations with Séverine, Roubaud decides to kill him and forces his wife to help. The murder takes place in Grandmorin's private car as the Havre express, to which it is at-tached, hurtles through the night. The following investigation leads to a satire of the judicial system and thereby to satire of the

Second Empire, for the government, obtaining reliable information concerning the real culprit, nevertheless fails to prosecute him lest the character of Grandmorin, an important figure of Imperial Society, be exposed and the revelations be embarrassing to the *régime*.

Except for the *décor*, the murder committed by Roubaud is a commonplace crime, the product of unreasoning jealousy. A far more interesting type of murder haunts the pages of this novel and involves Jacques Lantier, the brother of Étienne and Claude. Étienne was originally slated for this book, but as Zola proceeded with his planning, he realized that Étienne's character, as presented in *Germinal*, was inappropriate for *La Bête humaine*. Therefore, he created a new Lantier and gave him the name of Jacques. Jacques was to represent the hereditary criminal and the dark forces of violence which have persisted in men despite their upward climb from the cave to the modern world. "The locomotive is a wonderful invention," says one of the characters, "but savage beasts remain savage beasts, and even if better mechanisms are invented, savage beasts will not be eliminated." Jacques Lantier is not only a railroad man, an engineer, the driver of La Lison; he is also one of those human beings in whom the beast survives. His Macquart heredity has taken this turn; he has almost irresistible impulses to shed human blood, particularly the blood of a woman, for the blood lust is combined with a sexual urge. When we first see him, in the second chapter, he just barely succeeds in resisting the temptation to plunge a scissors' blade into the white bosom of Flore, the young, green-eyed, Amazon daughter of Aunt Phasie Misard. Minutes afterward, he glimpses the murder of Grandmorin as the Havre express rushes by. It seems like "an hallucination, born of the frightful crisis he had just undergone," and, indeed, this lightning-like vision, as a recent critic says, is "the mirror of his own unconscious state and lights up the abyss of his own passion." [7] As a witness of this murder he comes into contact with the Roubauds. Soon the wife becomes his mistress. They plot together to kill Roubaud, but in an upsurge of atavistic passion, he fulfills his dreadful need by killing Séverine instead.

All this and more is presented in a very complicated narrative which is quite skilfully arranged. Zola could have been a great success as an author of detective stories had he wished. He is concerned, however, with far more than plot. He seeks to plumb the dark depths of human nature. He is much more in the line of Lombroso's *L'Homme criminel* and Dostoevsky's *Crime and Punishment* than in that of Wilkie Collins' *Moonstone*. Lombroso's analysis of the "born criminal," often the product of alcoholics and criminals, reinforced Zola's notion that the descendants of Adélaïde Fouque or Antoine Macquart could include in their number a homicidal maniac. In Dostoevsky's Raskolnikov, Zola could see a man willing to "step over barriers." Jacques Lantier is not, however, a second Raskolnikov; he is not a man to whom an idea is more than human life, nor a man with a Napoleonic complex, but a tortured person, unsuccessfully seeking to control a terrible impulse inherited from the remote past.[8] The survival of the primitive in the midst of modern civilization is one of the themes of the book. As F. W. J. Hemmings says: "Zola seems to have had a premonition here of what would prove the greatest problem facing the coming century: the survival, in a race superbly equipped technically, of instincts and impulses which a new pattern of living has rendered obsolete and inappropriate."[9] Indeed, in the presence of the atomic bomb, this problem is more clearly seen and the reality of the peril more widely accepted than in 1890. Had Zola developed this idea—naturally minus the bomb —on a larger scale with fewer side issues, *La Bête humaine* would be a greater book.

It is not, after all, an inferior book. It contains an absorbing narrative, much dramatic suspense, and some admirable pictures. The Saint-Lazare station, with its activity, its noise, its clouds of steam, its light effects, acquires under Zola's pen, as under Monet's brush, an undeniable quality of beauty. The rush of trains in the night with their "hurricane of sound, smoke, and flame" past the crossing of La Croix-de-Maufras is also rendered most effectively, the trains disappearing into the adjacent tunnel as if swallowed in an abyss or emerging from it with gleaming headlights and deafening din. A less dynamic but appropriate style is found in the seventh chapter, which describes the *enlisement*, the bogging down, of La Lison in a severe snowstorm. After a long, determined, and courageous effort, the machine is finally buried in the accumulation of snow. "It was," writes Zola, "an *enlisement*, in which engine and cars were disappearing, already half covered, under the shivering silence of this white solitude. Nothing more stirred, the snow was spinning its shroud." Dynamism returns to

Zola's style in his description of the terrible derailment, caused by Flore in Chapter X, and in that of the final catastrophe when the train, no longer guided and controlled by man, but bearing a human cargo of soldiers bound for the Franco-Prussian War, rolls faster and faster toward destruction and death. The murder of Grandmorin and Jacques's struggles against his hereditary urge with his final surrender to it added to these descriptions show that Zola did not fail in his project of giving a nightmare (*un cauchemar*) to all of Paris.[10]

II L'Argent

L'Argent, next in the series, is not an hallucinatory book, in spite of the fact that it contains, in the character of Victor, one of those human monsters who appear in the *Rougon-Macquart* and produce a shudder. The novel was inspired by the desire to write about money as a social force and one of the basic themes of the book is that while money is the cause of corruption and vice, it is at the same time, the rich soil, "the dung heap," as Zola put it, in which tomorrow's humanity will grow.[11] For its central action Zola took the rise and fall of a banking institution, L'Union générale. The crash of this bank occurred in 1882, but as it could have happened just as well under the Second Empire, the anachronism is not very serious. For the novel's central character Zola chose Saccard, the speculator of *La Curée*, who becomes in this book an even greater speculator, one on an epic scale, "le poète du million," as his son Maxime calls him, a speculator who ruins countless people in the crash of his Banque Universelle, the name given by Zola to the establishment he launches.

Perhaps the most interesting thing about this book is the probability that in writing it Zola came to grips for the first time with the problem of anti-Semitism. The subject had been given great notoriety in 1886 by Edouard Drumont's book, *La France juive*. How anyone could have taken this absurd publication seriously is today a great mystery, but in the 1880's many people did. Zola must have known about it, and he had probably met Drumont for they were both well-known in journalistic circles in the early 1870's. Furthermore, Zola's correspondence shows that he was critical of Drumont. An allusion in a letter to Daudet, dated April 27, 1886, makes this quite clear, for while he denies having said that Drumont "worked in the latrines," he must have said something unfavorable about this man that aroused Daudet's ire. In any case, the subject of anti-Semitism was prominent during these years. Then, too, the failure of the Union générale in 1882 had been attributed by Bontoux and Feder, its principal officers, to the machinations of Jewish bankers and to Free Masons.

The chief character of the book, Saccard, is violently anti-Semitic and expresses himself in terms that Edouard Drumont might have used. While he is ruined on the stock exchange by the Jewish banker Gundermann, his financial destruction is due basically to his own folly, for had he not overextended himself, Gundermann would never have been able to profit from the situation. Zola's portrait of Gundermann, modeled on James Rothschild, cannot be labeled anti-Semitic. The man operates on the basis of shrewdness and intelligence, not through prejudice, malice, or evil. Two other Jewish characters in the novel, the Busch brothers, represent diametrically opposed types. One of them is, indeed, an unpleasant character, indulging in shady deals, but his brother Sigismond is a young idealist, a dreamer, and a convinced socialist. Zola's own position is made clear toward the end of the book through Madame Caroline, for when Saccard, arrested for gross irregularities, fulminates in his prison cell against Gundermann, calling him a "dirty Jew" and adding: "Yes, hatred of the Jew, I have it in me—oh! from way back, in the very roots of my being!", she says quite calmly: "To me the Jews are men like any others. If they are apart, it is because they have been put apart." This clearly represents Zola's personal view. His work-sheets show that he reached this position after careful reflection.[12]

The stock exchange, La Bourse, is comparable to the mine in *Germinal*, or the markets in *Le Ventre de Paris*. Seen from the outside in the first chapter and from the inside in the tenth, it becomes a temple of Mammon in which the innocent pay tribute, a building overflowing with speculators, "crowding and crushing together," creating a rumbling like that of a "steam-engine at work," which varies in intensity as a "flickering flame" may subside a moment only to flare high again. The tenth chapter, which relates the crash of the shares of the Banque Universelle from a high of 3060 francs to a low of 830, is full of technical details. It is, at the same time, an exciting narrative.

In spite of the ruin heaped on the innocent, all is not gloom in *L'Argent*. Offsetting the unpleasant characters are a number of sympathetic ones: the journalist Paul Jordan and his wife, Marcelle; the Princesse d'Orviedo, a model of Christian charity; Georges Hamelin and his sister Caroline; Sigismond Busch, already mentioned; Mme de Beauvilliers and her pathetic daughter. In the *Ébauche* Zola wrote: "I should like, in this novel, not to conclude with disgust of life (pessimism). Life as it is, but accepted, despite everything, for the love of it, in its strength." [13] This attitude toward life is embodied in Mme Caroline who serves as Zola's mouthpiece. At the end, stripped of illusions though she is, realizing that life, like nature, is often unjust and even ignoble, she can still find happiness in a beautiful spring day. "Ah! the joy of living," she reflects, "is there really any other? Life—life such as it is, however abominable it may be—life with its strength and its eternal hope." These are almost the closing words of the book. They have been connected by some critics with Zola's rejuvenation through Jeanne Rozerot. Undoubtedly he did find with her new life and new hope. At the same time, an invincible optimism underlies more than one volume of *Les Rougon-Macquart,* which Zola never intended to be an expression of defeatism and despair.

The same year saw two interesting events: the election of Zola as president of the Société des Gens de Lettres and the production of an opera based on *Le Rêve.* The former testified to widespread recognition of Zola's literary achievements. The latter, in which Zola took small part, for the libretto was written by Louis Gallet and the music by Alfred Bruneau, aroused great interest, and "was acclaimed," according to L. A. Carter, "as an important event in the history of French opera." [14]

III La Débâcle

Perhaps one reason why Zola contributed little to this opera is that he was hard at work on one of the most important novels of the series, *La Débâcle.* He had finished *L'Argent* at the end of January, 1891, and soon after he began his planning for the war novel he had long intended to write. [15] He wanted above all to give a true picture of war, to avoid glamorizing it, to show the hardships and sufferings of the ordinary soldier. He had already done a little of this in "Le Petit Village," in several of the "Souvenirs" published in his *Nouveaux contes à Ninon,* [16] and in "L'Attaque du moulin." For *Les Rougon-Macquart* he needed something on a much larger scale; and the Franco-Prussian War, far better than the Italian campaign of 1859, of which he had originally thought, met this need; it not only permitted a military narrative but involved the downfall of Napoleon III, his dynasty, and his government. It led also to the Civil War of the Commune, which Zola decided to include in his novel.

Everything was to go in. He wanted, first of all, as he wrote to Van Santen Kolff, "to tell the truth about the frightful catastrophe from which France almost died." He sought to have "the whole war: the wait at the frontier, the marches, the battles, the panics, the retreats, the peasants vis-à-vis the French and the Prussians, the snipers (*les francs-tireurs*), the bourgeois of the towns, the occupation with the requisitions of food and money, in short the whole series of important episodes which occurred in 1870." In another paragraph, he stated that the third part of the novel would include "the siege of Paris and above all the conflagrations of the Commune" which would permit an ending with "a blood-red sky." He went on to confess that all this was "not easy" to introduce into his plan. "My eyes," he wrote, "are always bigger than my stomach. When I attack a subject, I want to force the whole world into it. Hence my torments, in this desire for the enormous and for totality which is never satisfied." [17] In point of fact, he did most of what he wrote Van Santen Kolff, though his book is still not quite on the scale of Tolstoy's *War and Peace*.

He documented himself with his usual care, visiting the area around Sedan, reading articles and books, particularly memoirs (some unpublished), and questioning participants.[18] Because of his myopia and his dependent mother he had never been a soldier himself. He had never been a miner, or a banker, or a department-store owner either, and did not consider himself disqualified on any such grounds.

La Débâcle, which appeared in book form at the end of June, 1892, comprises three parts, each one containing eight chapters. The first part is devoted to the early defeats, the marches and countermarches, the changes of plan, the ignorance and incompetence of many of the officers, the incredible confusion that reigned throughout, and the resulting demoralization of the troops. The second part relates the Battle of Sedan, to which the defense of Bazeilles is a stirring prologue. The third evokes the prison camp in the Iges loop of the Meuse River, then moves into Paris where the siege, the pathetic attempts to break the Prussians' iron circle, and the Civil War of the Commune are described. There is a great deal of authentic history in this epic narrative.

The characters fall into two categories: historical and fictitious. The former include Napoleon III, some of his generals—MacMahon, Ducrot, Douay, Wimpffen, Margueritte—and the German Emperor, Wilhelm I. The French Army as a whole might be considered the principal character, and its terrible ordeal the main subject of the book. But Zola knew that readers are more affected by individuals whom they can easily visualize and to whom they can give their sympathy or their scorn. He therefore created for this purpose a number of fictitious characters through whose eyes one really sees the war and through whose reactions one responds emotionally and intellectually to it. In this sense they are more important than historical ones. Attention is focused on a squad of six men, headed by a corporal, Jean Macquart, who re-enlisted in the army at the end of *La Terre*. He furnishes the only link, and a very tenuous one, with the family whose history is given in this series of novels. He is still what he was in *La Terre*, a man not well educated, barely able to read and write, conscientious, calm, and practical. Maurice Levasseur, whom Zola contrasts with Jean, is in his squad. Maurice is educated, idealistic, and high-strung. The two men represent two important facets of the French character, and they are clearly the major characters of the book. The other members of the squad are minor in comparison. Another noncommissioned officer is present in the person of Sergeant Sapin, and above him are Lieutenant Rochas, Captain Beaudoin, and the commanding officer of the regiment (the 106th), Colonel de Vineuil. None of these men is historical, nor is the doctor, le Major Bouroche. Some of them are representative: Rochas is the type of the old-fashioned Napoleonic soldier convinced of the superiority of French arms, with a blind faith in the inevitability of a French victory; Beaudoin, a graduate of Saint-Cyr, the West Point of France, not in fact a good officer, a dandy in uniform, but a man who meets death with well-bred courage; Vineuil, a fine commander, a brave man, and a genuine patriot.

Civilians are not absent. Weiss, a Frenchman of Alsatian origin, is a clear-headed man who knows the area thoroughly and immediately sees the strategic errors being committed by the French command. He takes an active part in the heroic defense of Bazeilles. Weiss is foreman in the cloth factory owned by Jules Delaherche, a well-to-do bourgeois, Bonapartist in sympathy until the crushing defeat and his fears for his business lead him to turn against the Emperor. A third civilian of importance is Fouchard, a wily peasant, who profits shamelessly from the war. He is the father of Honoré, an artilleryman who dies heroically in the battle as his battery vainly tries to defend a strategic point, the Calvaire d'Illy. Old Fouchard is also the uncle of Maurice and Henriette. Pretty much against his will, his house becomes a refuge for Maurice and Jean after their escape from the Prussians. It is also the scene of the execution of Goliath Steinberg, a German spy, by three *francs-tireurs*. They cut his throat and let him bleed to death as they would a pig.

The dramatis personae include several women, four of whom have some importance. Henriette, Maurice's sister, married to Weiss, is the embodiment of feminine virtues; she is faithful, kind, tender, and courageous. Except for her blonde hair she is not unlike Jeanne Rozerot. Zola was thinking perhaps of his own lovely girl when he wrote: "She spoke but little, walked noiselessly, and displayed such skilful activity, such smiling gentleness, that she imparted a caress as it were to the atmosphere through which she passed." Somewhat comparable to Henriette is Silvine Morange, a servant to old Fouchard. A brunette, with big, beautiful eyes and an oval countenance, she too is kind, tender, and courageous. In love with Honoré Fouchard, she let herself, in a moment of weakness after his conscription in the army, be possessed by Goliath Steinberg in the time when he, too, was a farmhand at Fouchard's. A child, Charlot, resulted. But Honoré, meeting her now in the midst of the war, is prepared to forgive the past and to marry her when peace returns. Her trip to the battlefield to seek him out, her grief when she finds his corpse, and her return with his body to the farm provide one of the poignant sections of the book. The other two women are Delaherche's mother and wife. The former is a lady of the old school, disciplined, austere, courageous, and patriotic. The daughter-in-law is her opposite, flighty, pleasure-loving, faithless, kind-hearted, weak, but not really vicious. The civilians, women and men, help the reader to see other aspects of the war than the actual battlefield.[19]

Today, two world wars have eclipsed the war of 1870. A modern reader who prefers fiction to history but wishes the truth about war tends to turn to twentieth-century authors like Barbusse, Dorgelès, Remarque, Jules Romains, Stallings, Mailer, and Jones. But although the cannon are bigger and the rifles have a longer range; although airplanes have increased the destruction and the horror, in essence war is war, and Zola's narrative is both valid and decidedly worth reading.

The description of the defense of Bazeilles, universally admired, has become an anthology piece. The role of Weiss is central to it. While he lived in Sedan, he had acquired a house at Bazeilles. He goes there the night before the battle to protect it against marauders, and the next morning lingers on. The result is that the German attack finds him still present. He had never planned to take up arms, but his anger is aroused, his blood stirred. He picks up a rifle and shoots. From then on he is one of the prominent figures in the defense. In the last stage he, another civilian named Laurent, and a handful of soldiers barricade themselves in his house and defend it literally to the last cartridge. Caught by the Germans in civilian garb, Laurent and he are summarily shot, in the presence of Henriette, his wife, who came from Sedan to look for him. He achieves unquestionable distinction before the German firing squad, for he detaches Henriette's arms from around his neck, passes her to a Bavarian soldier, calmly places his eyeglasses in proper position, steps back, leans against the wall, and receives the fatal volley with stoic grandeur.[20]

The battlefield of Sedan is seen not only as a whole but also in detail through the experience of individual soldiers. Beaudoin's company finds itself anchored during the morning in a large cabbage field on the so-called plateau d'Algérie under fire from German batteries. Two examples will indicate Zola's method:

At that moment a shell splinter shattered the head of a soldier in the front rank. He was not even able to utter a cry: just a spurt of blood and brain-matter—that was all.

"Poor devil!" Sergeant Sapin, very calm and pale, merely said. "Whose turn next?"

But they could no longer hear one another; Maurice suffered above all from the frightful racket. The battery nearby was firing without pause, with a continuous roar which shook the ground, and the machine guns were worse, rending the air, insufferable. How long were they going to lie among those cabbages? There was still nothing to be seen; nothing known. Impossible to form the slightest idea of the battle; was it even a real, a great battle?

[157]

ÉMILE ZOLA

A little later things become worse:

The firing was now becoming more and more violent, the nearby
battery having been reinforced by a couple of guns; and in the increasing uproar fear, mad fear came over Maurice. At the outset he had
been free from the cold sweat he now experienced, from the painful
weakness he felt in the pit of his stomach, the almost irresistible need
to get up and dash, howling, away. Doubtless all this was but the result
of reflection, as often happens with delicate, nervous natures. But Jean,
who was watching him, read this crisis of cowardice in the confused
wavering of his eyes, and, seizing him with his strong hand, forcibly
held him close. Paternally, in a low tone, he upbraided him, trying to
put him to shame, for he knew that at times, strong words, even kicks
are needed to restore men's courage. Plache, tearful, was uttering low,
involuntary sounds, like the whimper of a small child, which he was
unable to restrain. And Lapoulle's vitals were so affected that he was
taken short, unable to reach a nearby hedge in time. Many jeered at
him and threw bits of earth at his nudity, exposed to the bullets and
the shells. Other men were taken in the same way, in the midst of
wisecracks which restored everyone's courage.

Neither Hugo nor Stendhal had written about war quite like this.
In the United States, Stephen Crane was to include the reactions
of the individual soldier in *The Red Badge of Courage* three years
after the publication of *La Débâcle*.

The order comes at last for the 106th to attack; they move up,
finally reaching, after heavy losses, the Calvaire d'Illy. Even with
the heroic support of Honoré Fouchard's battery, the position is
untenable in the face of the overwhelming German forces. In a
last desperate measure Margueritte's cavalry is ordered to attack,
and Zola relates the repeated attempts to reach the crest and drive
the Germans back. When this fails, the retreat begins.[21] Here
again Zola reports events through the experiences of individual
soldiers streaming to the rear, ultimately taking refuge in the
overcrowded city of Sedan.

Other things are worthy of note. The night before the battle the
106th regiment finds itself above the river looking down on the
ferry and the pontoon bridge over which the troops have to cross.
The darkness is broken by fires lighted on each bank. The whole
scene is an excellent example of Zola's skill in handling a vast
throng of men issuing from the blackness of the night into the red
light, then engulfed once more in obscurity. The passage of the

[158]

Cuirassiers is particularly striking: "Two by two, in endless files went the Cuirassiers [. . .] slowly emerging from the darkness on one bank, and passing at last into that on the other [. . .] all uniformly draped in long white cloaks, their helmets blazing with fiery reflections. They looked like phantom horsemen, with flaming hair, bound for the war of Stygian darkness." [22] As in certain scenes of *Germinal,* the colors produce a dramatic, hallucinatory effect.

During the battle itself, the calm bravery of the stretcher-bearers provides an eloquent and moving description. The blood and gore of the hospital improvised in Delaherche's factory inspire Zola to pages of realism and words of sympathy. The prison camp in the Iges loop where the defeated army is driven, without tents or rations, and where horror reigns for several days, is the subject of an unforgettable chapter. The fighting in Paris during the Civil War of the Commune and the burning of the city are rendered with all the colorful drama of which Zola was capable.

Glimpses of Napoleon III are scattered through the first two parts. To his credit, be it said, Zola does not vilify this unfortunate man. The facts speak for themselves. The novelist presents the Emperor as a man enduring physical suffering, as indeed he did. He was in excruciating pain from stones is his urinary system. His moral anguish, equally great, is also rendered by Zola, who suggests that Napoleon III acquiesced in a military policy of which he did not wholly approve and which he possibly realized would lead to disaster. The over-all picture is of a vacillating, unsure man too afflicted with physical pain to resist the pressures coming from his wife and ministers in Paris. That he bore much responsibility for the catastrophe is true, but Zola does not heap abuse upon him.

One of the central topics of the novel is developed through Maurice Levasseur and Jean Macquart, the two main characters. Hostile to each other at first, they become firm friends; and one of the tragedies of the book is the death of Maurice from a bayonet wound inflicted by Jean in the fighting in Paris when they are on opposite sides. In the heat of battle Jean does not recognize until too late the man into whom he plunges his blade. Maurice is the grandson of a soldier of Napoleon I. Theoretically republican at the beginning of the narrative, he has a certain sentimental attachment to the old, imperial glories. An excitable fellow, easily discouraged, tending toward extremes, he throws his lot in with the Commune after the siege is over. Jean Macquart, on the other hand, represents, as Zola put it in his preparatory notes, the reasonable side of the French, their capacity for work and economy, "all that will one day reconstruct the country." [23]

All this is clear enough, but the question arises as to why Zola gave such a poor impression of the Commune and why he placed Jean, whom he holds up to our admiration, in the ranks of the Versailles troops[24] who suppressed the Communards with far greater ferocity than was necessary. We know that although Zola was instinctively sympathetic in 1871 to the Commune, he refused to make common cause with either side. At the same time, he was appalled by the severity of the men of Versailles.[25] It has been suggested that in 1892, as a candidate for the French Academy, Zola did not wish to alienate conservatives whose vote he would need.[26] It is difficult either to completely refute this accusation or to accept it. In spite of the fact that Maurice is critical of the leaders of the Commune, finding them incompetent, it is nevertheless still true that he voluntarily joined the cause and that he continues to support it. On the other hand, while Jean Macquart is in the ranks of Versailles, his motivation is extremely simple. He is not a thinker, not a theorist. He has rejoined the army more or less automatically without giving any thought to the political situation in Paris. As a soldier in a given division of the army he has been ordered with all the others to retake Paris. He is merely doing what he believes to be his duty and cannot be said to symbolize the extremists of the Versailles camp. One suspects that in 1892 Zola's personal attitude toward the Commune and Versailles was: "a plague on both your houses."

If the last chapter points up the fanaticism of the Communards in massacring hostages and in putting the torch to Paris, it also reveals the ferocity of the men of Versailles, for their troops "were executing *en masse* the last prisoners they took." "At the Père-Lachaise cemetery, bombarded for four days and at last conquered tomb by tomb, one hundred and forty-eight captives were flung against a wall, the plaster of which was stained with huge blood spots; and three of these men, wounded, caught trying to get away, were finished off." It can scarcely be said that Zola was tender to the Versaillais. At the same time one could wish that

Zola might have indicated that the Commune, for all its serious faults, had a genuinely "patriotic, republican, and proletarian character" [27] which deserved some recognition from his pen.

The book's conclusion is twofold. There is the great catastrophe, so typical of many of the *Rougon-Macquart*, in the Civil War, in the conflagration of Paris, in the death of so many victims. Yet hope is not absent.

Then Jean had an extraordinary sensation. It seemed to him, in the slowly declining light as though a new dawn were already rising above the flaming city [. . .] Beyond the furnace, roaring still, in the depths of the great tranquil sky so supremely limpid, perennial hope was mounting once again. It was the unfailing rejuvenation of eternal nature and eternal humanity, the renewal promised to those who hope and toil; the tree which throws out a new and powerful stem when the rotten branch, whose poisonous sap was blighting the leaves, has been chopped away. [. . .]
The ravaged field was lying waste, the burnt house was level with the ground; and Jean, the humblest and the most grievous, took his leave, marching toward the future, to the great laborious task of building France anew.

The theme of death and rebirth is present here as in previous novels of the series.

Appearing twenty-one or twenty-two years after the events it chronicled, *La Débâcle* was nevertheless opportune. Enough time had elapsed to permit Frenchmen to review these events, not, of course, with detachment, but with lessened anguish. Furthermore, interest in army matters had recently (1886–89) been stimulated by the activities of General Boulanger and his supporters who included Bonapartists and monarchists. The possible danger of a "man on horseback" leading the country into rash adventures made recollection of the Second Empire's errors timely. Certainly, the public response was excellent. The novel outsold all the previous volumes of the series.

In army circles, *La Débâcle* was severely criticized. Many agreed with General du Barrail who wrote in *Le Figaro* that the book was "conceived in a shocking spirit" and gave "to the events which crushed France a philosophical explanation which is false." A German officer intervened to condemn the book, which in his opinion was lacking in "respect for misfortune." On the other hand, most of the literary critics in France and abroad were highly favorable, justly seeing in Zola's pages a magnificent and truthful picture of war.[28] Their judgments and the tremendous sale were gratifying, indeed. "The success of *La Débâcle* surpasses all my hopes," the novelist wrote to a friend, "and I should be happy, if a man ever could be." [29]

IV Le Docteur Pascal

Happy or not, Zola continued to work, though in the summer of 1892 he took a vacation during which he traveled to Lourdes[30] and later to Genoa. Soon thereafter he started on the twentieth and final volume of the series, *Le Docteur Pascal.* He began to write it in December, 1892, and finished it in June of the following year. The public dedication read: "To the memory of my mother and to my dear wife I dedicate this novel which sums up and concludes my whole work." Privately, he offered it: "To my beloved Jeanne, to my Clotilde, who has given me the royal banquet of her youth and restored to me my own." That Clotilde Rougon is none other than Jeanne Rozerot, and Pascal Rougon, Zola himself, is proved by this dedication. Yet proof is scarcely necessary, for the identifications are obvious.

Flashes of descriptive brilliance occur in this concluding novel. In Chapter III, for example, Zola admirably evokes the gorge of La Seille, "a narrow defile between giant walls of rock," which resembles "some spot rent by the bolts of heaven, some gully of hell [. . .] lying there in desolate solitude, disturbed only by the flight of eagles." Another impressive passage depicts, in Chapter XI, the mistral, the northwest wind of Provence, blowing with fearful violence as Clotilde prepares to leave for Paris. In general, however, the themes of science, social history, and love of life predominate. The first two permit a retrospective look at the Rougon-Macquart family and the social scene in which they have moved. The third emerges to some extent from this review but above all from the love affair of Pascal and Clotilde.

In this book, Zola returns to the question of heredity. Although it had played an inconsequential role in some of the novels, in the series as a whole it was far from unimportant. Apparently Zola still viewed it as a science, even though its laws were not yet fully and reliably established. In Chapter V, Dr. Pascal interprets to Clotilde the genealogical tree, maintaining that the voluminous files he has kept on the family are of the greatest scientific value. Then, too, he considers that the record of the Rougon-Macquart family is "an historical document; it relates the Second Empire from the coup d'état to Sedan." One finds there straight history, social studies, human experiences, even fanciful tales. It includes "the best and the worst, the vulgar and the sublime, flowers, filth, tears, laughter, the very torrent of life forever sweeping humanity along in its flow." Although Pascal admits that some degenerate characters have appeared in the fifth generation of the Rougon-Macquart, he refuses to despair. "Families represent eternal change" (*"les familles sont l'éternel devenir"*). New blood helps to reconstitute them.

Pascal's medical activity provides another interesting aspect of the book. He tries out some hypodermic injections of his own composition. Here Zola used information he got from a friend of his, Dr. Maurice de Fleury. In the end, Pascal tends to admit that medicine is less a science than an art. "Doubt has seized me," he tells Clotilde. "I tremble at the thought of my twentieth-century alchemy; I finally believe that it is greater and healthier to let evolution take its course." [31] Faith in evolution is still, of course, a form of faith in science. Pascal's attitude is a reflection of Zola's own.

The cult of life which is the essence of Dr. Pascal's philosophy is nowhere better illustrated than in the marriage, without benefit of clergy, of Pascal and Clotilde. "It was not a fall; glorious life inspired them; they possessed each other in full, complete joy." From this man, more than thirty years her senior, Clotilde learns the essential lesson: "Oh! to live, to live! that is the great task, the continued work which will doubtless be completed one day." We are told that after their night of love, "they opened the windows wide to let the springtime in. The April sun with its germinating power and its spotless purity was rising in the vast expanse of the sky, and the earth, stirred by the tremor of the seeds, celebrated their union with song." Before the end of the novel, Pascal dies of angina without having the supreme happiness of seeing the son he has engendered. The last paragraph depicts Clotilde nursing their child, smiling at the boy whose little arm is raised upright in the air, "like a rallying standard of Life."

Le Docteur Pascal is not a good novel, but it certainly "sums up and concludes" *Les Rougon-Macquart.*

V *Conclusions*

On June 21, 1893, a magnificent luncheon was offered by Zola's publishers, Charpentier and Fasquelle, in honor of the completion of *Les Rougon-Macquart*. Twenty-five years had gone into its planning and composition. Now the monument was finished, and a grandiose monument it was. To celebrate this event and to honor Zola, the publishers invited all the literary and artistic notables of Paris, headed by the Minister of Education and Fine Arts, Raymond Poincaré. It was recognized by all those present that Zola's achievement placed him in the front rank of European men of letters.

Les Rougon-Macquart are the work of a realist and a romantic, of a prose writer and a poet, of an objective historian and a visionary. They are the work of an acquisitive bourgeois with humanitarian and, on occasion, socialist sympathies. They reveal in their author certain obsessions: fear of disease, pain, and death; the attraction and repulsion of sex; admiration of fertility; faith in science and progress; acceptance and love of life. They combine pessimism and optimism, the former being as much a method as a philosophy. The black picture is often but a "fer rouge," a red-hot iron with which to cauterize a wound, or a scalpel to lance an infection. Pessimism may be unrelieved in *L'Assommoir* and *La Bête humaine;* it is modified in *Germinal* and *La Débâcle* by a vision of a better day to come, tempered in these and other volumes by the presence of some human beings in whom goodness is predominant. They may be temporarily frustrated, defeated, or crushed by men or forces more powerful than they, but the future belongs to them. A large measure of optimism underlies the series as a whole. The universe of *Les Rougon-Macquart* is essentially a materialistic one in which, as has been said in an earlier chapter, God is absent, but it is not devoid of idealism. It is not a lesson in despair. In reading this saga, men are not deprived of hope.

Certain myths arise from the author's capacity for poetic visions combined with his double tendency toward pessimism and optimism. A myth of increasing importance in the series is that involving a great catastrophe. The fire which consumes Mouret and Faujas, the rotting corpse of Nana as the crowds shout "to Berlin," the inundation and engulfment of Le Voreux, the suicide of Claude Lantier, the destruction of La Borderie, the railroad train hurtling to death and disaster, the burning of Paris—these somber denouements seem to indicate that Zola, like the decadents, was convinced of ultimate doom. They might even suggest a death-wish on his part, were it not for the myth of fertility and renewal which appears early in the series and continues, with some interruptions, to the end. *La Terre* has been called "an expanded Fertility image." This and other novels illustrate the cycle of birth-growth-decay-death-rebirth. The death of Pascal and the birth of his son at the end of the final volume emphasize the importance of this concept. Life is triumphant, and with it there is hope.

Les Rougon-Macquart are, as Dr. Pascal said, a history of the Second Empire. They are not, to be sure, a systematic or complete history arranged in chronological order; nor are they an impartial history. In his dislike of the *régime,* and above all in his desire to produce striking volumes, Zola tends to blacken the picture more than is necessary. Yet a great deal is authentic: the description of the working-class quarter in *L'Assommoir,* the strike in *Germinal,* the building up of a large department store, the existence of a corruptive demimonde, the political repression of 1858, the railroad as a modern activity, the Franco-Prussian War and the Commune—these are presented with great exactitude. A serious student of the period may need to be on his guard in reading Zola's volumes; if he is, he can profit from them, and, in any case, can enjoy the experience.

These events, these phenomena, these myths are recorded in powerful narratives frequently justifying the epithet "excessive" which, it will be recalled, Zola wished his books to be. *Les Rougon-Macquart* are written in a passionate, robust style which is often extremely eloquent. They are illustrated by pictures which rely on elementary colors and tones. White, black, and red tend to predominate, although blue, green, and gold are also found. The first group is sometimes used in depicting the beauty of a natural scene: the black and white of a moonlit night or the crimson of a gorgeous sunset. It also supports particularly well the violence and melodrama, the pessimism and the horror found in many of the texts. The more optimistic side, the fertility of the earth, and the joy of living are supported by the second group. Zola is not a great colorist in the sense that Chateaubriand is, but his use of color is effective and important.

Les Rougon-Macquart are, therefore, more than products of observation and documentation, more than examples of photographic realism. They realize Zola's own definition of a work of art: "a corner of nature seen through the temperament of the writer." They are a vast fresco created by a man of powerful imagination and epic talent.

CHAPTER 10

New Accomplishments and Controversies

The Dreyfus Case

Sudden Death

É MILE Zola was no man to twiddle his thumbs while resting on his laurels. He now had a new project, the initial idea of which had occurred to him in September, 1891. In that month and year he had happened to spend a few hours at Lourdes. Frankly surprised by what he saw there, concluding that it would offer material for a book, he returned in August 1892, taking care to make this visit coincide with the national pilgrimage of that year. He took copious notes during this second sojourn, began his *Ébauche*, and soon decided to write two books, one on Lourdes, the other on Rome. The first would contain "the naïve awakening of traditional Catholicism . . . the need of faith and illusion"; the second, "all of neo-Catholicism or rather the neo-Christianity of these last years of the century, [. . .] Rome trying to conform to modern ideas." A few days later a third book, to be entitled *Paris*, was added to his project. "My trilogy," he told reporters, "will sum up the century, will be less pessimistic than the rest of my work, and will be animated by a spirit of idealism and hope." [1] For a collective title he chose simply *Les Trois Villes*. *Lourdes* appeared in 1894; *Rome*, in 1896; *Paris*, in 1898. By the time *Paris* came off the press Zola was engaged in a far greater controversy than any provoked by his novels.

Not that the trilogy was noncontroversial. Given the general subject and Zola's ideas, it could scarcely be that. Throughout the second half of the century debate on Christianity, including the conflict between science and religion in general, was intense. It brought into the arena a good many Frenchmen, some of whom were and still are quite famous. Several were influenced by the positivist philosophy of Auguste Comte and the evolutionary concepts of Charles Darwin; others reacted against them. One of the most famous episodes in this running debate was the interchange in 1882 between Louis Pasteur and Ernest Renan on the occasion of the former's admission to the French Academy. Whereas the great scientist recognized the existence of an Infinite, of something beyond our knowledge and observation,[2] the author of *La Vie de Jésus* reminded his audience that the history of humanity shows that the field of the supernatural, of the unknown, is ever more restricted.

Debate continued during the next decade. Abbé de Broglie asserted in 1883 that "science has not destroyed religion; it has merely purged the thought of the faithful of a mixture of foreign elements and brought it back to the austerity of true monotheism."[3] On the other hand, the sociologist, J. M. Guyau, maintained that established religions would ultimately disappear and be replaced by philosophy.[4] The very title of his book, *L'Irréligion de l'avenir* (1887), was a prophecy. Ferdinand Brunetière was not slow in making his views known. After declaring (in 1887) Naturalism bankrupt, he stated in 1890 that "science [. . .] will never solve the riddle of the universe and of destiny."[5] In the same year, Renan finally published *L'Avenir de la science,* written much earlier, a work in which the author's reluctance to accept the supernatural was made fully clear. By the early 1890's Anatole France was joining the unorthodox group. Like others, he had been influenced by Darwin; he helped combat any form of blind faith which resulted in detriment to reason and observation. An example of liberal Catholicism may be seen in Paul Desjardins, whose pamphlet *Le Devoir présent,* published in 1892, preached a Galilean type of religion unspoiled by the dogmas with which the institutional church had complicated it. Émile Faguet dubbed it "Catholicism without faith."

Meanwhile, the revelation by De Vogüé (in 1886) of the Christian novelists of Russia, Tolstoy and Dostoevsky, combined with the pronouncements of men like Pasteur and Desjardins, affected the literary scene. Zola saw some of his friends slip away from Naturalism into a vague religiosity, into mysticism, or, in the case of Huysmans, into stranger tendencies. While he himself had seemed to recognize in *Le Rêve* the existence of an *au-delà,* of something beyond our ken, he had quickly reverted in the last novels of *Les Rougon-Macquart* to a belief in the positive, the real, and the scientific. The moment appeared to be ripe for a fuller treatment of the conflict between science and religion. As suggested above, this is basically the subject of *Les Trois Villes.*

I   Les Trois Villes

Let it be said immediately that the trilogy consists of bad novels but interesting books which contain, as often in Zola's work, some magnificent passages. In *Lourdes,* the descriptions of the white train carrying the invalids to the sanctuary of their hope, their arrival, the long column of the maimed and the ill on their way to the Grotto, and the candle-light procession of thirty thousand pilgrims singing the hymn of Bernadette and the *Ave Maria* are impressive and frequently moving. In *Rome* some of the evocations of the eternal city are admirably done. In the third novel, the vision of Paris as an "immense cauldron in which a whole human world is seething," from which Liberty has already risen to "wing its way over the globe," and where "Justice, in its turn," will emerge "to regenerate the nations" is accompanied by an eloquent, passionate statement of faith in Science as the force, indeed, the religion, which will establish "the kingdom of God" on this earth, unheedful of the "false paradise" of the theologians.

Pierre Froment is the link connecting the three books. In *Lourdes* he is already a priest who has lost his faith, but who wants desperately to recover it. He accompanies an old friend, Marie de Guersaint, a girl with whom he had once been in love, on the pilgrimage train. She is paralyzed and, like the other pilgrims, seeks a miraculous cure. She is cured, but Pierre alone understands that it is not a true miracle. It is one of those psychological phenomena, frequent enough, which great emotion can achieve. The cause of her paralysis was apparently organic but in reality neurotic. Her cure is acclaimed as a great miracle. Pierre can share her joy, but not her faith. As for the other invalids, compassion for them emerges from Zola's text. An immense pity for suffering humanity is contained in these pages. At the same time, Zola cannot resist a little irony. Some of his characters receive, during their sojourn at Lourdes, thoroughly mundane benefits and successes which the author amusingly but perhaps a little maliciously has them attribute to the intervention of the Virgin. Furthermore, he does not fail to flay the rampant commercialism which has seized upon the town and which inevitably offends people of taste. At the end of the book, Pierre Froment returns to Paris as unhappy as when he left it.

Another disillusioning experience awaits him in Rome. Between his return from Lourdes and his departure for the see of Saint Peter, he evolved a neo-Christianity, not unlike that preached by Desjardins, and put it into a book which he entitled *La Rome nouvelle*. Informed that his volume is threatened with being placed on the Index, he hastens to Rome to defend it, prepared, if necessary, to appeal to the Holy Father himself. For weeks he is forced to cool his heels in numerous antechambers, in a maneuver designed by Monsignor Nani, the Assessor of the Holy Office, to make him aware of his limitations and his impotence. Finally, he is granted a private interview by the Pope, something which Zola himself did not achieve. This Pope is Leo XIII who distressed many conservative Frenchmen by coming to terms with the Third Republic and who held liberal views concerning the needs and rights of the working class. He is not, however, liberal enough in Zola's narrative to approve Froment's book. On the contrary, he condemns it, and wrings from the young priest a statement of self-condemnation. The scene is extraordinarily interesting and extremely well composed.

Before seeing the Pope, Pierre Froment visits Rome in his spare time. The book turns into a kind of travelogue, some of which is brilliantly written but constitutes nevertheless a drag on the central action. Zola tries to enliven other chapters with the narrative of Benedetta and Dario. This girl is seeking an annulment from the man she was virtually forced to marry, hoping to wed her cousin Dario with whom she has long been in love. It leads to one of those odd, unlikely situations which crop up rather frequently in Zola's work. Although Benedetta's suit is successful, Dario is killed before the marriage can occur. The poisoned figs he consumes were intended for his uncle Cardinal Boccanera, a possible candidate for the papal throne in the event of Leo's death. This Renaissance motif, obviously inappropriate to the late nineteenth century, brings about the incredible scene in which Benedetta strips off her clothes and takes the dying and equally naked Dario in her arms. His death is followed within seconds by hers, for according to Zola, her emotions are so extreme that "she experienced in this embrace of death such a rush of blood to her heart that it burst." Once again, as in *La Fortune des Rougon* and *Germinal*, Zola has combined love and death in intimate and inseparable union.

Saddened by the death of Benedetta and her friend, disillusioned by the condemnation of his book, Pierre Froment leaves Rome convinced that reason is the only voice worthy to be heard and to be followed. "He swore that he would now always seek to satisfy reason, even at the risk of losing happiness."

Back in France, however, at the beginning of *Paris,* he still wears the cassock and performs his priestly duty. Two thirds of this long novel are completed before he musters up the courage to adopt ordinary civilian dress. He is aided in reaching this decision, which, of course, signifies departure from the Church, by his brother Guillaume and by Marie Couturier with whom he falls in love and marries before the end of the book. What Serge Mouret was unable to do, Pierre Froment achieves without the slightest feeling of guilt. Zola presents it as the triumph of nature over a form of death, a defeat of superstition by reason, a victory for life itself.

Space does not permit a review of all the elements of this complex novel. Some contemporary figures, thinly disguised, grace its pages. Bertheroy, the chemist, is clearly modeled on Marcellin Berthelot who succeeded Pasteur as secretary of the Academy of Sciences; the anarchist Salvat is obviously Vaillant, executed in 1893 for bomb throwing; Fonsègue and Sagnier are respectively Hébrard of *Le Temps,* and Drumont, author of *La France juive* and editor of *La Libre Parole.* Mège is none other than Jules Guesde, the socialist leader; Prime Minister Montferrand appears to be a mixture of Maurice Rouvier and Jean Constans, both well-known politicians of the period. The famous dramatic critic, mentioned in the second chapter of Part III, has been identified as possibly Sarcey or even Brunetière; but what man Zola really had in mind is uncertain.

The conflict between science and religion is indicated not only in the contrast between the two brothers, and in the struggle that takes place in the mind and heart of Pierre Froment, but also in the opposition between Paris, city of light and knowledge, and the church of the Sacré-Cœur, a symbol in Zola's eyes of obscurantism. That is why Guillaume chooses it for destruction and is prevented from blowing it up only at the last minute by Pierre who would have died in the blast if Guillaume had not given up the mad project.

Echoes of the old row of 1873[6] when the Archbishop of Paris requested from parliament a declaration of public utility for the

construction of a church on Montmartre are heard in these pages.
Take, for example, the passage in which the Sacré-Cœur is
evoked on the night of Salvat's execution: "Under the pale nocturnal sky, the structure loomed up like a colossal monster, symbolical of provocation and sovereign dominion [. . .] This wounded
him [Guillaume] so keenly that he could not help exclaiming:
'Ah! they chose a good site for it, and how stupid it was to let
them do so! I know of nothing more nonsensical: Paris crowned
and dominated by that temple of idolatry!'" Paris, on the other
hand, represents science and hope for the future. At the end of
the book, it is seen under the setting sun, which wraps the city in
splendor and evokes a vision of a magnificent harvest, "the great
future harvest of truth and justice."

II *The Dreyfus Case*

Paris came off the press in the midst of all the turmoil created
by Zola's intervention in the Dreyfus case, that terrible miscar-
riage of justice which shook French society from top to bottom.
It is such a well-known episode of this period that it need not
be related in great detail. Readers will doubtless remember that
Captain Alfred Dreyfus, a member of a wealthy Jewish family,
charged with having betrayed his country by selling military se-
crets to Germany, was convicted by a court-martial on December
22, 1894, degraded in a public ceremony on January 5, and sent
shortly after to penal servitude on Devil's Island off the Guiana
coast. His family believed his protestations of innocence, and before many months passed others began to have misgivings about
his guilt. Evidence was finally uncovered that the real culprit was
Major Walsin-Esterhazy rather than Dreyfus. The army authorities foolishly persisted in refusing the latter a new trial. They mis-
takenly thought the prestige of the army at stake. That some were
also motivated by anti-Semitism seems to be fairly well established. When Esterhazy was finally publicly mentioned by name,
he could not do other than request an investigation, which the
army authorities were compelled to grant.

Zola, meanwhile, was approached by the defenders of Dreyfus.
They were probably encouraged to do so by the article "Pour les
Juifs," published in *Le Figaro* in 1896,[7] in which he denounced
anti-Semitism as "a monstrosity." Conversations with Scheurer-
Kestner, vice-president of the Senate, and with others convinced

him of Dreyfus' innocence and made him decide to intervene. On November 25, 1897, his first article on the question appeared in *Le Figaro*. Entitled simply "M. Scheurer-Kestner," it was above all a tribute to this man's sense of duty and honor. It closed with the famous words: "Truth is on the march, and nothing will stop it" (*La vérité est en marche et rien ne l'arrêtera*). It was followed by two others: "Le Syndicat" (December 1, 1897) and "Procès-verbal" (December 5); whereupon *Le Figaro*, worried by the possible reactions of its conservative readers, closed its columns to the novelist, who immediately composed two pamphlets: *Lettre à la jeunesse* (December 14) and *Lettre à la France* (January 6, 1898).

Then, to the stupefaction of many, a court-martial acquitted Esterhazy on January 11. Zola at once decided that a direct, militant challenge was necessary, and wrote his famous letter to the President of the Republic. It was published on January 13, 1898, in *L'Aurore* under the title "J'accuse" chosen by the editor, Georges Clemenceau. The phrase began several paragraphs of accusations, accusations of such a nature as to make a libel suit inevitable. Naming various high officers, Zola charged them with either hiding the truth, or lying intentionally, or yielding weakly to others. He accused the officers of the Esterhazy court-martial of cynically obeying orders from higher up, and the war office of conducting in the press "an abominable campaign to lead public opinion astray and to conceal its own mistakes."

This letter and the libel suit that followed produced an uproar in Paris, and, indeed, throughout France. Friendships were ruined and even families divided. Zola's trial lasted fifteen days during which every effort was made by the court, whose presiding judge Delegorgue was far from a model of impartiality, to limit the issues and to hamstring witnesses for the defense. As a result, and in spite of the summation of Zola's lawyer, Maître Labori, in which the truth was revealed, the jury found the novelist guilty by a 7–5 vote, unanimity not being required as in the United States. He was sentenced to a year in prison and a fine of 3000 francs. An eyewitness has given the following description of this "criminal" leaving the courthouse one day during the trial: "He was awkward, he was nearsighted, he held his umbrella clumsily under his arm, he had the gestures and demeanor of the student. But when he descended one by one the steps of the Palais de Justice, amid cries of hatred, shouts of death, under an archway of threatening canes, it was like a king descending the great staircase of the Hôtel de Ville under an archway of naked swords. It was the greatest thing I have ever seen in my life." [8]

An appeal was promptly taken, and because of technical errors a new trial was granted. After some delay Zola again faced the court on July 18. Immediately, his lawyer announced that the defendant was defaulting, and they left the chamber. That night, on the advice of Labori, Zola bade farewell to France and took refuge in England. He did this so that the court's decision could not be served on him. Had he stayed in France and accepted such a notification, it would have been this time without appeal. Labori and Clemenceau were convinced of the need to keep the question of Zola's fate open as long as Dreyfus' case was not reconsidered. Zola reluctantly bowed to their views.[9]

His exile lasted almost eleven months, during which dramatic events occurred. Colonel Henry, one of those instrumental in preventing a review of Dreyfus' case, committed suicide. Esterhazy fled and confessed. A new trial for Dreyfus was ordered by the Cour de Cassation. This second court-martial brought in an absurd verdict: guilty with extenuating circumstances. President Loubet pardoned the man on September 19, 1899. He was not, however, completely exonerated until 1906.

III *The* Évangiles

As soon as the Cour de Cassation "broke" the decision of the 1894 trial and ordered a new one, Émile Zola returned to France. Not knowing on his arrival a word of English, not liking English food, compelled to stay pretty well hidden from view, he did not greatly enjoy his exile. He took advantage of it, however, to write the first novel of a new series, *Les Quatre Évangiles,* which he had already planned. This tetralogy was to consist of *Fécondité, Travail, Vérité,* and *Justice.* The hero of each novel was to be a son of Pierre Froment; and the four were to be named, respectively, Mathieu, Luc, Marc, and Jean, after the four gospels of the New Testament.

The three novels actually written show Zola as a propagandist even more than did *Les Trois Villes.* They are bad novels, and in this case only one, *Travail,* is an interesting book. *Fécondité* (1899), inspired in part by Zola's genuine concern over the declining birth rate of his country, in part by his attachment, apparent in *Les Rougon-Macquart,* to the theme of fertility, is mechanically constructed. Not only is it divided into six parts of five chapters each, but the central couple, Mathieu and Marianne, produce children at such regular intervals that the effect is more comical than impressive. In Part IV, for example, the first sentence of every chapter is a birth announcement. In the course of their lives this fruitful pair bestow twelve children on their presumably grateful country and become more and more prosperous. At their diamond wedding anniversary, one hundred and fifty-eight children, grandchildren, and great-grandchildren are present. When husbands, wives, and a few great-great grandchildren are added, an incredible horde of three hundred people, all relatives by blood or marriage, pays them honor at the large domain of Chantebled which they have built up over the decades. Meanwhile, those who have practiced birth control suffer disasters and come to sorry ends. The moral is only too clear.

Travail, published in 1901, can be taken more seriously, in spite of the fact that it embraces the outdated utopianism of Charles Fourier,[10] and in the last chapters becomes more and more incredible. An ideal community, modeled on Fourier's phalansteries, is founded by Luc Froment with resources provided by his friend Martial Jordan. Zola's account is, beyond doubt, a product of high-minded idealism. At the same time, it is, from the standpoint of both the capitalist and the Marxist, a piece of colossal naïveté. The former believes in the necessity of reward in the form of profit for individual initiative; the latter, in the need of a nation-wide application of socialist principles. The Marxist would view the narrative as sentimental. In particular, the notion that a class-less society can be produced even in part by intermarriage between sons of the bourgeoisie and daughters of the working class would strike him as laughable. The geographical and economic scope of this experiment would be judged by the Marxist as inadequate, and the project therefore doomed to defeat. He would, however, approve the criticism of capitalist society which is present in this volume. Some of the indignation, compassion, and fire of *Germinal* reappears in this second *Évangile.* The poverty of the many and the wealth of the few are clearly depicted in the first part of the book. Furthermore, the evocations of the metallurgical foundries with their huge furnaces and monstrous machines recall the descriptions of the establishment where Goujet worked in *L'Assommoir* and the mines in *Germinal*. Zola still possessed the power revealed in those earlier masterpieces. Nor had he lost the art of handling large numbers of people. The opening chapter depicts the working-class quarter of Beauclair on a Saturday evening just after the conclusion of a two months' strike which has embittered everyone. An atmosphere of sullen resentment is prevalent; threats of violence are heard; pilferers are feared by the shopkeepers, and the police are on the alert: "With a bleeding heart and a brain seething with dark forebodings, Luc went on walking in the sordid and now threatening crowd which kept increasing every moment in the rue de Brias. He became conscious that there was terror in the air, something indefinable which was felt by all of them, the result of the recent class struggle—a struggle not yet ended but which would break out again at the first opportunity." Specific characters and incidents—like that of a starving boy stealing a loaf of bread—skilfully chosen, portrayed, and reported confirm the general impression. In such passages the old maestro is once again at his best.[11]

Unfortunately, the same cannot be said of *Vérité*. The novel is inspired by the Dreyfus case, although Zola transferred the action from the milieu of the army to that of the school. Instead of a Jewish army captain, the victim is a Jewish schoolteacher by the name of Simon. His schoolboy nephew, Zéphirin Lehmann, is murdered; and Simon, accused not only of this crime but also of pederasty, is convicted. The counterpart of Esterhazy is a monk, Gorgias. Marc Froment, the real hero of the book, helps establish Simon's innocence as Zola did for Dreyfus. While the transposition permits the novelist to support the nonsectarian school system of the Republic, the *école laïque*, against the church school, in which young Lehmann, the son of a Catholic mother, had been a pupil, the change of milieu really diminishes the novel's effectiveness. Too many readers were and are familiar with the original drama of Dreyfus. The book, for all its sincerity, seems pale in comparison and, somehow, unreal.

Justice, in which Zola intended to treat the question of international peace based on social justice, was never written. On September 28, 1902, the Zolas returned to Paris after their summer's sojourn at Médan. That evening they ordered a fire lighted in their bedroom. The next morning, when they did not appear or ring for breakfast, the servants discovered them both unconscious. Zola was dead. His wife, still barely alive, was saved. The official investigation described the death as accidental, caused by carbon monoxide emanating from a blocked chimney. Since then, doubt has been cast on this interpretation; it has been charged that Zola was murdered by fanatical anti-Dreyfusards who hired a roofer or a chimney sweep to block the flue. Zola's son was inclined to accept this hypothesis,[12] which is not wholly improbable. Since the evidence is really insufficient, the official explanation is still that Zola's death was a tragic accident.

Do the six novels discussed in this chapter indicate a serious decline in Zola's literary powers, as many critics maintain? That they are inferior to the best of the *Rougon-Macquart* is evident. They demonstrate, beyond any doubt, the danger of attempting to put forth propaganda in the guise of creative literature. *Les Trois Villes* are in their way remarkable books, but they are very inferior novels. The three *Évangiles* are even worse. *Vérité* is not as foolish as *Fécondité*, nor as absurd as the last part of *Travail*. Only the first part of this last-named book suggests that in the midst of all the polemics of his final years, Zola still possessed some of the great literary talent of the earlier period. He, himself, recognized that he was writing books in which "the question of form [was] of secondary importance," [13] and social problems were the main concern. They should perhaps be judged from that point of view. If so, the opinions will be as numerous as the readers. All, however, will agree that these books are dominated by idealism and, in the last analysis, by an optimistic faith in the essential value of life.[14]

Conclusion[1]

Paul Bourget once made some comments on the novel of customs and manners (*le roman de mœurs*) and the novel of character (*le roman de caractère*). He suggested that the former is above all representative, depicting average people engaged in ordinary activities; the latter, analytical, placing before the reader complex, exceptional individuals who can be profitably studied. He found in Balzac an author who combined the two types and fused them into an artistic whole. He cited Benjamin Constant and Stendhal as examples of the analytical novelist; and, in Flaubert, the Goncourts, Daudet, and Zola, he saw writers who treated the *roman de mœurs* with marked superiority.

A number of ordinary activities in which ordinary people engage are, indeed, depicted in Zola's work. In *Le Ventre de Paris*, the selling of food by the Quenus and the Méhudins; in *L'Assommoir*, the operation of a laundry by Mme Fauconnier and by Gervaise Coupeau; in *Germinal*, the mining of coal by the Maheus; in *La Terre*, the cultivation of the land by Jean Macquart, Buteau, and Hourdequin; and, in *Au bonheur des dames*, the running of a department store by Octave Mouret (who is less "average" than the others) are described with much exactitude. In this respect, Bourget's definition of the *roman de mœurs* is fulfilled by these books.

Bourget's distinction, whether wholly valid or not, points to another conclusion concerning Zola. A number of characters in his work—Saccard, Faujas, Eugène Rougon, Claude Lantier, for example—possess a certain strength and dynamism. Saccard and Claude Lantier in particular are aggrandized beyond normal stature, Saccard ultimately appearing as the super-speculator, the "poète du million"; Claude Lantier becoming the super-artist, the "possédé de la peinture," in a word, the artist gone mad. Nana, too, is magnified from a mere prostitute into a voracious devourer of men. But in spite of such characters, it is fair to say that Zola's novels contain no real heroes, no inspired rebels, no splendid figures, no one really comparable to René, Julien Sorel, Rastignac, Vautrin, or Jean Valjean. In Zola's novels, as Bourget's distinction more or less implies, the group overshadows the individual. The young man in revolt, the noble woman defying convention, the seeker of the absolute, the complete miser, the redeemed man have been replaced by the people plying the above-mentioned trades, to which one might add bankers and stockbrokers, rank-and-file soldiers, small townsmen, and middle-class people in their middle-class beehive. The characters not only operate within their given framework but are a part of it. This does not mean that they seem unreal; on the contrary, Zola succeeds in infusing life into them, in arousing interest in their fate, and in holding the reader's attention to the end. What it does mean is that the characters are not analyzed in depth. Lacking in subtlety, they do not receive the minute inspection that Stendhal gives to Julien Sorel or to Mathilde de la Mole.

This general tendency of emphasizing the group over the individual accounts in part for Zola's descriptions of crowds. The horde of miners rushing over the plain in *Germinal;* the clash between these miners and the troops in the same novel; the packed theater at the premiere of *La Blonde Vénus;* the crowded stock exchange; the department store swarming with customers on a day of special sale; the thousands of soldiers treading the roads of northeastern France, crossing the Meuse river, manœuvering on the battlefield, retreating into Sedan, then herded into the Iges loop; the torchlight procession at Lourdes; the street scene in the early part of *Travail*—all these descriptions belong to the *roman de mœurs* but are also a manifestation of Zola's personal predilection and genius. His imagination tended toward the grandiose and the epic.

His imagination also led him into the symbolical, the visionary, and the mythical. "On the springboard of exact observation," he took a "leap into the stars." This oft-quoted phrase from a letter to Henry Céard in 1885 is a key—and, if not used to excess, a valuable key—to some of his descriptive passages. Le Paradou with its Tree, the mine in *Germinal,* the house in the rue de la Goutte d'or, Nana's gold-and-silver bed, the middle-class building in *Pot-Bouille,* Lantier's last painting, and La Lison in *La Bête humaine*

[*179*]

take on symbolic significance; and some verge on the monstrous or the nightmarish. Without ceasing to be realistic, the novels become impressionistic and subjective. Herein lies their greatest originality. Their poetry, frequently black poetry, is what most intrigues the modern reader.

This is not to say that Zola's work is not profoundly human. Violence, sex, and suffering abound in these novels which also contain compassion, sympathy, and love. Characters like Silvère and Miette, Florent, Catherine Maheu, Hennebeau, Gervaise, Pauline Quenu, Jean Macquart, Christine Hallegrain are not outside the common range of humanity. Their activities, hopes, and aspirations win the interest and arouse the sympathy of most readers. Of Hennebeau's difficulties with his wife, Zola wrote: "This banal adultery exists only to give me the scene in which M. Hennebeau cries out his human suffering in the face of the poignant social suffering confronting him." [2] The human element is never forgotten in Zola's novels.

In the order of the universe, death is a necessary part, and of this Zola is fully, even obsessively, aware. Death is, therefore, ever-present: death by accident, by starvation, by disease, death in combat and in war, death in all its terrible finality. To few does it come peacefully at the end of a long and happy existence. Yet, in the last analysis, it is defeated by life. If any positive credo emerges from Zola's work, it is precisely this: belief in the eternal force and value of life.

The news of Zola's death in 1902 was a sensation. People now saw in him more than a great novelist; they clearly beheld the man of action, the defender of Dreyfus, the champion of the innocent, and the upholder of justice. They appreciated the determination, zeal, and courage he had displayed in supporting that cause. To an American, Zola's attitude toward the question of Dreyfus' innocence recalls that of William Lloyd Garrison at the beginning of his campaign for the abolition of slavery: "I am in earnest—I will not equivocate—I will not excuse—I will not retreat a single inch—*and I will be heard.*" Such men may have a touch of megalomania in their makeup. One can only be grateful for it, for they arouse and rally public opinion as others are frequently unable to do.

At Zola's funeral, his casket was borne through streets lined with mourning people. At the cemetery, Anatole France delivered the principal oration. He spoke for thousands at home and abroad when he declared that, in defending the innocent, Émile Zola was for a moment "the conscience of mankind." In spite of the solemn surroundings, his words brought forth tumultuous applause. Numerous deputations then passed before the hearse, and cries of "Germinal" and "Glory to Zola" were frequent. The people of France revealed in this hour their convictions and their gratitude. Six years later, on June 4, 1908, Zola's mortal remains were transferred with impressive ceremony to the Pantheon where they were put beside Voltaire, Rousseau, and Victor Hugo, and where Jaurès and Anatole France have since been placed. It was too late for the French Academy to elect him to its membership. Its doors had remained obstinately closed to the author of *Germinal* and *La Terre.* Had he lived, his new luster might well have gained him entrance.

Notes and References

Chapter One

1. François Zola was partly Greek, for his mother was Benedetta Kiariaki from the island of Corfu.

2. *Nouveaux contes à Ninon*, "Souvenirs" VI (Bernouard edition, p. 398). See also M. Kanes, *L'Atelier de Zola* (Droz, 1963), pp. 68–70.

3. A. Lanoux, *Bonjour, Monsieur Zola* (Paris, Amiot-Dumont, 1954), pp. 32–35.

4. "Un épisode inconnu de l'enfance d'Émile Zola," *Mercure de France*, March 1, 1929, p. 508.

5. The text has not been preserved.

6. In a letter to Cézanne dated July 1860 he announced that he had quit, presumably the previous month. In this chapter my references concerning letters are to the *Correspondance*, Vol. I, in the Bernouard edition of the *Œuvres complètes*.

7. In the Bernouard edition, this letter is dated July 1860, but Professor Mitterand has shown conclusively that it must have been written in early September, 1860. See the *Mercure de France*, Feb. 1, 1959, pp. 351–59.

8. Apparently he did not finish it till the next year. See a letter to Baille, dated May 1, 1861.

9. This letter, too, is incorrectly dated in the Bernouard edition. Professor Mitterand dates it Feb. 10, 1861. Cf. note 7.

10. See his letter to Baille, June 10, 1861.

11. See "Trois textes inédits d'Émile Zola," by G. Robert, in *Revue des sciences humaines*, juillet-décembre, 1948, and in particular Robert's remarks on the importance of this early text, p. 184. It was published in the *Journal populaire de Lille*, April 16, 1864; see *Les Cahiers naturalistes*, no. 26, 1964, pp. 28–29.

Chapter Two

1. See H. Mitterand, *Zola journaliste* (A. Colin, 1962), p. 16.

2. P. Alexis, *Émile Zola. Notes d'un ami* (Charpentier, 1882), pp. 60–61.

3. Some writers on Zola have stated that Darwin's book was translated and published in France in 1864, but according to the catalogue of the Bibliothèque Nationale 1862 is the correct date.

4. *Documents littéraires,* "Dumas fils" p. 204 (Bernouard edition). He first formulated it in *Le Salut public,* 1865.

5. In this brief and necessarily incomplete discussion of the *Contes à Ninon,* I have used to some extent Professor Hemmings' article on "Les Sources d'inspiration de Zola conteur," *Les Cahiers naturalistes,* nos. 24–25, 1963, as well as Professor Lapp's comments in his *Zola before the "Rougon-Macquart,"* pp. 5 ff.

6. *Correspondance,* Vol. I, letter dated Feb. 6, 1865, to Valabrègue.

7. See H. Mitterand, *Zola journaliste,* p. 45. Cf. note 4.

8. Quoted by Henri d'Alméras, *Avant la gloire: leurs débuts,* 1902 ("Émile Zola," pp. 188–96). I have used Professor Hemmings' translation (*op. cit.,* p. 21). On *La Confession de Claude,* one should read J. C. Lapp's comment, *op. cit.,* Chap. 2.

9. See the critical apparatus in his edition, i.e., the Bernouard edition.

10. Quoted by F. W. J. Hemmings, *Émile Zola,* Oxford, 1953, p. 22; also by M. Kanes, *L'Atelier de Zola,* Droz, 1963, p. 41. See also Hemmings, "Zola's Apprenticeship to Journalism," *Publ. Modern Language Association,* June 1956.

11. Hemmings, p. 23. The French text can be found in G. Robert's "Trois textes inédits d'Émile Zola," *Revue des sciences humaines,* juillet-décembre, 1948.

12. Zola had used it before this. See Hemmings, *op. cit.,* p. 120, note 1.

13. See J. C. Lapp, *op. cit.,* pp. 74–87.

14. See É. Zola, *Salons, recueillis, annotés et présentés* par F. W. J. Hemmings & Robert J. Niess, Geneva, Droz, 1959, p. 15 and pp. 49–80. The editors have reproduced the original text which differs rather markedly from that published later in the same volume as *Mes haines.*

15. Reminiscences of Zola's association with the artists and his work as art critic will be found in his novel *L'Œuvre,* 1886, chaps. II and III in particular.

16. On the sojourn at Bennecourt in 1866, see the article by R. Walter in *Les Cahiers naturalistes,* No. 17, 1961.

17. The subject was originally suggested by *La Vénus de Gordes* by Adolphe Belot and Ernest Daudet, published serially in *Le Figaro.* Based on a real crime which occurred in 1861, this novel was a rather banal courtroom drama which recounted the murder of a husband by his wife's lover. Zola saw greater possibilities in it. He first wrote a short story, "Un mariage d'amour," which appeared in *Le Figaro,* Dec. 24, 1866. But not yet satisfied that he had wrung from the subject

all its potential, he determined to do something much more searching. Arsène Houssaye accepted the new version for *L'Artiste* where it appeared in three instalments in 1867. The volume was put on sale at the end of the year.

Louis Mandin suggested in an article in the *Mercure de France* (May 1940) that Mme Raquin was inspired by Tom Wil in Eugène Sue's *Atar-Gull*, 1831, and the cat, François, by Pluto in Poe's *The Black Cat*. These two suggestions seem to me very debatable.

18. Other rapprochements with *La Rabouilleuse* could be made. See in *Les Cahiers naturalistes*, nos. 24–25, 1963, the remarks of Pierre Citron, p. 25.

19. Ulbach wrote under the pseudonym of Ferragus (*Le Figaro*, Jan. 23, 1868). See Le Blond's critical apparatus in the Bernouard edition.

20. J. Michelet, *Œuvres complètes. L'Amour-La Femme* (Flammarion), *édition définitive*, p. 16. See also p. 254 and p. 344 where the same theory is repeated.

21. Dr. Prosper Lucas, *Traité philosophique et physiologique de l'hérédité dans les états de santé et de maladie, du système nerveux*, 2 vols. (Paris, 1847, 1850).

22. For further details on this aspect of the novel see J. C. Lapp, *op. cit.*, Chap. 5.

23. With the collaboration of Marius Roux, a stage version of *Les Mystères de Marseille* was composed and played in Marseilles in October. It was not successful.

24. Some of these "chroniques" and articles have been republished by Kanes, *L'Atelier de Zola*. They are very much worth reading; one finds in some a biting humor that is very effective. Furthermore, several articles of literary criticism reveal Zola's developing opinions at this period. See also by Kanes: "Zola, Pelletan, and *La Tribune*," *Publications of the Modern Language Association*, September, 1964.

25. J. Vallès, "Dickens et Zola," *Le Voltaire*, Feb. 11, 1880. I have used Hemmings' translation (*op. cit.*, p. 37).

26. *Correspondance*, Vol. I, letter to Valabrègue, Feb. 19, 1867, Bernouard edition.

Chapter Three

1. See respectively F. W. J. Hemmings, *Émile Zola* (p. 22), and his article in *Publications of the Modern Language Association*, entitled "Zola's Apprenticeship to Journalism" (1956) p. 348.

2. *L'Événement illustré*, July 4, 1868. The text is reproduced in Kanes, *op. cit.*, p. 88.

3. Interview with Zola in *Le Figaro*, March 6, 1893. Quoted by H. Martineau in *Le Roman scientifique d'Émile Zola* (1907) p. 75.

4. Ch. Letourneau, *Physiologie des passions* (Baillière, 1868), pp. 3, 86, 124–5.

5. See "Une campagne," Vol. 46 in the *Œuvres complètes*, Bernouard edition, p. X.

6. These documents are reproduced in the original French, of course, in the critical apparatus furnished by Maurice Le Blond in his edition of *La Fortune des Rougon*, Vol. 2 of the *Œuvres complètes* (ed. Bernouard). There are a few inconsequential misprints.

7. From the first document, "Notes sur la marche générale de l'œuvre."

8. *Le Rappel*, May 13, 1869. Quoted by H. Mitterand in his *Zola journaliste*, A. Colin, 1962, p. 111.

9. The term "innateness" is a translation of *innéité*, a "law" established by Dr. Lucas. See below.

10. Hemmings, *op. cit.*, p. 76.

11. From "Notes générales sur la nature de l'œuvre." See note 6.

12. "Le Naturalisme au théâtre," Vol. 42 of the *Œuvres complètes* (ed. Bernouard), p. 147. For the origins of the term, see the article on that question by F. W. J. Hemmings in *French Studies*, 1954.

13. "Le Roman expérimental," Vol. 41 of the *Œuvres complètes* (ed. Bernouard), p. 16.

14. *Ibid.*, p. 18.

15. *Ibid.*, p. 24. My italics.

16. *Ibid.*, p. 25.

17. *Ibid.*, p. 28.

18. For other details of the scheme, see *La Fortune des Rougon*, Vol. 2 in the *Œuvres complètes* (ed. Bernouard), pp. 357–61.

19. See the "Liste des romans" (MS. 10345, f. 129) published by Le Blond, *ibid.*, p. 361. The list, as published by Le Blond, is not strictly accurate for his includes *Retour sur les Mouret*, which is really a marginal note by Zola, and he has included *La Conquête de Plassans* twice.

20. For this early novel he called his preliminary outline "Premiers détails" rather than the *Ébauche*. The title, *La Curée*, has been translated in various ways. It's a hunting term and perhaps the best translation is either *The Kill* or *The Rush for Spoils*.

21. "Le Ventre de Paris," Vol. 4 of the *Œuvres complètes* (ed. Bernouard), p. 335.

22. "Germinal," Vol. 14 of the *Œuvres complètes* (ed. Bernouard), p. 557.

23. Bibliothèque Nationale, MS. 10313, f. 208, 212.

24. Cf. G. Robert, *"La Terre" d'Émile Zola*, 1952, p. 159.

25. "Au bonheur des dames," Vol. 12 of the *Œuvres complètes* (ed. Bernouard), p. 467.

26. Zola first met Céard in 1876 and through him Thyébaut.

27. My allusions are all to articles republished by M. Kanes in his *L'Atelier de Zola* or by H. Mitterand in his *Zola journaliste*.

Chapter Four

1. See H. Mitterand, *Zola journaliste*, A. Colin, for the account of Zola's contributions to these papers.

2. See in the *Correspondance* (Bernouard edition) a letter to Edmond de Goncourt, dated Sept. 7, 1870.

3. Quoted in H. Mitterand, *op. cit.*, pp. 135–36.

4. Plassans = Aix-en-Provence; see Chap. III. For the various sources of the novel see Mitterand's discussion in the Pléiade edition, pp. 1539–41, and also M. Kane's article, "Zola, Balzac and 'La Fortune des Rogron,' " *French Studies*, July 1964.

5. H. Mitterand suggests in the Pléiade edition (p. 1550) that Zola may also have read E. Deschanel's *Physiologie des écrivains et des artistes, ou Essai de critique naturelle* (Hachette, 1864).

6. For the sources, see also H. Mitterand, *ibid.*, pp. 1539–41.

7. In the work-sheets preserved in the Bibliothèque Nationale, we find the remark: "C'est décidément une nouvelle *Phèdre* que je vais faire" (f. 298, MS. 10282, "Premiers détails").

8. Also found in the work-sheets (MS. 10282, f. 240): "Ne pas oublier le côté de l'hérédité."

9. See Mitterand's excellent pages on the preparation of this novel, Pléiade edition, pp. 1608 ff.

10. In French: "Quels gredins que les honnêtes gens!" Zola expressed a very similar idea in one of his "Lettres parisiennes," published in *La Cloche*, July 6, 1872: "Ce sont de terribles gens, que les honnêtes gens," etc.

11. A. Wilson, *Émile Zola. An Introductory Study of his Novels* (New York, 1952), p. 108.

12. Republished in *La Tribune*, Dec. 26, 1869.

13. Zola's first idea, according to his work-sheets, was to have Faujas covet and take Mouret's wife. He wisely abandoned it.

14. Stated in the *Ébauche*.

15. *La Curée* was also published in Russia at this time.

16. For a complete list, see H. Mitterand, *Zola journaliste*, p. 295.

17. Some of the *contes* were modified from their original form as they appeared in the newspapers. For the original text of "Le Petit Village" and "Le Jeûne," see Kanes, *op. cit.* "Le Chômage," one of three added to the 2d edition, was none other than "Le Lendemain de la crise," published in *Le Corsaire*, Dec. 22, 1872 (see above, p. 58), though the political paragraphs were omitted in 1885. One of the best stories in this collection is "Le Grand Michu."

18. On this question, which lack of space does not permit me to treat, see J. C. Lapp, *Zola before the "Rougon-Macquart,"* Chap. I.

19. Suggested by a property called Gallice near Aix-en-Provence. The village of Les Artaud is Le Tholonet, also near Aix-en-Provence.

20. Just after this Albine plays the role of Eve a little too well, for like Eve she feels shame, a shame that is incompatible with her symbolic function as Zola sees it. See R. B. Grant, "Confusion of Meaning in Zola's *La Faute de l'abbé Mouret,*" *Symposium,* 1959.

21. I have used here Hemmings' translation, *op. cit.,* p. 87. The preceding translations are my own.

22. On the importance of the earlier stories, see F. W. J. Hemmings, "Les Sources d'inspiration de Zola conteur," *Les Cahiers naturalistes* (nos. 24–25), 1963, and J. C. Lapp, *op. cit.,* Chap. I. On the question of myth in this novel, see the interesting article by Philip Walker, "Prophetic Myths in Zola," *Publications of the Modern Language Association,* September 1959.

23. Stendhal's *Lucien Leuwen,* the second volume of which satirizes government bureaucracy, was not published until 1894.

24. On the sources, composition, etc., of this novel see R. B. Grant, *Zola's "Son Excellence Eugène Rougon"* (Durham, N.C.), 1960.

25. "Le roman devient ainsi une large page, sociale et humaine," *Ébauche,* f. 118, MS. 10292.

26. See the entries in Goncourt's *Journal* for May 31, 1874; Jan. 7 and Dec. 17, 1876.

Chapter Five

1. Quoted by H. Mitterand in the Pléiade edition of *L'Assommoir,* p. 1558.

2. See Mitterand, *ibid.,* pp. 1555–66; also L. Deffoux, *La Publication de "L'Assommoir,"* 1931.

3. An edition, in France, is normally a printing of one thousand copies.

4. Pléiade edition, p. 1535.

5. *Ibid.,* p. 1537.

6. *Ibid.,* pp. 1535–42 (particularly p. 1541).

7. See the *Correspondance* under the appropriate dates.

8. See Mitterand, Pléiade edition, pp. 1543 ff. Cf. also H. Massis, *Comment Zola composait ses romans* (Paris, 1906).

9. In my quotations in English, I have usually used Mr. Townsend's translation, but sometimes my own, and occasionally a combination of his and mine.

10. Cf. Turnell, *The Art of French Fiction,* p. 150 and Hemmings, *op. cit.,* p. 95.

11. As he did in "Le Forgeron"; cf. J. C. Lapp, *op. cit.,* p. 25.

12. Cf. Hemmings, *op. cit.*, pp. 95–97 and M. Turnell, *The Art of French Fiction*, pp. 147–53.

13. See Mitterand, Pléiade edition, pp. 1552–54.

14. The brutal treatment of Lalie Bijard and her death is one of the famous episodes of the novel. It was inspired by an article Zola read in *L'Événement*. See Mitterand, *ibid.*, p. 1542.

15. From the *Ébauche*, quoted by Mitterand, Pléiade edition, p. 1544. Also Massis, *op. cit.*, p. 103. Originally, Zola thought of killing her off "dans un drame" (Massis, *ibid.*, p. 102). He wisely gave up this notion.

16. For recent comments, see Turnell, *op. cit.*, and an article by J. L. Vissière, "L'Art de la phrase dans *L'Assommoir*," *Les Cahiers naturalistes*, No. 11, 1958.

Chapter Six

1. H. Guillemin, *Présentation des "Rougon-Macquart*," Gallimard, 1964, p. 154.

2. Cf. L. A. Carter, *Zola and the Theater*, p. 108.

3. *Ibid.*, p. 118.

4. In *Les Romanciers naturalistes*, *Le Naturalisme au théâtre*, *Nos auteurs dramatiques*, and *Documents littéraires*, all in 1881.

5. For those not familiar with French literature, the allusions are to Flaubert's *Madame Bovary*, *La Tentation de Saint Antoine*, and *Un cœur simple;* to Goncourt's *La Fille Élisa;* to Zola's *L'Assommoir.*

6. Chap. VII, in the paragraph summarizing Fauchery's article on "La Mouche d'or." In the "notes de travail," the preliminary portrait of Nana says: "Avec cela, finissant par considérer l'homme comme une matière à exploiter, *devenant une force de la nature, un ferment de destruction, mais cela sans le vouloir, par son sexe seul et par sa puissante odeur de femme,* détruisant tout ce qu'elle approche" [. . .] (MS. 10313, f. 192).

7. The first of these two quotations was penned a little later (*L'Œuvre*, Chap. 6). The second, according to Hemmings (*op. cit.*, p. 146), comes from an article in *Le Voltaire*, Aug. 5, 1879.

8. On the preparation of this novel, see Mitterand, Pléiade edition, pp. 1663 ff.

9. See his article in *L'Événement illustré*, June 6, 1868, quoted by M. Kanes, *op. cit.*

10. This particular detail was suggested to Zola, oddly enough, by Otway's *Venice preserved*. See L. Auriant, "*La Véritable Histoire de Nana*" (Mercure de France, 1943), pp. 125 ff.

11. Victor Hugo is a good example.

12. Another famous scene is the dinner in Nana's apartment, Chap. 4.

13. See Mitterand, Pléiade edition, pp. 1667, 1691. On the symbolism of *Nana*, see also an interesting article by F. M. Leonard; "*Nana:* Symbol and Action," *Modern Fiction Studies*, 1963.

14. In my treatment of *Nana*, I am indebted to both Hemmings and Turnell.

15. *Pot-Bouille*. The title is almost untranslatable. It refers to a very ordinary type of dish, like a stew. One English translator entitled the novel "Piping-Hot." The expression *faire pot-bouille avec quelqu'un* means *se mettre en ménage avec quelqu'un*, to set up housekeeping with some one. There is an extension of this meaning in Zola's title according to H. Mitterand (Vol. 3 of the Pléiade edition of *Les Rougon-Macquart*, p. 1638): "la *pot-bouille* devient ici la singulière fraternisation de ces familles de la petite bourgeoisie parisienne, qui, tout en se portant haine et jalousie, spéculent sur leurs relations mutuelles pour arrondir leurs revenus." On the preparation of this novel, see H. Mitterand, *ibid.*, pp. 1605–35.

16. Zola may have got this idea from a "chronique" in the *Gil Blas*, Jan. 16, 1882, entitled "Les Demoiselles de magasin" which told of such a case. Cf. G. Robert, *op. cit.*, p. 189. On the preparation of the novel, see H. Mitterand, Pléiade edition, pp. 1677–1703.

17. For the original text, see *Au bonheur des dames* (Bernouard edition), p. 467.

18. Even if this could not be deduced from the story itself, there is other evidence; see, for example, his letter to Baille, Feb. 14, 1860. In the *Œuvres complètes* "La Mort d'Olivier Bécaille" appears in the volumes entitled *Contes et nouvelles* along with some very good stories which we do not have the space to analyze.

19. See his letter to Céard, May 9, 1880.

20. P. Alexis, *op. cit.*, p. 126. Cf. also Mitterand, Vol. III of the Pléiade edition of *Les Rougon-Macquart*, p. 1744 ff.

21. Quoted by N. O. Franzén, *Zola et "La joie de vivre,"* Stockholm, 1958, p. 45. Cf. Mitterand, Pléiade edition, pp. 1740–71.

22. See, on this double tendency in Zola, H. Mitterand, Pléiade edition.

23. R. J. Niess, *Émile Zola's Letters to J. van Santen Kolff* (St. Louis, 1940), p. 27.

24. Space does not permit comment on other matters such as Pauline's first menstruation, the frightful *accouchement* of Lazare's wife, and the death of the dog.

Chapter Seven

1. MS. 10345, f. 129: "Un 2ᵉ roman ouvrier.—Particulièrement politique. L'ouvrier d'insurrection, [outil revolutionnaire], de la Com-

mune, aboutissant à mai 71." The words in brackets were written by Zola in the interlinear space.

2. See the Goncourt *Journal* under the date of Jan. 16, 1884.

3. V. Hugo wrote a poem on the Aubin strike. It was finally published in the *Œuvres posthumes*.

4. For those interested in this question, see the chapter on the sources of *Germinal* in my book, *Zola's "Germinal." A Critical and Historical Study*, Leicester University Press, 1962, and, of course, H. Mitterand, Vol. III of the Pléiade edition of *Les Rougon-Macquart*, pp. 1802 ff.

5. Cf. Ph. D. Walker, "Zola's Art of Characterization in *Germinal*," in *L'Esprit créateur*, 1964. This is an interesting, stimulating article, even though exaggerated.

6. E. Auerbach, *Mimesis* (Princeton University Press, 1953), p. 512.

7. For further comments on this chapter, see my study, *op. cit.*, pp. 31, 43–44, 114, 146–47, note 33.

8. The notion of introducing a socialist priest into the book doubtless came from Laveleye's *Le Socialisme contemporain*, 2d ed., 1883, but the idea of bringing him to this particular scene was, of course, Zola's own.

9. Zola took many of the details from Simonin's *La Vie souterraine*, Hachette, 1867. See note 4.

10. See M. Girard, "L'Univers de Germinal," *Revue des sciences humaines*, 1953, and Ph. D. Walker, "Zola's Use of Color Imagery in *Germinal*," *Publications of the Modern Language Association*, September 1962. I have made some comments on Walker's article in the June 1964, number of *Publ. Modern Language Association*.

11. In the volume entitled *Le Roman expérimental* see the article on the preface to Goncourt's *Frères Zemganno* (ed. Bernouard, pp. 216, 221).

12. Letter to J. Van Santen Kolff, Oct. 6, 1889. Reproduced in *Émile Zola's Letters to Van Santen Kolff*, edited by R. J. Niess, in the *Washington University Studies*, May 1940.

13. Quoted by W. H. Root, *German Criticism of Zola, 1875 to 1893* (Columbia University Press, 1931), p. 54. For additional critical comment, see the chapter on this question in my study (note 4, above). Throughout my treatment of *Germinal*, I have naturally made use of my study.

Chapter Eight

1. *Correspondance* (Bernouard edition), Feb. 23, 1886.

2. *L'Œuvre* in the *Œuvres complètes* (Bernouard edition), p. 409. Zola was fascinated by the theme of the growth, maintenance, or de-

cline of artistic genius. Cf. Laurent in *Thérèse Raquin* and the main characters in *Mme Sourdis*.

3. *Correspondance* (Bernouard edition), p. 218. See also a previous letter dated June 10, 1861, p. 201.

4. On this question see Lanoux, *op. cit.*, and Denise Le Blond-Zola, *op. cit.*

5. *L'Œuvre*, Chap. 2 (p. 32 in the Bernouard edition), translation by Walton.

6. Like Claude Lantier, Monet took to himself a mistress, had a son by her, and married her in due course. Monet tried in 1868 to commit suicide, though not for the same reasons as those which impelled Lantier to his action.

7. For this detail and other information, see P. Brady, "Claude Lantier," *Les Cahiers naturalistes*, No. 17, 1961; and see Lapp, *op. cit.*, p. 102, note 9.

8. Henri Gervex (1852–1929) was an artist of the period who acquired some reputation with his paintings on modern subjects.

9. *L'Œuvre*, Chap. 7 (p. 206 in the Bernouard edition).

10. Quoted by L. A. Carter, *op. cit.*, p. 129.

11. *Documents littéraires*, p. 179.

12. *Correspondance* (Bernouard edition), June 1886.

13. Cf. H. Guillemin, *Présentation des "Rougon-Macquart"* (Gallimard, 1964), p. 299.

14. See H. Guillemin, *op. cit.*, and G. Robert, *op. cit.*

Chapter Nine

1. Zola's daughter Denise was born on Sept. 20, 1889; his son Jacques on Sept. 25, 1891. Alexandrine Zola was informed of her husband's liaison sometime in the fall of 1891.

2. R. Frazee, *Henry Céard, idéaliste détrompé* (University of Toronto Press, 1963), pp. 46–47; and C. A. Burns, *H. Céard. Lettres inédites à E. Zola* (Nizet, 1958), pp. 27–30.

3. For a different opinion, see H. Guillemin, *op. cit.*, pp. 311–26.

4. See M. Kanes, *Zola's "La Bête humaine." A Study in Literary Creation* (University of California Press, 1962) and J. W. Scott, "Réalisme et réalité dans *La Bête humaine*," *Revue d'histoire littéraire de la France*, oct.-dec., 1963. Mr. Scott shows that while there is much accuracy in Zola's presentation of the railroad, there is some inaccuracy and some deliberate adaptation.

5. *La Bête humaine*, Bernouard edition, p. 48.

6. *Ibid.*, p. 149.

7. Antoinette Jägmetti, *"La Bête humaine" d'Emile Zola. Étude de stylistique critique* (Genève, 1955), p. 70.

8. Another character in the book, Denizet, the examining magis-

trate, was modeled on Porfiry, the police officer of *Crime and Punishment,* but according to Zola's work-sheets, he intended Denizet to be a satire on the clever sleuth. Cf. Hemmings, *op. cit.,* p. 217 and the Bernouard edition of *La Bête humaine,* p. 388.

9. Hemmings, *op. cit.,* p. 216. Cf. also a letter, dated June 6, 1888, written by Zola to Van Santen Kolff in the collection edited by R. J. Niess (*op. cit.,* pp. 28–30).

10. *Ébauche,* f. 338/1: "Je voudrais, après le Rêve, faire un roman tout autre; d'abord dans le monde réel [. . .] et comme sujet, un drame violent à donner le cauchemar à tout Paris." (Quoted in the Bernouard edition, p. 383.)

11. *L'Argent,* Bernouard edition, pp. 234 and 240.

12. See R. B. Grant, "The Jewish Question in Zola's *L'Argent," Publications of the Modern Language Association,* Dec. 1955.

13. *L'Argent,* Bernouard edition, p. 437.

14. See Carter, *op. cit.,* pp. 176–78.

15. See above, Chap. III, p. 50.

16. See, in particular, nos. XII–XIV of "Souvenirs."

17. *Correspondance* (Bernouard edition), Sept. 4, 1891, pp. 736–738.

18. Fragments of Zola's *Ébauche* are printed in the Bernouard edition, pp. 613–21, as well as some notes furnished by Fernand Hue (pp. 621–24), and some of the preliminary portraits that Zola wrote for his *Personnages* (pp. 624–31). Cf. also pp. 589–99 on his documentation. And see the preceding note.

19. There is doubtless some weakness of construction in the way fictional characters observe and overhear what the historical figures do and say, for rather incredible coincidences are required to bring this about. This may diminish slightly the literary achievement, but it detracts relatively little from the general interest of the book.

20. While Weiss is a fictitious character, it is historically true that civilians found with arms in their hands were shot. Cf. M. Howard, *The Franco-Prussian War* (London, 1962), p. 208.

21. A contemporary of Zola's, E. M. de Vogüé, who took part in the battle and was in fact in the cabbage field mentioned by the novelist, testified to the accuracy of his report: "*La Débâcle* de M. Émile Zola," *Revue des Deux Mondes,* July 15, 1892. (He also made some rather severe criticisms of other features of the book.)

22. Chapter 7, Part I.

23. Bernouard edition, p. 625.

24. The national government was sitting at Versailles. Its troops were therefore called "les Versaillais."

25. Cf. Mitterand, *Zola journaliste,* pp. 139–44.

26. H. Guillemin, *op. cit.,* pp. 375–76. Guillemin also claims that

Zola did not tell the truth about Bazaine, but on pp. 462, 472 (Bernouard edition, Chap. 4, Part. III), Zola is very severe toward Bazaine.

27. S. Bernstein, *The Beginnings of Marxian Socialism in France* (New York, 1933), p. 35.

28. See the Bernouard edition, pp. 636–60. The German officer's criticism is reproduced on pp. 600–604; Zola's reply follows.

29. *Correspondance*, Bernouard edition, p. 749.

30. He had spent a few days there the year before.

31. Chapter VIII (p. 192, Bernouard edition). On this whole question, see not only H. Martineau, *Le Roman scientifique d'Émile Zola*, Ballière, 1907, but also R. Ternois, *Zola et son temps*, Les Belles Lettres, 1961, pp. 271 ff.

Chapter Ten

1. Quoted by R. Ternois, *Zola et son temps*, Les Belles Lettres, 1961, p. 249. For the genesis and composition of *Les Trois Villes*, see Ternois, *ibid.*, pp. 147–655.

2. L. Pasteur, "Discours de réception à l'Académie Française," *Œuvres complètes*, Vol. VII, p. 338.

3. Abbé de Broglie, *La Science et la réligion: leur conflit apparent et leur accord réel*, 1883.

4. J. M. Guyau, Introduction, *L'Irréligion de l'avenir* (1887), pp. xi–xxiv. Cf. R. Ternois, *Zola et son temps*, p. 81.

5. F. Brunetière, "La philosophie de Schopenhauer et les conséquences du pessimisme," *Revue des Deux Mondes*, Nov. 1, 1890. His article on "La Banqueroute du Naturalisme" appeared in the same review, Sept. 1, 1887.

6. See above, Chapter IV.

7. It appeared May 16, 1896 and was one of a series of articles on diverse topics he wrote for the paper that year. See *Nouvelle campagne* in the *Œuvres complètes*.

8. Quoted by H. Barbusse, *Zola*, Gallimard, 1932, p. 252. The eye witness was Séverine, the well-known female political writer of the period.

9. This interpretation of Zola's departure seems to me supported by a recent publication: "Émile Zola. Pages d'exil, publiées et annotées par Colin Burns," *Nottingham French Studies*, May–October, 1964.

10. For the genesis and sources of these *Évangiles*, see G. Robert, *Émile Zola. Principes et caractères généraux de son œuvre*, pp. 156–65, as well as the critical apparatus at the end of the appropriate volume of the Bernouard edition of the *Œuvres complètes*.

11. Cf. Hemmings, *op. cit.*, p. 283.

12. See Gabriel Reuillard, "Zola, assassiné?" *Le Monde*, June 1, 1954.

13. See E. A. Vizetelly, *Émile Zola,* p. 498. Cf. Hemmings, *op. cit.,* p. 282.

14. Lack of space has prevented a fuller consideration of these novels and also a review of various operas for some of which Zola wrote the libretto. For this operatic activity, see L. A. Carter, *op. cit.,* pp. 179–210.

Conclusion

1. See my concluding remarks on *Les Rougon-Macquart,* at the end of Chapter IX.

2. From a letter to Edouard Rod, March 27, 1885, *Correspondance* (Bernouard edition), p. 637.

Selected Bibliography

Primary Sources

MANUSCRIPTS:

The manuscripts of *Les Rougon-Macquart* * and the *Évangiles* (*Fécondité, Travail,* and *Vérité*), including many pages of preliminary plans and notes, are preserved in Paris in the Bibliothèque Nationale, under the classification of Nouvelles Acquisitions Françaises, the call numbers running from 10268–10345. The manuscripts and preliminary notes of *Les Trois Villes* are preserved in the Bibliothèque Méjanes, Aix-en-Provence, under the call numbers 1455–1456, 1463–1465, 1471–1473.

A large collection of letters received by Zola is preserved in the Bibliothèque Nationale (Nouvelles Acquisitions Françaises, 24510–24524).

EDITIONS:

1. Complete works:

The standard commercial edition is published in Paris by Charpentier-Fasquelle in 48 volumes, or more, depending on whether some of the larger works are bound in one volume or in two or three.

Another edition, utilizing the same text as the above, with notes and commentaries by Maurice Le Blond, was published from 1927 to 1929 by the Typographie François Bernouard. The editorial apparatus is frequently useful, although the choice of material is often arbitrary. This edition is marred by many typographical errors.

2. Les Rougon-Macquart:

A new edition of this series is in course of publication by Gallimard (Paris), as part of its Bibliothèque de la Pléiade. Armand Lanoux wrote the general introduction, and Henri Mitterand has undertaken the task of summarizing the genesis of each novel and annotating the text. This Pléiade edition is by far the best available. So far, three volumes (up to and including *Germinal*) have appeared.

* One exception: the manuscript of *Nana* is in the Morgan collection of the New York Public Library.

[197]

ÉMILE ZOLA

Translations:

Most of the older translations, particularly those by Vizetelly, are so bowdlerized that they cannot be recommended. The following are satisfactory:

L'Assommoir, Tr. by A. H. Townsend. New York: New American Library of World Literature, 1962.
Earth (La Terre). Tr. by A. Lindsay. London: Elek, 1958.
Germinal. Tr. by L. W. Tancock. London: Penguin Classics, 1954.
The Kill (La Curée). Tr. by A. Teixera de Mattos. London: Elek, 1957.
The Masterpiece (L'Œuvre). Tr. by Th. Walton, London: Elek, 1950.
Nana, Translator not indicated. New York: Collier Books, 1962.
Zest for Life (La Joie de vivre). Tr. by J. Stewart. London: Elek, 1956.

SECONDARY SOURCES

1. General works:

Hemmings, F. W. J., *Émile Zola.* Oxford: The Clarendon Press, 1953; revised edition, 1966. This book by a British critic is an excellent piece of literary criticism, and, at the same time, is informative.
Lanoux, A. *Bonjour Monsieur Zola.* Paris: Amiot-Dumont, 1954. A lively biography.
Le Blond-Zola, D. *Émile Zola raconté par sa fille.* Paris: Fasquelle, 1931. An essentially factual biography, fairly objective considering the relationship.
Levin, Harry. *The Gates of Horn; a Study of Five French Realists.* New York: Oxford University Press, 1963. Contains a long and interesting section on Zola.
Robert, G. *Émile Zola. Principes et caractères généraux de son œuvre.* Paris: Les Belles Lettres, 1952. An excellent analysis of Zola's work.
Ternois, R. *Zola et son temps (Lourdes-Rome-Paris).* Paris: Les Belles Lettres, 1961. Ternois includes much more than a discussion of the *Three Cities.* He gives much on the intellectual background and Zola's reaction to it.
Turnell, M. *The Art of French Fiction.* New York: New Directions, 1950. Contains a long, interesting chapter on Zola.
Wilson, A. *Émile Zola. An Introductory Study of his Novels.* New York: Wm. Morrow, 1952. A brilliant essay; written, however, from a Freudian point of view.
Zévaès, A. *Zola.* Paris: Éditions de la Nouvelle Revue Critique, 1946. A highly sympathetic biography by a man who shares many of Zola's views.

[198]

Selected Bibliography

2. A few special studies:

Carter, L. O. *Zola and the Theater.* New Haven: Yale University Press, 1963. Several of Zola's works were adapted for the stage, and he sometimes collaborated in these adaptations. He was also a dramatic critic. Carter reports on these activities.

Franzen, N. O. *Zola et "La Joie de vivre."* Stockholm: Almquist & Wiksell, 1958. A scholarly study of the genesis, composition, etc., of the novel.

Girard, M. *"L'Univers de Germinal," Revue des sciences humaines* (1953). A very suggestive article on the vision of the miners' world in *Germinal* with details on Zola's use of colors, etc.

Grant, E. M. *Zola's "Germinal." A Critical and Historical study.* Leicester University Press, 1962. A scholarly study of the genesis and composition of this novel, with one chapter on Zola's art.

Grant, R. B. *Zola's "Son Excellence Eugène Rougon."* Durham, N.C.: Duke University Press, 1960. A scholarly study of the genesis, composition, etc., of this novel.

————. "The Jewish Question in Zola's *L'Argent," Publications of the Modern Language Association* (Dec., 1955). A scholarly, critical study of this question.

Guillemin, H. *Présentation des "Rougon-Macquart."* Paris: Gallimard, 1964. The volume contains a chapter (twenty in all) on each novel of the *Rougon-Macquart.* Guillemin is always interesting, though his ideas are frequently debatable.

Hemmings, F. W. J. & Niess, R. J. *Émile Zola. Salons.* Geneva: Droz, 1959. The authors present here the complete, original text of these essays by Zola. There is an interesting introduction by Hemmings.

Jagmetti, A. *"La Bête humaine" d'Émile Zola.* Geneva: Droz, 1955. This essay is primarily a study of stylistics.

Kanes, M. *L'Atelier de Zola. Textes de journaux 1865–1870.* Geneva: Droz, 1963. A useful collection of some of Zola's early newspaper articles.

————. *Zola's "La Bête humaine."* Berkeley: University of California Publications, 1962. A scholarly study of the genesis and composition of this novel.

Lapp, J. C. *Zola before the "Rougon-Macquart."* Toronto: University of Toronto Press, 1964. This good little book is devoted to the early stories and novels written by Zola. It seeks to show that they contain themes, imagery, attitudes which reappear in Zola's mature work. It sheds light on Zola's creative genius.

Leonard, F. M. *"Nana: Symbol and Action," Modern Fiction Studies* (1963). An interesting essay on some of the imagery—particularly that of the theater—in *Nana.*

Matthews, J. H. *Les Deux Zola*. Geneva: Droz, 1957. Treating primarily the question of style, this book demonstrates that Zola's language combines the objective and the subjective, the scientific and the personal.

Mitterand, H. *Zola journaliste*. Paris: A. Colin, 1962. A succinct, valuable account of Zola's journalistic career.

Niess, R. J. *Émile Zola's Letters to J. Van Santen Kolff*. St. Louis, Washington University Studies, 1940. Contains letters which give information on many of the novels.

Robert, G. *"La Terre" d'Émile Zola. Étude historique et critique*. Paris: Les Belles Lettres, 1952. A scholarly study of the genesis, composition, etc., of *La Terre*.

Walker, P. D., "Prophetic Myths in Zola," *Publications of the Modern Language Association*, September 1959. A very suggestive article on some of the myths which exist in Zola's work. Walker is always interesting, though some of his ideas are debatable.

Index

Place names and names of fictional characters are not included. In listing alphabetically, definite and indefinite articles, and the prepositions *à* and *de* have been ignored; *Le Bien public,* for example, is listed under B.

Index

Index

Index